AN OHIO SCHOOLMISTRESS

AN OHIO SCHOOLMISTRESS

The Memoirs of Irene Hardy

edited by
LOUIS FILLER

The Kent State University Press

Frontispiece: Photograph of Irene Hardy in 1871, courtesy of Antiochiana, Antioch College Library

Portions of the memoir have appeared in *Ohio History* and *The Antiochian* and are reprinted with permission.

Library of Congress Cataloging in Publication Data
Hardy, Irène, 1841–
An Ohio Schoolmistress.

Bibliography: p.
Includes index.
1. Hardy, Irene, 1841–   2. Teachers—Ohio—Biography. 3. Education—Ohio—Biography. I. Filler, Louis, 1912–   II. Title.
LA2317.H423A36   371.1′0092′4 [B]   80-17242
ISBN 0-87338-242-0

Contents

Introduction

Irene Hardy, schoolmistress, poet, and early Stanford University professor, was born July 22, 1841, in Eaton, Ohio, the eldest daughter of Kentucky and Virginia parents. Her father, Walter Buell Hardy, was a schoolteacher of culture whose four daughters—he also had a son, Lewis—all taught school successfully. Irene was so named from a character in Bulwer's novel *Rienzi*, with conscientious regard for the original Greek pronunciation. Her mother was an enthusiast for education, who declared that if she had twenty daughters, she would send them all to college if she could.

Irene early became a school teacher, as the following memoirs recount, and saved money to enable her to enter Antioch College. As she had occasion to write (June 19, 1921) in a letter to the later president of Antioch College, Arthur E. Morgan, who had recently taken on the all but defunct institution and with it begun a new career for himself and it:

> I entered Antioch in September, 1861, as partial freshman. My preparatory school had given me no Latin, no Greek, and no ancient history. I had, therefore, to do three years' work in these subjects, which I did in two years. At the end of that time, owing to conditions brought about by the war, the College classes were suspended for one year and the faculty gave all their time to the preparatory school.
>
> I went home to teach. To shorten my story—I was in and out of the College a number of times to teach, until 1867, when I was nearly ready to take my degree. Although I was matron of North Hall and teacher in the preparatory school from 1874 to 1876, I did not care to take my degree, notwithstanding I had done work enough to entitle me to it: nor was I ever afterward

a student there. In 1871 I came to California,* and on a return visit in 1883-4, when Dr. David Long was President, he urged me to take my degree at the next commencement. I could not return to do so, but the degree was granted in 1885—eighteen years after it was mainly earned. . . .

At the college, Miss Hardy was of an era of notable students: among the women Olympia Brown, known as the first regularly appointed female minister in America; Susanna Way Dodds, a pioneer physician and reformer, who had refused to accept her Antioch degree because she had not been permitted to wear her Bloomer costume for the occasion; and Ada Shepard, who had accompanied the Nathaniel Hawthornes to Europe as governess for their children, and who figures in Hawthorne's *The Marble Faun* (see Robert Lincoln Straker, *Horace Mann and Others, Chapters from the History of Antioch College [1963]*).

As Miss Hardy says, she then went west, primarily for reasons of health, but stayed to develop a California career, interrupted then renewed, as a schoolmistress. As such, she was influential in developing standards for composition and the teaching of literature for the entire state, publishing a textbook which was used in the public schools. She was influenced by the poet Edward Rowland Sill, of the University of California, and herself wrote much verse. Some of it appeared in magazines and in collections: a 1892 volume, privately printed in Oakland, and one published by a San Francisco firm in 1902. These and her teaching activities gave her considerable local and regional prestige.

In 1894, she joined the Stanford University faculty, and gave courses in American literature, composition, and short story writing. The honor she accrued is exemplified in an article by a colleague of hers, Melville B. Anderson, who memorialized his deceased son ("Malcolm Playfair Anderson," *The Condor*, XXI, May 1919, pp. 115-19). Miss Hardy's teaching, he believed, "did much to repair the devastation wrought by the German method upon his soul." Herbert Hoover was among many of her former students who remembered her with affection and respect. In 1919, Hoover, then at the height of his pre-Presidential fame, opened the assembly at

*She returned to Antioch College, as indicated, for the years 1874-76, then left permanently for California.

Introduction

Stanford University with a talk on the Peace Treaty, which had recently been consummated. Miss Hardy received from him a copy of his talk.

In 1901, she retired from active teaching duties to a cottage "built for her by appreciative students" (*Palo Alto Times*, June 5, 1922). In 1908, she became blind. That year she undertook the preparation of her memoirs, "The Making of a Schoolmistress." It was completed in 1913, and comprised 530 pages of manuscript, which took her up to the initiation of her Stanford University career. It included such matters as her meetings with John Muir and Dr. Edward Everett Hale, a vignette of Horace Mann, whom she saw during a visit to Antioch College, a reception to General U.S. Grant, and friendship with the widow of John Ross Browne, the humorist, traveler, and government official. It was dedicated "To my Kindred and other friends of my early life in Ohio, and to the many friends of my later life in California."

Her seventy-fifth birthday in 1916 brought numerous letters and felicitations from students and friends. She succumbed to pneumonia at her home in Palo Alto, June 3, 1922.

She was survived by her sister Adelaide, also a poet and teacher, and her brother Lewis, who had settled in Yellow Springs, Ohio. He made efforts to get published his sister's "The Making of a Schoolmistress," but failing to obtain support, gave the manuscript, plus other material of both Irene and Adelaide, to the Antiochiana section of the Antioch College Library. There the poems, letters, clippings, as well as the memoir are preserved, thanks in large part to the good offices of the late Miss Bessie L. Totten. The present publication is made with the kind permission of Antioch College and the invaluable cooperation of the present Curator of Antiochiana, Mrs. Nina Myatt.

LOUIS FILLER
OVID, MICHIGAN

[ix]

Note on the Manuscript

Irene Hardy's mind was an all but fabulous repository of memories of the world in which she had lived. Her capacity for total recall of endless scenes and people she had encountered ensured that they would not only be recalled, but remembered individually, in detail and in depth. The reader is drawn into a world of conditions and goals which moves as naturally as though it has not been thoroughly superseded by time and revolutionary changes.

Miss Hardy's exceptional memory and fond recollections inevitably resulted, in her manuscript, in repetitions and observations that interfere with the essential flow of her narrative. In the interest of the modern reader, such impediments have been deleted, as have been some of her homilies and views which, it should be emphasized, are sufficiently represented, but which gain no new strength from elaboration or addition.

Paraphernalia of older school-essay writing have been eliminated, to bring out more firmly the integrity and clean lines of her story. Other details of inadvertent error and of arrangement and presentation have been edited, but without infringement on Miss Hardy's basic statements. Spelling, capitalization, and punctuation have been modernized.

One repeated element which was edited out of the published version of the manuscript was Miss Hardy's practice of footnoting the Latin name of just about every flower and tree she mentions in the text. This seemed unnecessary baggage for a smooth narrative, but it is an interesting reflection of the meticulous detail she expended on those things that were important to her.

Missing from this memoir, but not because of editing, is any great amount of the inner reflection or self-analysis we have come to expect in more recent self-portraits. We never know, for instance, whether she had any interest in or prospects for marriage. Or what she thought of her role as a professional woman in the partiarchal Gilded Age. Or very much of anything regarding political or social questions of the day. Only about education does she allow herself to get philosophical. This may be her own private nature; even her poetry is largely external descriptions of nature with little of the poet's emotional response. Or her reticence about private matters may be because the manuscript was written with publication in mind, and public confession was not a feature of autobiographies in that day.

Nevertheless, Irene Hardy has left us a clear picture of the life she knew, from the details of a rural childhood through the classrooms of nineteenth-century America, the people she met, the places she saw, the changes that took place over the years. It is all the more valuable for being objectively descriptive. Our view of the times is clarified through the eyes of Irene Hardy.

A PIONEER CHILDHOOD

1

Family

The pioneer settlers' cabins had already begun to appear in southwestern Ohio at the opening of the nineteenth century. Before the end of the first decade the virgin landscapes of this beautiful region of thick woods and bright streams were diversified by these compact little dwellings. They were built of rough unhewn logs, roofed with handmade clapboards and flanked by big chimneys, at first of sticks and mud, or of such stones as were near at hand. They bore in their very existence signs of the courage and hope of the pioneer men and women, and of their faith in themselves and in the land which God had given them.

Not until the middle of the century had these temporary monuments of the conquering spirit of man given place to the more commodious and comfortable squared log houses or the more pretentious pebble-dashed frame structures. But not even then had they entirely disappeared, for many of them still served as summer kitchens or as loom houses. Not infrequently these out-grown dwellings began a new interior history for themselves by receiving again a bride and groom, the first to leave the family hearth and take up life in this respect as their parents had done.

It was to such a dwelling and such conditions that my father brought his bride in the early autumn of 1840, and there July 22nd. of the following year I was born.

The house was a very primitive one-room log cabin and stood in the edge of an open maple grove whose yearly sweet ministrations to the family had saved and still saves it from the ax. The cabin was torn down soon after my father's removal to another settlers' cabin at Banta's Lane, near my maternal grandfather's. I was then six months old.

When I was eleven years old I once went with a cousin, while I was visiting at her home to help gather up the wooden bowls and other vessels used in the open woods at the maple-sugar "camp." I recalled afterward having seen a place where a house had stood on the edge of the wood; this was the spot where I was born, my mother told me. Not far away was the pebble-dashed house of my uncle-in-law, James McCown, surrounded by its orchard and garden. The farm of which these places were a part adjoined the little village of New Westville, lately renamed "Progress," Preble County.

My parents removed to their own home in the hewn log house which they built on a little piece of land belonging to my mother as a gift from her father. I was then between two and three years of age. To this place belong most of the recollections of the first ten years of my life and the greater part of my outdoor and indoor education, as well as the greater part of those influences which determined what kind of a creature I should be physically, morally, and spiritually.

To the fact that my father had recently read Bulwer's *Rienzi* and greatly admired a character therein described, I owe my Christian name, pronounced as in the original Greek. For the time and place this seemed fanciful, as the plain old-fashioned names for women as well as for men were the rule. My mother wished to name me Margaret Elizabeth, but my father's wish prevailed. Their former teacher, George W. Daly, insisted on the spelling and pronunciation Irena, and always wrote it so, having periodical disputes with my father on the subject. They both agreed, however, that the name should be pronounced with three syllables, not in the abrupt American fashion Ireen, to which I have been subjected nevertheless most of my life.

My very earliest recollection is of my mother, kneading bread at a table by a window, with the feeling that her cheeks were of a lovely pink and her eyes blue. My grandmother sat by the fireplace holding her baby (my Uncle Francis, six months younger than I) on her knee. My baby sister lay in the old-fashioned wooden cradle near the middle of the room, which had a bare floor. I could not have been more than twenty-two months or two years old then. Three or four other memories of that house while we lived in it I have: one was of a cold morning standing up in the high bed to look out of the high window at its head, to see what the noises outside meant. I saw men, my father among them, scalding great hogshead laid in a hollow in the ground and saw the steam rise and heard the water slosh in the barrel.

Another memory is of a return late at night from somewhere with an aunt and my mother and going into the dark house and waiting for the lamp to be lighted; of hearing someone on another night, as my mother thought, walking about outside; of being stood in the open door to hold the tin lamp of lard oil, while she took a candle and walked around in the dark to see what it was; of her finding nothing and going in and to sleep. One other time after moving to our new log house, I went with some children into the old home and climbed the winding stairs to the loft overhead. This house, it was said, harbored the ghost of a young soldier who had come home from the War (of 1812) and had died there. He was a bugler and it was said that his bugle was sometimes heard on still nights. This house was also soon after torn down, when I was four or five years old.

My first recollection of my father is that of seeing him through a window early one frosty morning, as I stood up in a high-posted bed to look out. Other early recollections merely recall his figure and his personality as my father. I do not remember his face as a young man until I was five years old or thereabout when I saw him bending over a singing book containing music which he was practicing with some neighbor. He had a beautiful tenor voice and was very fond of singing. Later, after he had acquired the ability to read "round notes," I remember hearing the singers laugh when my mother thought the sound of *do, re, mi* rather silly, compared with the "*mi-fa-sol-la*" system of the old "Missouri Harmony."

To a time somewhat later than this, 1848 or 1849, belongs the memory of the beginning words of two anthems, "He shall come down like rain upon the mown grass," and "How beautiful upon the mountains are the feet of him that bringeth good tidings." These gave me, I do not know why, for I did not understand them very well, excepting about the rain on the mown grass, a great deal of pleasure, and I always stayed by when the singers practiced and afterwards had "long, long thoughts" about the words, and sometimes took down *The Psaltery* (1848) and read them for myself. All this practice with neighbors and sometimes with my Aunt Eliza was in preparation for a sacred concert. This was to be given in the public church in Eaton at the end of a course of singing lessons by a locally distinguished singing master named Mr. Fiske, of Richmond, Indiana. I was able to understand enough of the talk at these times of practice to know that it was a great privilege to be taught by Mr. Fiske and that there had never yet been so great a concert in this part of the country.

My father was the youngest son of Rev. John Hardy and his wife, Rachel Downing, who had moved from Kentucky in 1808 to Preble County, Ohio. There he was born May 5, 1818, and was named for the old family physician, Walter Buell. He was five feet ten inches in height, well proportioned, and was considered handsome in his youth, even by persons less prejudiced than my mother. He had very thick dark-red hair, fair skin, with good color and blue eyes, while his forehead and nose gave to his profile a poetic dignity. A very retired man, exceedingly shy, with a good deal of what might be called moral pride, he disliked coarse and vulgar people and held himself aloof from the dull and uninteresting.

Before my recollection of him he had read every book that could be had by borrowing in neighborhoods far and near, history, fiction, and poetry. In his twenty-second year he had begun one or two blank-verse poems, one of which he continued to a considerable length.

In my sixth or seventh year, I went to a night singing school made up mostly of grown-up young folks to whom my father taught what was called the "Buckwheat notes." My father played the violin with considerable facility, but entirely by ear; this, however, he had given up after his marriage, as in the common opinion of the neighborhood and especially of church members a violin was a fiddle and a wicked instrument played at dances and other worldly festivals. When he began to play the clarinet and flute I do not know, but probably some time after giving up the violin. He played both these instruments beautifully and was especially proficient on the clarinet. I remember moonlight nights in which he took his instrument to the orchard and played for hours. He had been the fifer for the yearly "Muster Day."

One such day I distinctly remember because of his fife playing. Late in his life I brought to him the novel *Charles Auchester* by Elizabeth S. Sheppard ("E. Berger") in which there is a great deal of violin talk and violin music. Somehow, this book seemed to justify to himself his love of the violin which doubtless he would have taken up again if the book had fallen in his way. He played the clarinet at intervals to the end of his life.

His knowledge of history was prodigious, as he read widely and retained well. He was very fond of mathematics and worked at various problems all his life. Nothing pleased him better than to get hold of a problem no one else could solve, and he never met a greater scholar in mathematics than himself without positively pestering him with knotty problems. He had a good deal of inventive ingenuity and was often interested in making some new thing. He loved wood carving and though untaught fashioned many useful things, all of which were beautified by a little touch of decoration.

My father's business in life was teaching, which was mostly done in district schools. He was considered one of the best schoolmasters of his time, and was often called to larger and more difficult schools on account of his scholarship and powers of discipline. He preferred the country school, somewhat to my mother's chagrin, as she wished him to take places more in accordance with her opinion of his ability and deserts, but he disliked towns, and his natural shyness and reserve made him prefer the country schools among the woods and fields. He had many friends among former pupils and their parents, some of whom I met afterwards when I began to teach. A number of these often spoke to me of their affection for him. The present (1908) governor of Ohio, General A.L. Harris, and his wife were among these.

My father had a quaint dry humor, which disclosed itself sometimes in odd rememberable sentences quoted by his friends and neighbors; now and then it took the form of biting satire, especially in relation to conduct he disapproved of, but I believe never to his pupils.

Such ambitions as my father had were for his children and their intellectual developments. He would have been glad, for instance, to see me delivering a lecture in a public hall. He wished too, as I knew late in his life, to see a book of mine in print, and thought I might easily have published one. When I said that I had not the strength after teaching for such mental effort, he did not understand. It is a matter of grief to me that he did not live to see the poor little books I wrote later. A partial loss of hearing before he was fifty interfered with much that my father did and would have done. He died at the age of sixty-nine years and ten months.

My mother, Mary Ann Ryan Hardy, was the eldest of a family of fourteen children, the daughter of James Ryan and Elizabeth Chrismore Ryan of Frederick County, Virginia. She was born near Winchester, September 18, 1817. Her childhood was spent in the country there, and later until she was twelve near Newbern, on New-River, West Virginia, where her father had removed his family a few years before his emigration to Ohio in 1829. She grew up with a fondness for woods and mountains. So vivid was her memory of plants, flowers, and trees, and their seasons of flowering, that her talk about these things made the principal subject of her stories to her children around the evening fire.

My mother's schooling in Virginia was under one of those severe masters who punished with a rod or the ruler, for the slightest fault. She herself was once whipped on the hand with the ruler until her palm was blistered, for no worse a thing than eating some sweet birch leaves behind her book, because she was hungry. An ill-conditioned boy named Henry told the master, who called her out on the middle of the floor. Many of the masters of this time were of this severe type. They had brought their ideas of school discipline from the old country, where most of them had been educated. In these pioneer schools and later in the Dooley District in Preble County, my mother learned reading, writing, spelling, arithmetic, and a little grammar. As she was the eldest of a large family, her school days were soon cut short by the necessities of a pioneer home.

She had inherited a perfectly sound constitution. She was tall and slender, with blue eyes, brown hair, and very fair complexion. She was quick and energetic of movement, and possessed the family trait of being a notable walker. Of course, like all the women of the country settlements in those times, she was mistress of the various crafts necessary to living, spinning, weaving, dyeing, and all that went to make these possible. Her ruling and care of her children were based in the belief that prompt obedience was the foundation lesson to be taught. She gave us the largest liberty, but required instant obedience to such commands as she made. We must come at once when called, we must not touch what did not belong to us; these two rules were absolute at home and away from home.

My father and mother were wholly agreed as to measures of discipline. I had never seen my father angry, nor heard him speak severely until one day in my fifth or sixth year I went out to ask him if I might do a certain thing. "Go and ask your mother," he said. "I did ask her." "What did she say?" "She said 'No.' "What do you mean then by coming to ask me?" I never repeated the offense. A similar thing happened when I tried it the other way.

The following will illustrate my mother's way of dealing with her children. One day when I was out playing in the snow with my sister, making beautiful round snowballs, my fertile five-year-old mind suggested to itself and then to my sister that boiled snowballs would be something very good to eat. Whereupon we ran into the house to ask mother if we might have some. She smiled and said, "Yes, sometime." A few days after, when the iron kettle full of boiling water hung over the fire, we reminded her of her promise. She said we could have them then, and we went out and brought in our aprons full of big round balls. She took them one by one and dropped them into the kettle as we stood by her, amazed to see each one disappear into nothingness.

Another incident of the kind a year or two later recalls the recollection of a desire to please and surprise mother when she came back from a short errand at my grandmother's. She had left the little cedar churn, washed and scalded after using, standing in the sun in the yard and half full of water. I had often stood on my little chair and helped to churn. Looking into the churn at this time, I suddenly thought that it would be such a fine surprise to mother if we could make some water butter. My sister always followed my lead. We brought out the little chair and took turns in churning for I do not know how long, looking in now and then at the foam and bubbles and saying, "Yes, it's coming." I saw in my imagination a plate of transparent butter, fresh from the churn. When mother came home we told her about our disappointment, which, however, had not convinced us that the thing could not be done, because we had sometimes seen a churning of milk fail to bring the butter. Neither then nor at any other time did my mother laugh before us at our mistakes.

Sometimes on my father's infrequent absences from home at his singing school or when he had gone to take a lesson at some distance from home at night, my mother would allow us to sit up later than usual, perhaps for company. At such times she would entertain us with stories of when she was a little girl. It was to evenings like these that I owe the remembrance of our little brown cricket on the hearth. My mother would pause in the middle of her story, say, "Listen!" draw us very quietly close to the right jamb of the fireplace, and lay some crumbs of bread down near a crack. Then we too would sit breathless at her knee, waiting for the little chirp which had told her that the cricket was there. In a few minutes he would creep out, stand still and move his long antennae delicately in front of him; then his little silky brown body would move forward an inch or two and repeat the motions of his thread-like feelers; forward again, then a few more inches till he reached the bread crumbs. And we would sit with mute delight watching him eat. I never saw any other like this dear and silky little creature. The field crickets about us were much larger and were always black, and were very undesirable in the house.

Another recollection of these days is of one Sunday morning during an illness of my mother. We had been dressed by an aunt who was taking care of her and sent out to play. We began to run up and down on a great log in the woods behind the house where we often played. After running up and down once or twice I wanted to be in front both ways instead of in my turn. When I tried to make my three-year-old sister let me run in front of her, she objected, and I reached out and pinched her on the bare arm, just below her ruffled short sleeve, whereupon she went crying into the house. When I went in sometime after, my mother called me to her where she lay on the front of the bed with the side of her face on the pillow. She said nothing but drew me to her, pinched my left ear sharply, and said, "That's the way it feels when you pinch your little sister." I was so astonished at the light that this let in on my brain that I forgot to cry.

My mother had a small singing voice, very soft and sweet, but I seldom heard her sing. She did not hum about the house, but if she sang it was perhaps the words of some familiar hymn. I remember hearing her while she sewed by the fireplace, singing, "How firm a foundation, ye saints of the Lord," and wondering what *firma* could mean. She was fond of reading, and all her life read in the scanty moments when household business permitted.

Sometimes, about my tenth and twelfth years, she read books to us at night around the open fire, when my father was away teaching. My mother had had a great desire for learning in her young womanhood, and her ambitions for herself became ambitions for her children, so that she sacrificed to the end of her life in order to further her children's advancement. Her reward and happiness expressed themselves in the loving pride with which she saw us gaining what she herself had missed. Once when criticized for encouraging us to go to college, she said, "If I had twenty girls, I would send them to college if I could." My mother's intuitions about people were very strong, almost infallible. I have often found it to my own advantage to follow first impressions myself, knowing that she believed so strongly in them, and acted so generally upon them.

My great-grandfather, Curtis Hardy, was of English descent. He emigrated with his wife Mary and children to Kentucky from Dinwiddie County, Virginia, where November 17, 1779, John Hardy, my grandfather, was born. The emigration was made when my grandfather was a child, and during Indian hostilities. John Hardy devoted himself early to the Christian ministry in the denomination called by its deriders "New Light," by its adherents, Christians, Antioch Christians, which must not be confused with the later sect known as Campbellites or Disciples. He married Rachel Downing, March 1, 1803, and in the autumn of 1808 removed to Preble County where he bought a farm on Paint Creek four miles from Eaton. He farmed, took care of his increasing family, spoke and "exhorted" in the church meetings, and was observed to have had a peculiar gift for public speaking, modest and unassuming as he was. In 1810 he was ordained to the ministry by David Purviance, the leader of the New Lights, Hugh Andrews, and Richard Clark, called "Elders," instead of "Reverends." (Richard Clark was my great-uncle.)

Educational advantages were lacking in those days and places, so that my grandfather had had limited opportunities; but his natural gifts were so uncommon that he was soon known as a good popular preacher. It is said that no other man of that time and region was so enthusiastic and constant a student of the Bible. I have heard my Aunt Laurinda say that it was his nightly habit in winter to lie by the fire studying the Book. He was called by people of his time one of the "sons of consolation." He was said to be methodical and systematic in his discourses and spoke with "a soft and harmonious voice," and easy, graceful gestures. "In reality," says his biographer, Levi Purviance, "his manner was eloquent and interesting; well calculated to entertain and edify all classes, particularly those of a refined taste."*

His ministerial work was in the main in southern Ohio, but he often went to Kentucky. He was pastor of the church at Eaton at his death, which came untimely in the autumn of 1819, October 25, from a fever. My father was then but eighteen months old, but I have often heard him say that he remembered distinctly having seen the funeral procession, through the window to which he was held up by his sister Laurinda. I have been told that my father resembled his father very much in looks and natural gifts. They were both slenderly built, with very fair complexions, blue eyes, abundant dark-red hair, and good voices.

My grandmother, Rachel Hardy, was, as I remember her, a stout, not very tall woman in caps. She had large dark eyes, and a brunette complexion, and when I knew her her hair was still dark. She was often at our house for months at a time. I never knew her very well, and remember very little about her, except that like most Kentucky and Virginia women of all ranks, she smoked a pipe. When she was with us after we moved to the suburbs of Eaton, she used to go down our garden path and sit on a certain bench there, while she smoked—silent, thoughtful, with dark eyes glowing and contemplative. Both my Grandfather Hardy and my father loathed tobacco, but that subject was never discussed in our house in my grandmother's time. She died at about sixty-three of paralysis, at my Aunt Laurinda's in New Westville, Ohio.

My mother's parents were James Ryan and Elizabeth Chrismore Ryan. James Ryan was of Scottish and north of Ireland Irish parentage. His father, Derby (or Darby) Ryan, and his mother, Nancy Symmes Ryan, were born in America. He was the youngest

---

*I am indebted for some of these facts about my Grandfather Hardy to the sketch of his life by Reverend Levi Purviance contained in his "Biography of Elder David Purviance." (B. F. and G. W. Ells, Dayton, Ohio, Publishers, 1848).

[12]

of eight children, born in Dinwiddie County, Virginia, in 1792, and was brought up in Frederick County, Virginia, near Winchester. His mother was descended from a Lady Margaret Symmes. He was a soldier in the War of 1812, and one or two of his brothers, who were likewise men of great stature and extraordinary strength, are said to have fought in the Revolutionary War. He died in August, 1849, of cholera. I have many recollections of seeing him at his own home and ours and in the fields at work.

My last recollection of him is a vivid picture of a group of wheat harvesters sitting on the grass of the roadside, after the day's work, resting in the shadows before they went home. He sat on the ground, the center of the group, bareheaded, with his sleeves rolled up, his arms resting on his drawn-up knees. I remember distinctly his dark hair, strong featured face and his even teeth, as he looked up, talking to my mother, who was on her way home with her four children. The talk was of cholera, that terror of my dreams. Other recollections of him are of seeing him drive by on a load of hay toward town and having some pieces of peppermint stick he had brought.

Ever present in my thought of him was the knowledge that he had to be minded when he spoke. In politics he was an old-time Democrat. As my father was a Whig and later a "Black Republican" and abolitionist, they often had political discussions. He was a successful farmer and had put two eighty-acre farms under good cultivation in the twenty years between his emigration to Ohio in 1829 and his death. He had been brought up a Roman Catholic, but although he had had his first two children, my mother and my Aunt Margaret, christened by a priest, he seems not to have had connection with the church later than that. He read whatever came into his way on religious subjects, and among other things, Josephus, Rollin's *History of Rome*, and the Bible. His family all grew up Protestants.

After I was twelve or thirteen years of age, I heard it said in our family, as something not to be talked about or told, that my grandfather had read Paine's *Age of Reason*. But I never saw the book or heard of it in my grandfather's house; and as I had been many a time allowed to climb up to look at the books on the middle shelf of the glass-doored cupboard in the "big room" where all the books were kept, I should have seen it if it had been there. No other books besides those I have mentioned, and a dream book, and a few odd school books, and some of the earliest numbers of the *Godey's Lady's Book* sewed together, were there. I heard my mother say that my grandfather was fond of theological arguing with my father, whom he sometimes walked down to see on Sundays. She said also that if the discussion sheered off into politics my father would say no more, as he would not talk politics on Sunday and more particularly as they did not agree.

When I think of grandfather, I am also reminded of two or three of his contemporaries and neighbors who had much to do with the settlement of this region. Silas Dooley, Sr., for example, had cut his farms from the virgin forest here, as had both my grandfathers, one on a northwest and the other on a southwest section of the same region; he was, as I remember him in 1865 and a little later, a large, strongly built man of more than six-feet stature, straight even then; he died soon after at the age of ninety-six. I have often seen him hoeing his little patch of turnips in his son's garden ground for exercise. Curiously enough, in this connection, I remember that he had allowed to remain among his turnips two or three plants, known to us as the Lady-fingers, which he carefully hoed along with his vegetables, evidently cherishing the common belief that the plant kept out weeds. This beautiful plant, with its slender jointed and collared stock, its gracefully poised, rather wide-spreading branches, with their pendant plumes of bright red, was often seen about the gardens and farmyards. It was sometimes called Kiss-me-over-the-fence, alluding to its habit of swaying in the least wind and touching you on the cheek as you went by. Its common bookname is Prince's Feather.

My grandmother, Elizabeth Chrismore Ryan, was born of German Lutheran parentage in Pennsylvania. She was brought up in Frederick County, Virginia, near Winchester, where her parents had moved in her infancy, and where she was married to James Ryan in 1816. Her father was Anthony Chrismore, a combmaker. Her mother was Anna Cole Chrismore, the only child of wealthy parents who had disowned her because she married against their wishes. She had but one other child besides my grandmother, a son John, who died a young man. She herself lived to be a hundred years old. My grandmother's grandmother, Elizabeth Chrismore, came from Germany, and lived to be one-hundred-ten years old. My

grandmother was a little below medium height, slender and energetic. Of her fourteen children, the thirteen who grew up were all
tall except one who was a little above medium height. She had somewhat abundant hair, which was long and brown as early as I remember seeing her, but which had been a bright yellow until after her
marriage. This was also true of my mother's hair and that of several
of her younger sisters. My grandmother led an active life full of all
the experiences of a large pioneer family and did not lay aside household interests until her eighty-fourth year. She died at the age of
ninety-seven, in full possession of all her faculties.

Among the pleasantest recollections of seeing my grandfather
and grandmother together is of a beautiful Easter Day in my
seventh or eighth year. It was their custom to walk out on pleasant
Sundays to look at various parts of the farm and to drop in a while
on their way at our house. I had gone out to the Little Woods with
my sister to play in the warm sunshine. There we found grandfather
and grandmother sitting on a log quietly talking. They had just
salted a small flock of sheep then in the woods, and, infant as I was,
the quiet and beauty of the spring day, or whatever it might have
been, impressed this picture on my mind. Perhaps it was the beautifully colored Easter eggs which grandmother gave us, one of dark
purple with a goose-foot pattern scraped all over it, another with the
pretty flowers of a piece of calico impressed on it by boiling the egg,
tied up in print, in weak lye; but I remember myself as standing
looking at the two on the log, my grandmother in her best drawn
sunbonnet, the bare beech trees full of buds, with the blue sky
beyond.*

*Added, November 6, 1905, Palo Alto:

Day before yesterday, a cousin whom I had seen only once, and that when I was
thirteen and he eight, came to see me. I was greatly interested to find a remarkable
family resemblance to my mother's father and mother. Indeed in no other of my
grandmother's numerous descendants is the family likeness so strong as in this
second child of my mother's oldest brother. The huge straight frame, the magnificent build of my grandfather, the complexion and eyes of dark brown, and even
the little and very peculiar "tuck" in the corner of the right eyelid, which is not
repeated in the left, as in some of my mother's sisters—all are there. Last year
a broken right wrist and the surgeon's verdict that he could never work anymore
laid him by. But the sound constitution he had derived from our grandparents came
to his aid, although he is nearly sixty years of age. This is another surprise, one

[15]

The home of my Grandfather and Grandmother Ryan was at this time in the hewn-log and weather-boarded house built after their settlers' log cabin could no longer accommodate their increasing family. It was a one-story oblong building of two large rooms with two front doors at equal distances from the ends and middle of the house. A large brick chimney stood at either end. The two rooms were divided by a matched partition of thick planks with a door in the middle. All the doors of the house had iron thumb-latches, excepting the front door of the big room, which had a lock and key. The "Big Room" was one-third larger than the living room and had on one side of the wide fireplace an enclosed winding stair leading to the large attic which was used as a room for beds.

On the other side of the fireplace was a built-in cupboard with glass doors. On either side of the front door was a small-paned, two-sashed window with white curtains. A door and a window on the opposite side opened to the backyard and orchard. The furniture of the big room was of the simplest and most necessary character; it consisted of two beds next the corners of the living room, a mahogany bureau with glass knobs, a candle stand of the same kind, a settee with rockers, a cherry-wood chest against the front wall between a window and the door, and several "Windsor" chairs. The floor at first was bare but afterwards covered with a rag carpet laid in overlapping widths. The only other article of furniture in the room was an old-fashioned clock, which was about three feet high and stood against the wall above the bureau. The lower part of its glass door contained one of the two pictures in the room, a colored lithograph of Robert Burns and his Highland Mary, which represented a loving interview between the poet and the lady of his song. This picture, although the object of some wonder to me, remains in my memory connected with one of two very dim recollections of my uncle-in-law, Nelson Jones, who sat in front of it with his face to the back of his chair, teasing my aunts with remarks about

---

of very many which the Ryan blood has given to the medical profession in various parts of the country. Dr. Pliny M. Crume, a locally distinguished physician of earlier times in Eaton, Ohio, once told my mother that he had never had in all his practice— and he was an old man then—a family so absolutely sound and without taint as my grandfather's. But not all were able to conserve that splendid heritage. Indeed, most were prodigal of strength and health, expending in various ways what might have made them nonagenarians at least.

it and their beaux. I should not otherwise have remembered seeing it as a child. The only other wall decoration was a framed lithograph of a very astonishing young man named William in a dress suit and a satisfied simper. At that time I supposed it to be a portrait of my Uncle William, though I could not see any resemblance.

The logs with plaster between showed only on the sides of the room, as the wooden partition was at one end, and the fireplace, cupboard, and staircase filled up the other. The big room was continually in use, at least at night.

The living room differed very little in its appointments from the other. It was smaller and had but one bed and a large dining table with let-down leaves and six legs. A high wooden mantel of simple design decorated the wide fireplace, and was flanked on one side by a built-in cupboard and on the other side by a closet door. The hearth was of flagstones at first, and the floor was bare. A large hand-wrought shovel and tongs stood on the hearth by the fireplace, in which was a pair of andirons. I do not remember exactly the dimensions of this fireplace, but it was wide enough and deep enough to take in a back log which had to be rolled into the house and into the fireplace because it was too heavy to be carried by the man who was making the fire. On top of the back log was laid the back stick. The andirons were put into place and the fore stick was laid across; then with "curious art," described by Whittier in "Snow-Bound," the crooked branches were laid and fitted in between with a few quick movements by the skilled architect of the family altar fire. Many a time I have stood by and watched the building and waited for the sudden blaze to spring up among the crackling sticks from the great bed of coals beneath. This was a familiar sight in my own house as well as at my grandmother's.

There were a window and a door at the front and back of the room. The only wall decorations in this room were a small looking-glass between the front door and the window, and some wooden hooks high up on the partition wall for holding the rifles and shotgun. Some Windsor chairs and a candle stand completed the furnishings. The beds in both rooms were generally covered with blue and white hand-woven coverlets, and sometimes with elaborately designed patchwork quilts.

When I was about five years old a kitchen and a bedroom with a long wide porch between were added to the back of the house. A square log smokehouse, set up two feet from the ground on cross sections of a tree, stood not far from the house in the backyard. Two large corn cribs, with a roofed space between for wagons and plows, stood at a little distance from the backyard in a corner of the orchard. Not far from the smokehouse near an apple tree were the ash-hopper and the place for the outdoor fire. The front yard was a wide grassy lawn with a straight path from the living-room door to the front gate. On the right side of the front were an apple tree and a damson plum tree, on the other an apple and a cherry tree. In the left hand corner of the yard was the well with its wooden pump and the milk house nearby shaded by young sycamore trees. All the grounds, at the front, at the ends, at the back, were grassy and always neatly kept. There were no flowers in them excepting a bunch of red peonies, some yellow lilies, and a damask rose at the big-room end of the house. Snowballs, lilacs, and thousand-leaf roses looked over and through the palings of the garden into the grassy front yard.

2

Early Recollections

So early as to be that of a twenty-six-months-old baby is my memory of a trip in a covered wagon, then the only means of long travel in that part of the country. My grandfather took grandmother and her baby, mother and her two babies (my sister Laura was then but a few months old) some eighty or one hundred miles to visit his sister, Mrs. Elizabeth Miller, who lived in Shelby County, Indiana. The summer's work had been "laid by" and the autumn operations of a farm life had not yet come on. One circumstance of the going, that of all having to get out of the wagon, so that it could be drawn from a mudhole in which it was "stalled," is all that I remember, except that while we waited I saw dogwood trees with red leaves and bright red berries, and a sassafras tree. A dim recollection of seeing Great-Aunt Betsey and being in her house is all that remains of the visit itself.

On the return a deeper impression came from a want, crying about it, and punishment for the crying. In the wagon just behind my grandfather's and my mother's chair was a box of peaches, which filled the wagon with their odor; I could see into the box through a large crack. I wanted a peach and to be let to sit between my grandfather's knees to look at the "horsies." I had no language to express all these wants, being still but a baby with merely a vocabulary of words not yet formed into any sentences, and so I cried. Through sympathy or for some weary reason the little baby set up a cry also. My mother, sensitive (as I afterwards heard from her) as to her children's conduct, fearing that my grandfather would be annoyed, and being unable to find out what ailed me, took me, spanked me soundly, and made me lie down in the back of the wagon near my grandmother's chair, with my head on a bundle of clothes. There I wailed out my poor little griefs, which were greatly increased by the interest and laughter of my baby uncle, who enjoyed the noise I made, crying and flopping about on the floor. Not until I was twelve years old did I happen to tell this to my mother. "Why child," she answered, "why didn't you say what you wanted? You could have had the peach and sat in front. I always wondered what made you cry so."

Corduroy bridges were still in use in some of the byroads of our part of the country as late as 1851. Corduroy roads, or bridges, were made by laying eight- or ten-inch logs close together across wet or swampy spots in the new roads cut through the forest. In some places where it was possible, the earth was thrown up on the road a little from either side before the logs were laid down. Riding over long stretches of such road in springless farm wagons made some impression on the memory, to say the least. The larger part of the otherwise impassable places in the forest roads of our county and the adjoining Indiana border were built in this way.

When I was six years old, my father and mother took their family of three children, the youngest but two months old, to visit my Uncle Curtis Hardy in Jay County, Indiana. It was in late September, 1847, and our covered wagon was sometimes our only shelter from the frosty nights. For along those unfrequented roads there were few houses, and except once where we came to a crosscut of a main road, no taverns at all. We two older children were kept in the back of the wagon, or rather in the middle, behind the chairs of the two in front. The straw bed which made our comfort at night was a sort of cushioned floor to us. Even so the jolting of the springless farm wagon must have tried my nerves, for I remember looking ahead apprehensively over my mother's shoulder as I stood on the rounds of her chair to see if there were any corduroy ahead of us. A mingled memory of riding between brilliant bushes and trees, among which I saw dogwood with red leaves and bunches of berries, wild grape vines with purple grapes, and oaks with ripe acorns, remains of that time.

One night on our journey out, we were obliged to camp at the woodside, another we stayed with a newly married couple in a cabin in a lonely corner of the wood. They seemed glad to have us and allowed us to bring our beds in to spread on the floor of their single room, which had a partition across one half of one end, where their own bed was. A long bench by the wall was their table, which they gave up to us; a shorter one on the other side they themselves used. Two or three short high-benches served as chairs—they had but one real chair, a splint bottom one. Some open shelves against the wall held a few plates and cups. The huge fireplace had a fire, and the clean floor was white. There was not another bit of any kind of furniture or other belongings.

The man was in his shirt sleeves and wore a broad-brimmed, home-braided straw hat; he had a violin ("fiddle") which he and my father discoursed on by the wide open door in the evening until dusk. We had our own provisions with us, so that we were not too great a burden to our entertainers. The next morning before we started, the young woman with pride showed to my mother her wedding dress, a coarse lawn with wide blue and narrow black stripes, of a floral pattern. A simple pathetic life was hers, happy and proud with so little.

Another episode of that trip was the stopping for the night—I do not know whether going or returning—at a tavern on a crossroad, a farm house by the roadside, with a large orchard behind. We arrived at dusk and were obliged to spread our beds on the parlor floor, as the place was full. Two very low-voiced women moved about as they seemed to be baking pies in the stove in the parlor. Dim lights, a wide, clean, bare floor with beds spread in one end, and a big-eyed staring child in a dusky corner on the floor taking note of everything. Then sleep, to be waked in the middle of the night by men tramping back and forth, swearing at the accommodations, at "the sour pies," at what else I did not understand.

Next morning I went out to look around; my sister Laura, about four, following me. We went into the orchard where the grass was almost up to our shoulders. Trees with long boughs bending low to the grass with dark red apples, a tall apple tree with golden russets all over it and on the grassy ground beehives at one side, and— O bliss!—two snow-white rabbits with pink eyes, the like of which I had never seen or heard of. They ran from us, of course, leaping through the high grass. The quiet-voiced women, a spinning wheel on a back porch, a broad-brimmed hat on a bent man, a little plum tree on the opposite side of the road—and the picture vanishes.

In my uncle's low log house was the usual one room, containing two beds, a trundle-bed, and plenty of children with whom I played in the daytime. Not far away was a big barn where there were owls and a big snake to catch rats, a new hewn log house on the hill above, just begun, with walls, a roof, a place for a door and other places for windows, a terrifying flight of wasps inside when we went to see it, a spring among some trees down below—these are my main recollections of the place. Playing on the banks of the Salimony River, which ran nearby, seeing my cousins slide down the bank to the water's edge to get some blue clay to make marbles of, wanting to slide down and being afraid to, shiveringly doing it and bringing back a handful of the precious stuff, seeing Cousin Phoebe make a clay wagon and a boy of clay sitting in it: O what joy! In an afternoon we went to the wood nearby to get some chinquapins, and brought back besides some branches of the black hawthorn with half-ripe berries. These we laid in the open on some "Jimson weed," so that they would have all the frost and ripen faster, my cousins said.

I noticed enough of the conversation around me there to know that it was about people—who married whom, how many children they had, where they lived, and who had died. One phrase of my uncle's I picked up and wondered at; of someone's son he said, "O he's a right smart chunk of a boy, maybe ten or twelve."

My uncle's agreeable voice, his blue eyes like my father's, his stout figure, all so pleasant to remember. I saw and heard too little of them thereafter as the way was long, the roads rough, and our visits and theirs infrequent. The time of this visit is easily fixed in my memory because my sister Adelaide, who was born in July, 1847, was then a very little baby, and part of the time wore the same little striped calico dress in which I had first seen her.

One very cold and frosty night, on the way out to Salimony, I remember, we had gone on a little later than usual in the hope of finding shelter. A big house showed its roof and barn some distance from the road. Father left us by the roadside, and went in to inquire for a place to sleep. The house owner said he could not take anyone in; his wife was sick. Could we go into the barn? No, we might set it on fire. Father put the horses into an old unused stable by the wood's edge, built a fire outside, and we made ready to sleep there in the wagon by the side of the road. After my mother had put us to bed, I was cold and went out in my stocking-feet to warm myself at the fire walking down the wagon-tongue to where father was standing. When I came back I stepped into the bucket of water set inside, whereupon my father came and got my stocking to dry it by the fire; holding it too close, he scorched it across the white stripes at the top—my best Sunday stockings, knitted of the finest "cross-banded" yarn, dark blue, and soft, and warm.

There is perhaps no better proof of the strong affection existing between the members of each of the two families from which I am directly descended than these long and hard wagon journeys, taken once a year to visit some far-distant brother or sister. When the difficulties of travel in those days are considered, these journeys even seem heroic. Wilderness roads, unbridged streams to be forded, no wayside taverns or but few, probable storms to be encountered, the springless farm wagon with its bows over which was stretched the canvas cover—house by day and bedroom by night—frosty nights, for late August and September were the only months in which the farms could be left: all this made a visit something more than a mere outing for pleasure. Other visits to his family connections were made by my Grandfather James Ryan, and by them in return.

On one occasion in the late thirties or early forties my grandfather walked from his home near Eaton to visit his sister Sally, Mrs. Jacob H. Kern, who lived near Fincastle, Virginia. He in turn was visited by the Kerns, who came in a covered wagon, bringing with them a slave woman named Jin. This black woman aroused great curiosity among my grandfather's younger children, who had never seen a black face nor known a visitor who did not sit to eat with the family. The Kerns made a fortnight's stay, and later their son Jacob Kern, who had recently married a Miss Nancy Legget, came with her and stayed for several months. He afterwards went to Indiana to settle. Another aunt who married an Englishman named Sidebotham came to visit from a long distance also, and her son Henry later spent part of a year at my grandfather's home. I remember two or three incidents of this cousin's visit; one of these relates to a great iron pot of ink which he was making over the living room fire, of logwood, oak bark and I know not what else. Two of his cousins, my aunts, were teasing him, and interfering with his chemistry in some way which caused a good deal of laughter. I thought he must be making ink to last all his life. I think he was a student at the time.

In those regions of the country which were distant from the natural highways, the navigable rivers, mails were uncertain and infrequent so that people seldom heard from each other. Those who traveled, for whatever reason, often carried news by word of mouth to people along the way, of their friends in other parts. I suppose it was with others of the time much as it was with my great-grand-father's large family. Of the ten brothers and sisters, some went south and some went west. My grandfather's family lost track of his three oldest brothers, George, William, and Samuel, soldiers of the Revolutionary War, nor have we any record of two of the sisters.

The first house my father owned was a hewn log building of one big square room with a large brick chimney and fireplace on the north, built inside. The floors were of ash; the kitchen was a lean-to built on the whole of the east side, and at first with a puncheon floor. In the further end was the place for the loom, which my father had made. The front door of the house opened on the middle of the west wall with a window of two sashes and small panes on either side of it. At first each door had a wooden latch with a leather latch-string, later replaced by an iron thumb-latch. Rude wooden steps led up, as the floor was three or four feet from the ground. A shed at the further side of the kitchen made a place for wood and farm utensils. A ladder at first and a narrow staircase afterwards, led to the loft above, which was made by laying rough wide boards on the beams overhead. A smokehouse in the backyard for curing meats for family use, a milk house in front under some cherry trees and near the well, both made of small round logs, a log stable at some distance to the north with its corncribs attached, made up the conveniences for living. The house and appurtenances stood in the south end of a two- or three-acre lot, which my grandfather had given my mother, but to which she had no deed.

The living room had in it two high-posted beds with the usual feather mattresses and under mattresses of straw laid upon cords tightly stretched from side to side and end to end. Handmade linen, quilts and blue and white coverlets, valances, "canopies" with curtains netted by my mother, completed the bed furnishings. A trundle bed was pushed under my mother's bed during the daytime and drawn out at night for the children. By the window nearest the fireplace was the table, a square one with let-down leaves, of walnut,

I think. On the left of the chimney was the cupboard of some hard dark wood. Between the two beds against the south wall stood the cherry-wood bureau with deep drawers and glass knobs, a place of great interest to us babies, when we were allowed to look into it as our mother put away or took out things. By the door leading to the kitchen on a shelf stood an old-fashioned clock, three or four feet high, which had once had a looking glass in its lower panel, I was told, but which in my memory had a colored lithograph of "The Crucifixion." Under this stood the cherry-wood candle-stand, and usually between it and the best bed (there was a third one in the loft) was the walnut cradle, made and carved by my father for me, and used for all my sisters. A pair of andirons and a hand-wrought shovel and tongs made the furnishing of the fireplace.

The well was surrounded by a wooden curb, about five-feet high, and made from the cross section of a hollow gum tree, and had a sweep for drawing water. This with the little log milk house nearby, covered in summer with blue morning-glories and shaded by a cherry tree, made what I know now to have been at least one picturesque bit in our surroundings.

Not far to the north of the smokehouse, in the backyard, was a little shelter for two or three bee-gums, that is, beehives made of a cross section of a gum tree of smaller diameter than the well curb. The gum tree was a rare tree in southwestern Ohio, as it belongs much farther south. The only one of the kind which I remember stood in the edge of Banta's Woods, two or three hundred yards from our corncribs. Its leaves were very shiny and of a brilliant red in autumn. Its habit of decaying throughout its healthy looking trunk, to within about three inches of the surface, so that while it was fully alive it might be toppled over by a sudden wind, made the gum tree a peculiarly useful kind of timber to the settler, as it supplied him with ready-made well curbs, big wooden buckets, and beehives with little labor in the making. Hence the word bee-gum came to be used for beehive.

Near the beehives was an oblong garden patch, not unlike in its arrangement to my grandmother's, even to the tree moss, rue, saffron, and Johnny-jump-ups, these last being the little *Viola tricolor* which had a look about them that none of their aristocratic progeny, the pansies, have ever contrived to get, through all their evolutions. But our one most precious flower was a damask rose, planted by my mother at the corner of the house, just as my grandmother's was. I used to stand on tiptoe, in admiration and wonder, to look at its first open blossom, with its bright red petals and its circle of thickly set yellow anthers, and to smell its fragrance. We had no other flowers excepting those that came over from the woods into our grounds. Somewhere on the back fence each year, were gourd vines, bearing large, long-handled gourds used in making dippers for wash day, or large round ones, cut into vessels for holding soft soap, or small, curved-handled ones for drinking dippers; sometimes too, pretty little striped ones for children's play things.

A large and tall beech tree stood just outside the southeast corner of the house yard and an equally large and tall linden tree shaded the southwest corner and was a delightful personage, I might say, in our surroundings, on account of its myriad sweet-scented blossoms in the spring, where innumerable bees hummed as they pastured. The widespread roots of the same tree harbored in a hole in one of their angles a great toad, which used to come out at dusk and feed on angleworms we offered to him, and stick out one fat side when we tickled the other with a stick, and blink at us with his golden eyes.

By the linden tree, or "linn-tree" as we called it, opened the gate into the lane through the Big Woods, which lane led off eastward to the West Road from town and by the brick house of some people named Wellborn; they had a beautiful daughter with curling black hair and red cheeks named Derexy, who was a friend of my mother.

At ten years of age I left this log house life. This came about partly because my father and mother wanted better opportunities for their children's education, and partly because the land upon which our house was built was taken by the administrators of my grandfather's estate, as he had failed to give my mother a deed for it, simply through neglect.

3

Schools and Schoolmasters

Dooley's Schoolhouse as I first knew it was a little, square log building of the pioneer fashion—built of unhewn logs "daubed and chinked," a door in the middle of the front side, a window of small panes in either end and a long narrow one, occupying the space made by leaving out one or two logs in the side opposite the door. The furniture was a long slanting bench made against the wall for a desk, and a high puncheon, or plank, bench without a back, in front of it, to sit on. When writing one sat with face to the wall and at other times facing the other way. A lower bench of the same kind stood in front of that, serving as a seat for the little children and often as a footrest for those behind them. This arrangement held for the two ends of the room. Parallel to the long, narrow window and facing the middle of the room was a high, wide bench, behind which was a lower, narrower one to sit on. This was for the older scholars; a high and low bench, similar to the ones along the ends of the room, in front of that completed the furniture for the children, except a cross section of a log, or beam used as a dunce-block.

In the middle was a large stove. The open space between the door and the corner was occupied by the teacher's desk and chair, both handmade of thick, yellow "poplar"* plank, the chair sometimes of the variety known as "split-bottom," or hickory bottom. This description fits in every respect the pioneer schoolhouse built in every district of this region. The name of the schoolhouse was taken from the name of the owner of the land upon which it stood. Dooley's Schoolhouse stood on the upper bank of Paint Creek, which ran along one side of a piece of open wood, with a large elm in

*Tulip tree, *Liriodendron tulipifera* as lumber called yellow poplar.

the end nearest, and grassy meadow-like spaces among the scattered trees where we played at noontimes.

My first teacher there when I was five was Lucy Wilkinson, a widow with one little girl, whose pretty clothes were the admiration of the other children. I do not remember learning anything in the few weeks that I was there except what I learned at play: that it was a sad thing to be ugly, and have freckles; that it was nice to lock arms with another girl who liked you, and walk up and down singing,

> The last lovely morning,
> All blooming and fair
> Is fast onward fleeting
> And soon will appear,
> While the mighty, mighty trump sounds,
> Come, come away,

which I suppose now to have been the remnant of some camp meeting hymn.

Nancy Crane had freckles and was "ugly," so said the other girls, who did not choose her to play, although she brought "pretty pieces" (scraps of calico) as everyone had been asked to do by the big girls, who had been planning to play "house." Although I had not been allowed to bring the pretty pieces, they let me play no doubt because I was the youngest. But what made me feel so bad that I crept off to the upper end of the wood to sit down upon an old burnt log, beside poor Nancy who sat there raining tears down her freckled cheeks, into the pretty pieces in her lap? But so I did, and we comforted each other and looked at the pieces. This must have been about the summer of 1846.

Dooley's Schoolhouse was then in its last days, as it was torn down in 1848. It had been the pioneer educational institution of the time of my father's and mother's schooling. There they had met under George Washington Daly, who was later my own teacher in the new Dooley's Schoolhouse. This stood a quarter of a mile beyond the site of the old one in the corner of a beautiful beech wood, and near fine fields of meadow and wheat land. Samuel S. Young, who afterwards married my father's sister Eliza, had also taught in the old schoolhouse.

The Dooley's were in my time three brothers, sons of Silas Dooley, Sr., mentioned earlier; two of them had adjacent farms, on one of which stood the old schoolhouse called by their name. The new schoolhouse was in use until 1877, when it was replaced by a more modern building with the same name. It was, when built, a good "weather-board" wooden house with plaster walls, a high platform, a little blackboard above it, wooden desks, and backless benches all ranged on the sides of the room like pews. Winter and summer a big stove stood in the middle.

My first real schooling, however, outside of my own home was at Bailey's Schoolhouse, two miles southeast—a log building like that described as Dooley's Schoolhouse and built, as were all pioneer schoolhouses by intention, near a piece of woodland. I went as a visitor with my Aunt Juliet, a girl of eleven, for a few days in the spring of 1846 to a teacher named Frances Acton, a maiden lady who was considered to know enough to teach a summer school, as it consisted mainly of small children beginning to read and spell. The next summer I went for a month or two to the same schoolhouse to a young man teacher. I remember nothing of this school except an incident or two of the playground. The going to and from across the fields and woods was the main part of the schooling to me. The paths inside the field fences were safest, and had the added attraction of being full of entertaining objects along the corners of the worm-fence—in spring, elder flowers, blackberry blossoms, wild violets, later in midsummer, berries and the late wild flowers. Here and there a most desirably thickety place full of birds, and maybe birds' nests—wrens, hairbirds, and robins.

I suppose I spelled in the earlier pages of *Webster's Spelling Book*, which was *the* book of the log schoolhouse. Children were not permitted to have readers until they could "spell through" the spelling book, from cover to cover. I was reading at home for myself before I was allowed to at school. When my father and mother discovered that I was enjoying the reading lessons—mostly fables—in the back of the book, and trying newspaper paragraphs, they bought me a new *Second Reader*. In the same way later I was advanced far more rapidly than my understanding justified because I could handle polysyllables without winking. From McGuffey's *Second* to the *Fourth Reader* is a long step, which I took unquestioningly without knowing much about the things I read there. However, my memory of these things and of an education really begun belongs to the first winter school in this schoolhouse, to which I went with my father, who was the teacher. Young men and young women, big boys and girls, and only two other little girls were my schoolmates. Everything in the house was exactly like that in the Dooley Schoolhouse, excepting that there hung on the wall, to the left of the door, a flat wooden paddle, on one side of which was printed in large black letters OUT, and on the other IN. When one wished to leave the room he did not disturb the master, but if the word IN was toward the school, he reversed the paddle and went out, again reversing it on his return.

Webster's Spelling Book, as I have said, was the chief instrument of primary education in Ohio in the forties and fifties. In our districts it was a matter of course that children should be able to spell every word in that book from a-b, ab, at the beginning, to such words as *impenetrability*, and the definitions and abbreviations at the end, besides the numbering to one thousand in Roman letters. Then one might take the *First* or *Second Reader*. I never had the *First Reader*, except to read as a story book between whiles by borrowing in school. The *Second Reader* was soon done with, and I read a little in Wilson's *History of the United States* until I went to the Dooley School, where Mr. Daly put me at once at eight years of age into the *Fifth Reader*, very little of which I understood then, except that I had soon found all the stories in it for myself. At the Bailey School, while I was still under eight, I read through *Colburn's Mental Arithmetic*—read through, I say, because I had not one mathematical idea, and merely said over the analysis and solution of all the problems after my teacher, word for word, a harmless exercise. Thus I was saved from the mischief which might have been the result had I been put through "grades" after the present system, and been compelled to cram problems for the understanding of which I had as yet not reached the mental development.

At the Daly School I made an effort to learn the multiplication table, as desired, from the back of my writing book. But as nobody thought of explaining *how* 7 times 8 was 56, I did not get beyond the 2's until after I was ten, in the town school in Eaton. There I saw for myself, by counting, the mysterious truth of so-many-times one thing being another thing, and all was easy enough. After this I learned in two or three years all the arithmetic I ever knew, practically, until I began to teach it. As a matter of fact, I was, as they

[30]

said, "good in arithmetic," but not until I could understand the reason of everything. The let-alone method in the district school saved my intellectual life, I am convinced, in every direction. I should have been an utter dunce if I had been subjected to some of the irrational methods of the present.

In my seventh or eighth year, under what teacher I do not remember, but at the Bailey School, I learned what it was to "speak a piece." It was, I believe, always a voluntary exercise. As none of the children had any books except their school readers, they selected little poems and other pieces from these. I could not memorize except with the greatest difficulty. Words I remembered easily whether I understood them or not, but my memory refused to take hold of sentences, at least by any conscious effort of mine. I listened with admiration to some of my mates who stood up and recited "Casa Bianca," "The Hollow Tree" or even "Lazy Sheep, pray tell me why?" But I envied most the little girl who recited "We are Seven." I saw the hair, thick with many a curl, that clustered round the head of the little cottage girl, and made a picture of the churchyard to which she took her little porringer to eat her supper there. Thus, unconsciously, I began to know my Wordsworth. After much painful effort I was at last able to stand up and recite this four-line stanza, which I now remember was quoted in some didactic prose of the *Third Reader*:

> With books or work or healthful play
> Let your first years be passed,
> That you may give for every day
> Some good account at last.

Strange as it may seem, I did not understand what this meant. One of the big girls of the school, Hannah Banta, an orphan niece of Peter Banta, recited a piece of prose from the *Fourth Reader*, of which I have a dim recollection of thinking that the complaint expressed in it about being misunderstood was personal to the girl herself, although she was a gay, happy, carefree young person. Also I wondered why she did not select verses.

At the Bailey School the custom of studying aloud was still a matter of course even in the winter school taught by my father in 1847. The children and young women and young men of all ages studied aloud whatever lessons they were next to recite at the master's knee, or standing before him in a class of three or four. Thus, anybody passing on the road could hear whether the children were kept at work by the master. A school in full operation was likely to be heard at least a quarter of a mile from the house. This was especially true of a time when everybody was preparing a spelling lesson, just before noon. Then each had his own speed, his own pitch of voice, and with his greater or less skill in spelling or pronouncing, spelled over the lesson from *Webster's Spelling Book.*

At other times of the day one might hear a definition in grammar, or bits of parsing, or the reading of a *Second Reader* story, or scraps of the multiplication table. But these were the last years of the loud schools. So far as I know, the first quiet school at Bailey's was in 1849 or 1850. George W. Daly had introduced silent study in the Dooley School a little earlier. The change was rather hard, as the children thought, at the first school of this kind at Bailey's, and by special favor we were permitted to study aloud on Friday afternoons.

In looking back over my schooling in these early years in the two district schools which I have described, I find that the greatest differences between the methods there practiced and those of the schools of the present time lie in the fact, first, that the teaching was individual, and, second, that there was no attempt to teach more than three subjects at a time. Iteration characterized the elementary lessons taught from books. Obedience was the chief moral lesson and was unvaryingly exacted.

George W. Daly (pronounced Dal-ly), my father's and mother's teacher for the little schooling they had, and also my own teacher for two or three school years, was an Irishman, probably American born, without an Irish accent at least. He had often been at our house before I was of school age. When I first knew him as a teacher in my seventh or eighth year, he was white-haired except for a single jet-black lock on the very crown of his head, had blue eyes, always a clean-shaven face, inclined to redness, and often very red, a straight, large, commanding figure, and decisive agile steps and movements. He was a notable man in that region and in that day and was considered one of the best disciplinarians of his time— severe, but just. As I remember, there seemed to be very little "discipline" in the school sense, as all went on quietly as he would have it, without words. It was known that he had a thick beech switch and that he could easily be made to use it—severely—if any dared to transgress. I do not remember when he taught us "manners," but we always stopped to curtsy or bow at the door as we were dismissed one by one.

If he happened to be looking away, which I think he did purposely sometimes, each child stood still in the door until he looked up. We could not bear to lose the "good evening" and the bow he gave to each of us. Besides all that, we did not like to be reproached by our mates as we left school with, "You didn't make your manners." He used to walk about the room in the summer in his woolen-stocking feet, which seemed proper and right to us, as his shoes troubled him. My mother told me that he usually went barefoot in summer, at his farm, which was somewhere in Indiana. He was very fond of me, which came from the fact that I was a sort of grand-pupil of his. He brought his stockings to my mother to be darned, and often spent evenings with us. If he came after I had been put into my trundle bed, he always had me haled out, dressed, and brought to the fire, where he stood on the hearth and read to me, usually from McGuffey's *Fifth Reader*, which in its early edition form, was (and still would be if it were in print) one of the best reading books yet made for schools.

I was at that early age (eight, nine, ten) reading that book at school, without understanding much of what I read. Southey's "The Cataract of Lodore," some notion of whose meaning I did have, was a favorite of mine. Usually, however, Mr. Daly read Hood's "Ode to an Infant Son," or Dimond's "The Sailor Boy's Dream," or Southey's "The Maid of the Inn," all of which poems his reading made me understand; even Hood's "Ode," with its droll humor, got through my infantile understanding, when he read it. There was something wonderfully fascinating in his voice, to which my father and mother, and even infant I, would have been glad to listen till midnight. He had the reputation of being the best reader in the area, a distinction which he retained past his eightieth year, when I heard him read at a teacher's examination immediately after his hurried arrival from a train and climbing a long flight of stairs. He called at my father's house then, which must have been about 1855 or 1856. We heard of his death not long after, at his home in Indiana.

[33]

It was not until after I was grown up that I understood why we had school on Saturday forenoons frequently, and occasionally no school on Mondays. This had been true, as I was then told, throughout his teaching years in this district. The man's character was so admirable, his scholarship so exceptional, and his teaching so thorough that the neighborhood had long before my time tacitly agreed to overlook the fact that he had occasional fits of drinking. But the children were never allowed to know that this was the reason for his Monday absences. I have still a card written by him and given to me as a prize for being head of the spelling class at the end of the week. It had on one side my name, "Irena Hardy"; on the other, "Head, Saturday afternoon, July, 1851."

Books were very scarce and precious in the log schoolhouse days of my time. Our neighbors had seldom any but the Bible, possibly a copy of Flavius Josephus, and, besides, as in my grandfather's case Rollin's *History of Rome*. Such other books as they had were a few school books which were handed down in turn to the younger children as the older ones staid at home to work. *Webster's Spelling Book*, as I have said, was the chief instrument of teaching spelling and reading. In the forties, McGuffey's *Readers* had come in, and some of the older young people of the winter schools read in the *Fourth* and *Fifth Readers*. Others brought such books as they had, sometimes the New Testament, or a history.

In most families the newly bought book for school was covered with figured calico or stout gingham and usually had attached by a thread to the top a neatly folded paper, which was held under the thumb at the bottom of the book, while the child studied his lesson. Whenever he turned the leaf he moved the "thumb paper." Even the young men and young women in the winter schools used the thumb paper, which was sometimes elaborately decorated and shaped by the scissors. I remember seeing some spelling books, first readers, and arithmetics dog-eared, dirty, and worn where the thumbs had held, until they had worn through nearly to the back. I still recall an uncomfortable feeling of childish judgment about children who used their books so badly. Certain families had the idea that arithmetic was the essential part of knowledge, that you must be able to "go through the arithmetic" or you had no learning. So that not infrequently a boy would come to school with an arithmetic only, and devote his whole time to that, "ciphering" from morning to night. The common question was, "How fur you got in cipherin'?" He took no other part in the school exercises unless he chose to go into the spelling class, which included the whole school. Copy books were made of foolscap paper cut in halves and sewed into a cover. The master set the copies and made the goose-quill pens. He sometimes had to be careful about the sentiments he wrote in their alphabetical order for copies; as for instance, I remember a young woman being angry because the schoolmaster (who happened to be my father) set for the copy in E, "Evil communications corrupt good manners." I sat next to her and wondered why she was mad at that. I suppose she knew.

Some of the patterns of the calico covers I have mentioned became a part of the furniture of my memory; one in particular belonged to a little red-headed boy named Nathan D. It was of a deep orange color, thickly sprinkled with oval white spots, about which I was curious, as I had heard two of the young men and my father talking about Nathan and praising his cleverness. One of the young men said, "Yes, Nate sees everything; he is all eyes." I concluded that the white spots on the cover of his book, which usually faced me on the other side of the room, must have something to do with the number of his eyes, which I could not see differed from those of other people.

Nobody studied geography and there were no maps. I never saw a map in a schoolhouse until after we had moved to Eaton, nor had I ever seen a map until I was sent to the geography school in Berea Chapel. About 1849 my father walked to Dayton, Ohio, twenty-eight miles away, bought a pair of large hemisphere maps, and carried them back on his shoulders. He used to study these after hanging one of them at a time from a beam in the living room. They reached from the low ceiling nearly to the floor. At these times of study, my little sister Adelaide used to go to the maps and put her fingers on a very bright-colored country named Thibet and the next one to it called Little Thibet. Her gurgles of delight at the brilliant blues and yellows so amused my father that he nicknamed her Tib, and the six-months-old baby Little Tib, which names he used for them for some years.

The geography school to which I went in the summer of my seventh year was taught by a travelling teacher who brought a pair of hemisphere maps to the neighborhood and opened a class for lessons in "singing geography." The children and young people went to Berea Chapel, sat on benches, looked up at the wall map, as the teacher pointed, and sang over the names of the countries and their capitals, and of all natural features of the continents and islands. The teacher pointed, for instance, to the river farthest north on the east coast of Asia and so on down in order to all the rivers of the coast, chanting each twice over, with the class. Thus we chanted all the rivers, mountains, deserts, bays, lakes, oceans of the big round world, but learned nothing except the curiously fascinating names, shapes, and colors of the countries on the map. The geography man took his leave at the end of the eight or ten lessons, and went to the next district. Later my father gave similar lessons after he had bought his own maps and studied them.

Among the books of my earliest recollection was my father's own arithmetic book, made, as was the custom when he was a schoolboy, by himself at school. This consisted of a copy in a large blank-book of every word, and of every worked-out example in the printed arithmetic. It meant also the making of a great many ornamental capital letters and headings of the various kinds of examples, in large letters adorned with color. On many pages were elaborate initial letters beginning a new subject, sometimes of fantastic invention, sometimes outline copies of a picture in pen drawing. Of these, one which I often looked at and pondered over was an outline of Raphael's "Madonna of the Chair," drawn in the large exaggerated curve of a capital script E. Where my father had got this, or seen it, I do not know, as I never saw the picture in our own house nor in the homes of our neighbors; nor had we any books with such pictures in them. And curiously enough, our neighbors would have said, "Why that's a Catholic picture! What do you want of that?" They really did say this of the picture in the clock-front, which was "A Crucifixion." Every schoolboy of the backwoods in my father's boyhood made such a book of arithmetic, if he arrived at such a stage of learning as to be permitted to attempt it. Unfortunately, the book was destroyed in our ignorance of its historical value, when I was a young girl.

At the Bailey School, in the early years of my school life, when we did not play in the woods nearby, or in the corners of the field

[36]

fence, we usually played games in the open yard about the school-house. "Black Man" and "Pizen" were always popular, as all the children could take part at the same time. A few other games, as "Sun and Moon," "Fried Eggs," "Chicky-Me-Crainy-Crow," and "Tag" were favorites. Most of these are still played by children in schools all over the land.

"Sun and Moon," however, I have not seen otherwheres as played then. Two of the largest and strongest girls would agree secretly to be Sun and Moon. They would stand eight or ten feet apart facing each other, and the players in a group to one side would come up, one at a time, within eight or ten feet of the line between the Sun and Moon, stop and call out: "How far is it to Briley-Bright?" "Three score miles and ten," answered the leaders. "Can I get there by candle light?" "Yes, if your legs are long and light. But look out for the old witches on the way." Then she would start to run between the two leaders, who would run to catch her. Then both leaders clasped their arms around her, whispering in her ear: "Which will you be, Sun or Moon?" When she had chosen, she was told to stand behind the luminary of her choice. When all had gone through the ordeal and stood behind the two leaders each with her hands clasped round the waist of the one in front, the two leaders grasped hands and there was a trial of strength, the weaker side tumbling over on the grass with laughter. I do not remember any quarreling or cross words in dispute about which side had won in any of these games. I do remember that the fun of the game was in playing it and not in winning it.

The only count outs of this time that I remember were:

> One - ery, oo - ery, ickery, Ann,
> Villison, Vollison, Nicholas John,
> Queevy, Quavy, English Navy,
> One, two, three,
> O - u - t
> OUT!

And:

> Wire, Briar, Limber, Lock,
> Three geese in a flock;
> One flew east and
> One flew west,
> And one flew over the cuckoo's nest.

[37]

"Keeping house" always involved a good deal of work in cleaning up the grounds. Every leaf and twig was picked out of the grass plot outlined by rails or logs for the house. Other games played about the fireside at night were such as could be played with the hands or fingers, and sitting still. Besides those commonly known now were one or two taught us by our parents and probably handed down from generations reaching back to England. "William o' Trimpity" was evidently "William of Trinity" and was in the nature of a count out, though it was itself a part of the game. It ran thus:

> William o' Trimpity,
> He catches hens,
> Puts them in pens
> Some lay eggs,
> And some lay none,
> Underfoot, Specklefoot,
> Be gone.

This was said over the fingers of one hand of each player, laid on the knee of the leader, until all the fingers were doubled under. It ended with: "Whoever speaks a word, or laughs, or shows his teeth, shall have a box and give nails," which meant a box on the ear and five slaps. The game "fist-stock" had much the same ending after a long preamble of questions and answers; the last hand is asked:

> What you got there? Bread and cheese.
> Where is my share? The cat's got it
> Where is the cat? Behind the door.
> Where is the door? In the house.
> Where is the house? In the field.
> Where is the field? In the woods.
> Where is the woods? The fire burned it.
> Where is the fire? The water quenched it.
> Where is the water? The ox drank it.
> Where is the ox? The butcher stuck him.
> Where is the butcher? The rope hung him.
> Where is the rope? The rat gnawed it.
> Where is the rat? The cat's got it behind the door.

Fee, faw, fun! The first one who speaks or laughs or shows his teeth will get a box and five nails.

When all was said, however, the favorite play was play in the woods. All the settlers' schoolhouses were built near a piece of woodland, which of itself gave better nature teaching than any modern systems or books can possibly do.

In the country districts in the forties, school privileges were very greatly prized, and losing a day of the short terms was avoided if possible. The comparatively slight importance attached to Christmas Day at that time favored the custom of keeping school without any break for holidays, from September until the term ended very early in the spring. The custom of Christmas treating had been established long before, whether in the time of my parents' childhood or not I do not know, but stories of struggle to establish it had come down to us from them. For instance, of a teacher having been taken out and ducked in a hole cut in a frozen pond because he refused either to treat or give a holiday, which alternative was conceded. But in my time the treat or the holiday had become a matter of course, and the teacher good naturedly agreed to whichever the school chose, which was usually the treat. This consisted of candy, gingerbread and apples, or sometimes of apples, sweet cider, and doughnuts; though this last was not satisfactory unless apples and cider had been made more desirable by scarcity that year.

Lessons went forward as usual on Christmas Day, until near noon, when the ginger cakes and the candies were passed around in the schoolroom to every one, old and young. The part of the treat most enjoyed by the older members of the school was the distribution of what were called sugar-kisses, little squares of caramel wrapped each exactly in the same way, in white paper which contained some sentimental couplet. The fun of exchanging, then opening the sweets and reading the sentiment, afforded not a little amusement. Young as I was then, I remember seeing sly exchanges of these verses, and blushes and conscious looks. The noon recess was usually a little longer, and the afternoon was taken up with a spelling match. The leaders in the spelling match were chosen by the teacher, any two of the older pupils, who each in his turn chose from the best spellers first, and from all the others afterward, until the whole school was divided into two sides. Who should have the first choice was determined by a stick thrown by one leader and caught by the other, and then overhanded alternately, until the stick was left in the hand of one or the other leader, who again threw it to be caught in the same way by his opponent, with whom it was measured off by the hand again, and a third time thrown. He in whose hand the stick remained at the end of the third time made the first choice.

The school having thus been divided into two parties, the leaders stood out in the middle of the floor facing each other, each in front of the contrary side in case someone should become too anxious and prompt when his champion showed signs of uncertainty before his one chance of spelling the word. These two spelled alternately until one or both missed, when the first one chosen on each side took their places, in their turn trying the word which had slain the first one or two. And so on in turn, as each one missed he sat down and the next in the line came out to spell. It sometimes happened that the best spellers at the heads of the divisions were so hard to defeat that the master had given out most of the hard words in the spelling book before the upper halves of the divisions had been sent to their seats by a missed word. The lower halves, or last chosen, were usually soon put to rout by some harmless polysyllable or knotty disyllable. It also sometimes happened that one whole side would be spelled down before half the other side had been called out. Or, in other words, it might happen that a champion speller would spell down the whole of the opposite side, and could not himself be defeated by any word in *Webster's Spelling Book*. Of course that meant victory for his side. If time enough still remained before four o'clock, another try was made by giving out words, the whole school standing, each one sitting down as he missed. He who stood last in this test had won the day. Sometimes during the winter school, a neighborhood spelling match would be held in the schoolhouse at night, to which grown people and older children went. As nobody was excused from taking part in the match, there was a good deal of fun for everybody. Once in a while, too, a match was arranged between schools of adjoining districts, the two masters taking turns in giving out the words.

I once went with my father, who was then teaching in the Hendricks District on the West Road, to a Christmas Day treat and spelling match. It was two miles away by the lane through the woods, and there was a deep crisp snow on the ground. I wore for the first time a beautiful new moss-green, homespun flannel dress with singlethread stripes of cochineal red, all woven and made by my mother. I came home happy in the evening to tell my mother how the big girls had noticed my pretty dress and how I had spelled down a long row of big boys and girls in the spelling match.

4

Feelings and Experiences

It was near our cribs and barn on the edge of the Big Woods, looking up at the budding or "flindering" beeches and maples, and hearing a peewee singing in the trees a little distance away, that I became conscious of the ME, and knew that this was *I*. I do not know how old I was, certainly not much above four. I translated the peewee's song as "Felix, felix," a name I had heard once or twice. But then it seemed to ring with an infinite sort of something which must have been sadness. The name was afterward connected otherwise with a sorrow of my later child life at school in Eaton. The peewee's song forever after had that first note in it for me.

Under the age of six I was for two or three years a sickly child, subject to nervous nights, sleepwalking, and dreadful dreams, much of which I now attribute in part to malaria. It was at this time that I experienced at night, after waking in a sweat, and often wandering out of my bed in some remote part of the room, the feelings which are so accurately described in A. W. Kinglake's *Eothen* (Chapter XIX). These constituted the most terrible moments of my life. I lay in my bed in the same room with my father and mother, speechless and trembling in every fiber of my body—frozen with something more awful than fear, wet with my own sweat from head to feet— thinking of that Awful Thing, Time and Extension, but without any consciousness of its name, seeing the line stretch away and away, right and left Forever. I had no words to tell my trouble; I did not know how to escape it. The sensation—I was always wide-awake— came to me at intervals through early life, long after my recovery from that weak state, which grew worse until it culminated in a long illness through the summer of my sixth year, after which I had again to learn to walk.

Somewhere in the neighborhood of my eighth year, there began to be talk about cholera, and I read for myself in the *Cincinnati Gazette* accounts of the ravages of that disease in the cities of Europe and Asia. Later when the epidemic appeared in American cities, the fear of the country people about me communicated itself to me, and I began to lie awake nights thinking about it, or wake dreaming of it. One of my dreams was of going in a sleigh, as fast as horses could be driven, to get away from the cholera, and knowing that it was following us, for we saw that all the leaves were dropping from the trees as the cholera came. To prevent myself from thinking of it when I went to bed, I tried to imagine something pleasant and beautiful. Nothing seemed so good at this time as to recall the face, blue eyes, and pink cheeks of my Aunt Mary, my Uncle John's wife, whom I admired violently. I said over her name scores of times, "Aunt Mary, Aunt Mary," until I fell asleep.

In 1849 the cholera did come—even then the vagueness of the monster did not get shaped into what it really was.* My grandfather died after a few hours of sickness, in the prime of a splendidly strong physical manhood. Several of his children were stricken, one of whom died on the day of his funeral. My youngest sister also had the sickness. Many of the townspeople in Eaton, two and a half miles away, died, and many fled. One little village in our neighborhood of eight hundred inhabitants, Boston by name, was entirely depopulated, except for one solitary man, who stayed in his home and lived through to tell the tale. I have still the recollection that the neighbors of my grandfather's region never hesitated to help all they could without fear, when the sickness really came. My mother and father scarcely left my grandfather, who wanted "Mary" (my mother) only to wait upon him. I was left to take care of my three sisters—one, the baby Caroline, not yet six months old, my mother running down home to see to us for a few minutes every few hours. Changing all her clothes in a shed behind the house, she hung everything in the open air away from the house, came in to nurse the baby and feed us, and went back again.

We saw the funeral cortege of neighbors go by across the field

---

*"The Cholera Season of 1849" is described in *History of Preble County, Ohio. . . H. Z. Williams & Bro* (W. W. Williams, Cleveland, Ohio, 1881), pp. 122–24; hereafter noted as *History of Preble County*. [Ed. note]

and knew that grandfather was gone, we knew not how or why. My sisters Laurinda and Adelaide and I went behind the house, climbed the high fence, the better to see across the fields, looked at each other silently, looked at the funeral train, and knew that we should weep, and as for me, I felt like weeping, but went dry-eyes back into the house to the baby. A few weeks later after all was over, we were allowed to go up to grandmother's to play in the orchard, but not to go into the house. The ground under the peach trees was covered with over-ripe fruit; a smell of peaches was in the air; a few quilts still hung on the garden fence, left there since the sickness. A feeling, mercifully undefinable, again came over me of the heaviness of Space and the Awfulness of Time. I can still see the pitiful little image of the child *ME* there helpless in the hot sunshine which was full of the odor of over-ripe peaches—standing still and feeling and thinking, or, rather, struggling to think.

Just how or where I picked up any notions of religion when I was a little child I do not remember; some I had of my own, however. My parents were church members and churchgoers. Sunday was scrupulously kept in that no work more than was necessary was done—to sew on Sunday was especially wicked and besides disgraceful. To visit and receive visits was customary and not ill thought of in the community. To work in the fields on Sunday was a clear defiance of God and the opinions of one's neighbors. The neighborhood consensus about lying, swearing, card playing, and dancing was well agreed that all these things were bad. When the preacher or church members came to dinner, everybody had grace said; but in no families that I knew before I was ten was that observed as a daily custom. I went to church and Sunday school, and learned "verses" for next Sunday. I read and got notions from Sunday school books by scores—little, thin coarse-print volumes bound in marbled boards with red-leather backs.

Some theories I worked out for myself: as that the good—and I was one of the good—would have wings (when? I did not arrange that) and be able to fly up above the beech woods, where I often saw myself in fancy floating just below the bright summer clouds. The bad would be down on the earth and look up to see the floating angels with wings—just the same gingham-aproned little girl I was,

I saw bewinged, and looked up to by the naughty boys and girls that did bad things—swore or lied.

"O the Bad Man'll get you if you do that; my mother says so," was a speech common enough, at school or at play, with neighbor children. "Bad Man" was the circumlocution easily fitted to childish lips and used generally by children as well as by those talking to them with threats.

After our removal to Eaton, I went to the Christian Sunday school in the old Public Church in the mornings, and later both to that and to the Methodist Sunday school in the basement of the Methodist Church on Main Street. The result was not wholly to my advantage, as I had already begun to think about what I heard. Trying to learn the Methodist Catechism (which of course was all true, certainly, I thought) and gradually getting at the New Light Christian point of view pretty generally mixed up my theology, so that I never got it untangled to any degree until I went to college, where Dr. Thomas Hill's sermons, the college prayer meetings, and the general atmosphere of thoughtful common-sense views made a leading out of the maze and amaze.

My father and mother, and, for that matter, most of those I knew, were reticent people on most things relating to the inner life. The people in the Christian Church did not ask you if you were "one of the saved." They seldom mentioned the name of the Lord, and never in that familiar, unctuous way sometimes heard from others. They prayed publicly in the prayer meetings, but with a reserve and simplicity born of a personal sense of humility. Nor were they often excited in an emotional way over religious matters. "Shouting" and "Amen" and "Praise-the-Lord's" were seldom heard in the churches of the New Light. I remember that my mother thought them all indecorous and out of place. Possibly the Catholic blood in her and the Puritan blood in my father were at one in this particular. Be that as it may, my own choice was to be silent on many things that other people at times saw fit to be free about. And not that only, but certain other personal reserves were carried further in our family— my mother's and her mother's—than in any other I knew when I was young, or have known since. I do not say that this was better; I only say that it was.

Outward observance of religious forms there was not at any time

[44]

in my home life, but a general feeling of the presence of God, and a sense of responsibility about what one was told to do or not to do made good air to grow in. Promptness to the hour set for coming home when we went by permission to grandmother's or to a neighbor's was exacted. "When the long hand is at twelve and the short hand is at four, you must start home" was the order. Failure to be on time brought punishment, so surely that infringement was rare. But long days of freedom in the woods and fields, few restrictions, and a large amount of delight and liberty made life a long joy.

Dolls were not part of my education. To be sure, I made dolls of rags, of hollyhocks, of sticks and leaves in the woods to serve for inhabitants of my stick towns, but a real doll I never had until I was six or seven years old. Then a cousin who had outgrown such playthings at fourteen or fifteen gave me, reluctantly, as I remember, and at her mother's command, her own best doll, a creature of wood, sawdust, and plaster of Paris as head. She wore a carefully made canary-colored gown, with neat tuck for outgrowing, on which was sewed some edging. Her sleeves also were finished with edging and her handmade underclothing—of course handmade; there were no machines—were examples of my cousin's work.

My doll never rose to the dignity of a name in my mind, and was never played with much, usually reposing in a bureau drawer. My sister Laura had a smaller doll of the same kind, and we always played with them at the same time, hardly knowing how. Once we played after a rain, out by the currant bushes, standing the dolls up on the bushy tops, and dandling them from one branch to another. A sudden outcry from Laura made me look at her doll whose face had fallen off and left the empty head staring in a most fearful way, as if the whole thing looked out at us. The horror of that empty face I shall never forget.

Nor had we other playthings except the best that any children could have: all the wood treasures were at our call and touch. Kittens of course we had, but also toads, harmless snakes, beetles— a big "horn bug" (*Lucanus*), the "Bess-Bug" (another *Lucanus*), the velvet-spotted Spring-beetle, frogs in the ponds, tadpoles— all these live things, with innumerable adaptations of chance objects found in the woods. And fantastic bits of bark or stick,

[45]

chips, strips of pawpaw bark, puff balls with their clouds of "smoke," as we called it, hard wood fungi with white undersides on which we drew clock faces to make timepieces for our playhouses among the roots of the elms and beeches. And still more: acorn cups and saucers, flowers, berries, nuts, sweet sprouts of berry vines, young hickory-nut growths, beech-nuts sprouting—the whole "Big Woods" and "Little Woods" full from winter to winter, from summer to summer—all these we had.

Before I was ten years old, my reading consisted of such books as we had and the two or three weekly papers, the *Cincinnati Gazette*, and another paper. At intervals I also read the *Ohio Cultivator*, old numbers of which I found in the loft in an old well-cleaner. This was, I may explain, a cross section of a red gum tree, with a wood bottom put in, and a wooden hoop bail—a large bucket used to go down into the well in the times when it was necessary to clean it; not in use it stood in a corner of the loft serving as a receptacle for various kinds of castoffs. It was in this old bucket that I found, one memorable day, when I was seven and a half or eight, an old book with faded, muslin cover, undervalued because it seemed mere idle tales, I suppose.

The Club Book, another copy of which I have never seen or heard of, was a collection of tales of various kinds, two or three of which contained Scottish dialect. These I read over and over again, and evidently to such purpose that when Scott's novels fell into my hands I was at home in the style. The two tales of this kind that I remember were *Gowden Gibbie* and *The Deerstalkers*, the latter a story of the Scotch Covenanters, with whom I was ever after in sympathy, though understanding then little of what their troubles were all about. I think there was also a tale called "The Covenanters." The other, and, to me, the most delightful, was "The Gypsy of the Abruzzo," a romantic love story with a gypsy, a Lady Constanza, a gallant lover, a desperate escape, and a happy ending. I would give much for a copy of this book now. Our own was burned for fire-lighters when I was about thirteen. My father had a copy of Robert Pollok's *Course of Time*, into which I sometimes looked with baffled curiosity. Young's *Night Thoughts* was there also. *The Universal Traveller*, a book of travels all over the world, compiled, I think, and sold by a peddler, was offered to me by my father, as soon as I would read it through—seven, I think I was. I read it, over and over again, in parts that I could understand, but nothing would induce me to read *words* that had no meaning. Legends, stories, marriage and burial customs, and the like were given at length and these I read, but laws and government and so on—no; so that I did not come into possession of the book until I was a big girl.

Before I was ten, a cousin, William James McCown, who loved books and had a good number, gave me a copy of Campbell's *Poems*, which I read, read and re-read, even *The Pleasures of Hope*, extracts from which I had read in the school books. Campbell was long my favorite poet. I generally read poems in newspapers without understanding much. Besides these were the Sunday school books, from our own little Berea Chapel library—some travels, especially missionary, and a number of thin little goody, goody stories, about good children who died young, or curious tales of English life which were so foreign in the society they depicted that they made little impression except that of "special wonder." In my eighth and part of my tenth year reading was fortified by the books taken from the Presbyterian and Methodist libraries in town, to which my cousin Claribel, two years and more older than I, went, and who kindly sent them every week to be returned before the next Sunday. Many of them were of the good-die-young type. Also at this time Claribel sent fairy stories and other stories to me, which I eagerly read and re-read.

Before I was allowed at school to have a reader, I used to sit in my little chair in front of my father's knees as he read the *Weekly Gazette*; this I had just brought in from the crossroad sign-post which I had the habit of watching for an hour or two from the fence of our yard to see the neighbor who brought our mail leave it in the sign-post box. Then I would "streak it" (as the common saying was) down the road and bring it up, triumphantly, enjoying the newspaper-y smell of printer's ink as I ran. I sat before my father as he opened it and read it, and patiently read the turned-over top while he read on unconscious of what I was about; so that I soon was able to read with the page upside down as well as right side up—an accomplishment I made use of in my earliest teaching experiences.

5

Growing

Very early, somewhere between four and five, I came to learn what a Lie was, at least that it was something unnamably bad. And this was the way of it: My mother had left me and my sister at home alone for a short time while she ran up to grandmother's on some errand. By some chance, I do not remember how, I came to think of the sugar-keg that stood full of fresh brown maple sugar—our usual supply of sweetening made at home—by the wall in the living room. One lesson I knew pretty thoroughly and had known for a long time—not to touch what did not belong to me. But fresh sugar was so good and there was the baby wanting some too with her wordless way of asking—for though she was nearly four she did not talk in intelligible words at all—and we both went into the sweet brown stuff and ate all we wanted. When mother came home she saw signs, and said to me, "Did you take some sugar?" "No," answered I promptly, with what behind the answer I do not know, except possibly the fear of slapped hands. Little Laura clung to my dress, and I am sure we looked a pair of culprits with our mouths smeared with the brown stuff. I do not remember whether my mother whipped me or not—I think not—but I do remember learning from what she said and the way she said it, and her shame and sorrow, what a dreadful thing a *L I E* was— a most awful word, as bad to say as to swear. I had heard people accused of telling "a story," which had the bad meaning of an untruth, or at least of something not right, and distinctly bad, but a lie!—and I had told one! It was a shameful thing.

And not because of fear; I was seldom punished by whipping. Indeed, so little did that kind of punishment enter into my early training and that of my sisters that I have no memory of more than two or three instances. Obedience had been *given me* as a precious possession very early and to that I owed the docility of mind and the open-eyed happiness over all that was around me, which made the learning of things a delight. It was easy enough to believe that my parents knew best about what I did not know. They never failed to answer every question of my questioning mind rationally, that is, if they did not know, they said so. If they knew and did not wish to answer they said, "When you can understand that, I will tell you," in the meantime telling me whatever was to be told then—always satisfying, so far as that could be done.

But of course there were many puzzling things which I never asked about for reasons I did not know myself. As for instance, "Why was the moon so pale in the daytime?" "What was that moaning sound, soft and plaintive, heard in the fields on summer afternoons?" Perhaps that was the moon, sad because it was so pale. Long after I found that it was the sound of wild doves. I could read in the *Third Reader* before I found that out—which fact I recalled by another conjecture of its source. I had seen in that book the picture of two giraffes, one standing straight up with his head in the air near a tree top, the other with his head twisted back so that his neck looked to be in a loop. This struck me with awe and wonder, and a real pain at the pain I thought the creature suffered. So impressed was I by this, that I often thought of it when I was playing, and at last imagined I saw a giraffe with his neck twisted over a fence, making the moaning sound I had once thought the moon's. Why I would not ask, I do not know. This delusion slipped away when I had learned where giraffes lived, and that one could not be standing with a twisted neck over a staked-and-ridered fence somewhere beyond grandfather's woods.

Some preachers were dining at our house once when I was under six or thereabouts. It was customary when company was present for children to wait until their elders had finished dinner before they had theirs, and we had not been called in from the woods. But in the middle of the meal we came in delighted with some new thing we had found—a green butternut, I think—and brought it at once to the table to show to mother. I held it in my two hands made into a cup while with a laugh of delight I said, "See what we have found," and without paying any attention to the guests. My mother, a little annoyed, said, "O that's nothing but a butternut," and went on serving. Suddenly aware of the visitors, I hung bashfully by my mother's chair knob—swinging half round, and staring, I suppose, when one of the men suddenly said, "Who was the first man, little girl?" and I answered as promptly as unexpectedly, "George Washington," much to the mortifying and scandalizing of my father and mother. A very immediate lesson on Adam and Eve, the Six Days of Creation, and the Flood followed this display of heathenish ignorance.

In my early childhood I came to hear a great deal about mad dogs. No real cases of madness ever occurred in our immediate neighborhood, though several suspicious dogs had been seen. So great was the fear of them, however, that most children had thoroughly learned the lesson of suspicion with respect to strange dogs, or of any dog running alone on the road. I was taught to climb the fence at once at sight of a dog coming on the road, and to stand perfectly still until he had passed by. The long distance from school often left little children on their way to and from, unprotected for a mile or two. In the Dooley neighborhood, one or two cases of bitten horses and cattle justified the common fear.

In a little valley on Lower Paint, some seven miles away from Eaton, the people of the farms about the hills were on their way home from the little church in the valley. A twelve-year-old boy was ahead of the crowd on the road; a dog foaming at the mouth ran up and bit him before he could defend himself; but he, thinking of those behind, caught the animal and called out to them to get out of the way while he held on. The brave lad, whose name was George Schrackengas, was bitten many times, but was presently relieved by a man who ran into a house nearby for a gun and shot the dog. The boy died an agonizing death in a few weeks. In that little country neighborhood George Schrackengas was long a name revered.

This story told to me at the time and often talked of in my presence made an impression of deeply mingled colors on my mind. I often thought of it when I was alone and went over the terrible details, fragmentarily gathered from the lips of those who talked it over before me and not to me. If it had not been for the woods and fields, and freedom to live and play there, I should never have righted myself from any of the tragedies that befell in the neighborhood. I can yet recall an indefinable sensation of tottering off into nothingness—a sort of mental fainting fit, that now and then obsessed my childish spirit, as if something were laboring to bring it into the place of understanding and not fearing, such as grown-up minds attain to.

But the only terror connected with my outdoor life was the fear of lightning. Before I was seven I had once been stunned to insensibility by a bolt out of a nearly clear sky, which struck and splintered a staked fence near where I lay rolling in the grass in my grandmother's yard, and had seen a maple tree in the Little Woods torn to splinters, and a tall dead trunk near the Bailey School set on fire by lightning, and could therefore not be persuaded out of most abject terror even at the mere appearance of thunder clouds. I could not be made to hold up my head at school, but hid my face on my arm or crept into the darkest corner of the room. I had the added unhappiness of feeling that my playmates thought me a baby because I was afraid. This unreasoning fear of lightning never entirely left me, though I was quite able to control it by the time I began to teach.

When I was seven or eight years old, my father and mother took us one evening to the home of the Bantas, neighbors who lived three-quarters of a mile away, if you went through the woods—the Big Woods, which belonged to them—or a mile by the road and lane; mother took her sewing to sit with Mrs. Banta, and father went to help gather and husk corn by firelight in the field nearby, where big fires were built at intervals down the corn rows. We children played about the big fireplace, told riddles, ate nuts, and burned bits of dried bladder in the fire.

Presently we went into the yard out to the garden fence to look over into the fields to see what the men were doing. We saw big fires, men jollily husking and talking in their light, and a big dog amiably moving about among them. When we turned to go back into the house I was behind because I had the care of my one and one-half-year-old sister, Adelaide, who could not walk fast. All the others had left me, and I thought I saw my father jump over the stile and go down the lane toward home. I was not sure enough to speak to him, nor did I stop to think that he would not go without my mother, but followed on as closely as I could.

The baby began to complain to be taken up; how I got her forward on the road so fast I do not know, except that I took her on my back with her arms around my neck, and carried her as fast and as long as I could; then sat down to rest, keeping my eyes on the dark figure in front, for I had decided that if it was my father he would turn down the road where the lane came into it, instead of up. When we came to the end of the lane, I saw him turn up the road, but it was too far to go back, and seemed easier to go on home.

I had no thought of what would be the effect at the farm house, but started on home by the road. A quarter of a mile from the lane, I had to pass a swampy place thick with trees, brush, and brambles, where the big girls told us there were mad dogs—for their own ends, as it appeared after, as there were berries to be had by walking on the logs into the swamp. I sat down opposite the dark spot, on a rail under a dead tree, to rest myself and the baby, whom I kept quiet by whispered "Hushes!" I looked up consciously, perhaps for the first time in my life—to the starry skies—there was no moon—and sat and said, "I don't believe there are any mad dogs—no!"

Then I went on over a piece of corduroy bridge, which led over a pond and a swampy place in the road and between the Little Woods and the Big Woods. Here I carried Addie on my back and comforted her by saying, "Nearly home now." I heard a screech owl down in the Big Woods but said to myself, "I ain't afraid o' you. I saw you once on the well curb, and you're nothing but a little bird, not so big as a hen." I was uncovering the fire to rekindle it when my mother and sister arrived in hasty fear; they had come around the road, and father had gone through the wood path to look for us. Much relieved they were to find us; they had looked the farm over, and called us everywhere with our neighbors' help. I was unconscious, wholly, of having made trouble, as I had no fear of the road, or of the dark, and I did not understand their not knowing.

My first acquaintance with death came in the Big Woods. Our old mare, Dinah, with her year-old colt had been turned into the woods for pasturage—a good place, as it had grass, water, shade, and shelter. As I was playing in the woods not far from the house with my sister one day, I saw Dinah lying down, and the colt standing with head over her. I went nearer, and understood that something had happened that I did not know about. The colt stood still, but turned to look at me. I went away without understanding why Dinah lay so still with her head stretched out so far and so low.

But sometime before this, I do not know how long, our young mare, Sally, a beautiful, cream-colored, dappled creature with long white mane and tail, had disappeared. I remembered that my father and mother had taken a lantern out at night to see her and that somebody had come to help give her medicine because she was sick, and they said that she had died. Old Dinah was her mother, and the two were so gentle that my sister and I played around them without fear, even pulling long hairs out of their tails to string beads on. I had sometimes ridden behind my mother on Sally's back when she went to town.

Our little dog, Tige, was the brother to the Arrasmith's Plato, though he showed no mark of that relationship. He was short and thick, with thick legs and a thick tail. His hair was stiff and nearer dust color than black. He was lame in one leg. He had no graces excepting very white teeth and a good disposition, which later was the unmaking of him, for he could never be taught to catch chickens or pigs or anything else upon which he had been set. He seemed to think we never meant him to hurt anything, and always came grinning back from the chase, with his mouth open and empty. It was after one of these futile runs to catch a chicken, which my mother wanted in a hurry for some unexpected company, that I heard my mother say, "Tige, you good-for-nothing thing! I wish you were dead." Sometime after this when I was playing in my grandmother's woods with Elly and Frank, Henry Clay, my grandmother's big mastiff, snarled at Tige, who had followed us as usual, and seemed about to take him by the neck. The children scolded the large dog and drove him away. It was at this point that my seven-year-old memory recalled what my mother had said to Tige, and I said to the others, "Oh, mother doesn't care if Tige is dead. I heard her say so." Whereupon one of the children set the larger dog upon poor Tige, who was killed in a few minutes. My conscience has carried the scar ever since, and the picture of poor Tige lying among the dead beech leaves, with his little legs sticking up in the air. But not until I went home and told my mother, in answer to her question as to where the dog was, did I begin to understand what I had done. When mother remonstrated with me for allowing it, I said, "But you know, mother, you wished he was dead; I heard you say so." She answered nothing, but I know that the lesson to her sank deep.

The farm next to my grandfather's, on the southeast and on the same side of the road, belonged, in my childhood, to Wm. and Susan Arrasmith, who were our nearest neighbors and lived opposite to us, beyond a flat-iron-shaped field. Their long, one-storied, white, weather-boarded house fronted the main road, which made an angle at the point of this field with the Brookville Road, on which our house stood. Several large elms grew in the small field, which sometimes made a play place for us. The Arrasmiths were pioneer people and had a family of sons and daughters, mostly at home. Two of them, Richard and Harvey, went to school to my father at the Bailey School in the winter of '47. Richard, whom I liked best among the big boys and young men, used to pick me up, set me on his shoulder, and carry me over wet spots in the edge of the woods, as we went home. I saw little of him after that time until after he was married and living in a little house on one side of his father's farm.

My mother sometimes took me to visit his pretty wife, Martha, and afterwards when I was older told me the story of their runaway match. Richard and Martha had made up their minds that they would marry each other. Her father and mother had made up theirs that they should not because they did not like Dick, and besides they wanted Martha at home. Martha lived at some distance from our neighborhood, I do not know where, but I think across the Indiana line. The young people had met somewhere and agreed that they would take the very first chance to run away. The parents suspected and kept watch. But one day when the family were at the dinner table, Martha rose and went to the kitchen to look at a pan of biscuit she had left in the oven. Glancing out of the back door, as was now her frequent habit, she saw in the edge of the field just beyond the yard a hat and face and pair of shoulders, which immediately disappeared in the forest of corn. In a few minutes she had also as completely disappeared in the same forest, bareheaded and dressed in a calico gown and kitchen apron. Whether he had a saddle horse concealed in the woods on which they made their escape to the parson, I do not know. All I do know is that Martha was a pretty woman and made a happy home.

Jacob Arrasmith, the eldest son, was a schoolteacher for some years in the county. I have very little other recollection of the family or the place, excepting that they had beehives on one side of the large grassy yard, which made me afraid to go to the orchard beyond them; that they had their small, shiny black dog named Plato, which used to stand on the stile in front of their house and bark at me till someone called him off.

Our only other playmates besides my little Uncle and Aunt Frank and Elly were the two youngest daughters of the Reverend Peter and Mrs. Keziah Banta. These good people had six daughters and one son, most of whom went to school at the Bailey Schoolhouse some part of the year. Mr. Banta was a preacher in the Christian Church of which Mrs. Banta was a prominent member. She always wore a white lace cap, and covered her white hair on her forehead with a black band under it. She was kind, and seemed to be one with her daughters as they were together in the household work.

I was once there when Mary and Josephine were putting into practice a curious and newly learned art. They drew roses, bud and leaves, set conventionally on long straight stems, very much like what I long afterwards knew to be Persian design; these they painted red and green and afterwards placed in homemade frames. But the kind of paint used was interesting enough to me to make me remember all the rest. The green was made by stirring unroasted coffee grains into a small quantity of soft soap. The red was made from pokeberry juice.

The orchard at Banta's with its many climbable trees, good apples, and one old pear tree, was a favorite play place of us all. The big barn halfway down the lane was chiefly interesting for its clouds of barn martens that chattered and circled and hung to their masonry under the eaves. It gave me a delightful sensation to see their little heads at their little round doors, while their mates flashed their steel-blue, white, and tan bodies over and around the barn.

When people talk to little children they often fail to realize that many of their words and sayings have ceased to have their original figurative meaning, and that many words known to the child in their literal sense have taken on a figurative force. I was once at my Aunt Laura's in New Westville, where my mother had driven us for a short visit. Soon after our arrival I had taken off my slippers and stockings, as it was a warm day and I was used to being barefoot. When I got tired playing about the backyard and porch, I asked mother if I might go and stand in the front door and look up and down the street. My aunt said, "No, not without your stockings and slippers."

After I had been properly arranged as to my hair and my feet, I stood in the door looking up and down the pavements. A little girl about my own age came to the front of the house, stopped before me, and said in a critical tone, "What did you come up here for?" I looked at her without replying, too shy for words, and with a feeling that there was something wrong about me, then went back to the porch to my mother and aunt and told mother what the girl had said. She and my aunt laughed and my mother asked, "Why didn't you tell her you came up here to see her spin street-yarn?" I went back to the door, looked up and down, could not see the girl, but in imagination I saw her at the head of the street with a big spinning wheel, spinning a long thread down the street. By then I knew that this was not at all my mother's meaning, though I could not understand what the real one was, and did not ask.

I may illustrate this further by another childish recollection. I had started home one afternoon from my grandmother's, when, a short distance down the road, I came upon my little Uncle Frank sitting by one of the posts of the bars letting into a field. The men were hauling grain into the barn, and had called the boy down to keep stray pigs and cows from going in while the gap was open. I had heard one of my aunts tell Frank, a little before I started home, to run down to the field as they wanted him to "keep the gap." "Come on," he said, as I passed, "Come and help me keep the gap." I stopped, but said I couldn't stay, "Because the long hand is at twelve and the short hand is at four." I sat down a few minutes, however, and said, "Where is the gap?" "Here," he said, pushing his fist down into a bunch of grass and making a little round nest of it, "this is the gap." I hardly think he knew any more than I did what the gap was, although he understood what his business was there. He was probably driven to the subterfuge of making the nest in the grass for an answer to my question. I went away none the wiser, wondering why it was necessary to keep that little hole in the bunch of grass.

One late spring day after the farmers had waited impatiently for a chance to plant their corn, we all went out into the field north of the Little Woods to help grandfather to get in his corn crop. Everybody old enough to hoe, or to drive horses for marking off furrows, or to drop corn was marshalled for the day's work. I was the youngest of those who dropped corn. I filled my apron from the sack at the end of the long row beginning at the woods fence, and dropped four grains into each marked-off hill down the long row to the end of the field and back again. By this time my apron was empty, and I went to get some more corn for my next row up and back.

Somehow after filling my apron with corn, I spilled it all at the end of the row I was about to follow. I scooped it up in handfuls as well as I could; knowing that I could not wait to pick up every grain, I covered the rest of it with the earth at the end of the furrow and went on about my business. Whether I forgot it or feared a scolding or was ashamed of it I do not remember, but I did not speak of it. Certain it is, I forgot it for a time till late in the summer when one day, playing in the corner of the woods near the old well, I looked over the fence and saw a great bunch of cornstalks crowded in one place. With something quite like a sudden accusation I knew how they came there, nor did I explain except to myself. There grew near this bunch of corn in one of the fence corners a clump of elder bushes, the white blossoms of which could be seen from our play places in the Little Woods, and even from our front door, as they stood on a slight elevation and the wood was open. I never there-after saw the white blossoms of that clump of elder bushes, near or at a distance, without thinking of the apron full of spilled corn and what came of it.

Among the stories told to us by my Grandmother Ryan was one of her early childhood in Virginia. It was of an old beggar named Witheroe who used to make periodic visits at her mother's house as he went his twice-yearly rounds in her neighborhood. Grand-mother remembered seeing him approach the house once, somehow reflected in a looking glass at which her mother stood combing her hair. Grandmother, then a mere baby, hid her face in her mother's dress, clinging to it as the old man came up. He was a fearsome-looking creature to her. He sat down and told how he had slept in an old empty cabin somewhere, and had been waked by a bird sitting on the rafter over his head, singing, "Poor old Witheroe! Poor old Witheroe!" and had come there to get away from it, but could not. "Poor old Witheroe," it still sang.

He told further then, or after, how he had been in the barroom of a tavern, one night not long before, when two travelers came in. Presently noticing him, a mere piece of wreckage as he was, they began to talk about him in a foreign tongue. After they had said all they wished to amuse themselves, he answered them in the foreign language they had used. Whereupon a little confused and curious they spoke another tongue with some further disparagement of a man who could know so much and thus become so degraded. When they had concluded he rose, answered in the new tongue, and stood for a few minutes reeling off quotations from the classics, and went out. This last story grandmother heard from her mother after she was older, and after she had seen Witheroe many times.

Certain very early but distinct recollections I have concerning the effect of voices and names of people on my feelings and imagination. The soft, gentle, and refined voices of my Aunts Laura (Laurinda Hardy McCown) and Eliza (Eliza Jane Hardy Young) made so deep an impression that I seem to hear them perfectly at any moment of recalling, although both my aunts died many years ago. I seldom saw my Aunt Laura, and more seldom still her brother, my Uncle Curtis, whose voice had much the same gentle quality, all three resembling the lower notes of my father's speaking voice. The very resonant richness of my Uncle James McCown's voice associates itself oddly enough with the smell of brown sugar and raisins in his general merchandise house, where I saw him when we visited their home in New Westville, Ohio. Several of my cousins, on the Hardy side, inherited these voice qualities.

I may observe in general that the log schoolhouse training had no bad effect on the voices of children. They usually recited their lessons in natural tones, in a small room, and at the knee of the master, so that there were not then any examples of the "public school voice." Moreover, the life spent in pure air, day and night, knew nothing of that nervous tension which tightens the vocal chords and contracts the throat. Although the people of our neighborhood knew no more about caring for the voices of their children and paid no more attention to them than do women of the present time, there was not the habit of that loud high-keyed talk in the houses, which ruins the voice, as one hears so often in these days. Anyone who will listen will see that even among the educated mothers of college towns children's voices are entirely neglected. If the children go to the public schools the trouble is increased, because they are required to recite in classes of fifty or sixty, in large rooms, and at a distance from the teacher. Their head tones are hard and sharp, with a wiry edge. The notes of their lower registers are thick and throaty, and they manage their consonants very badly in the mouth and on the lips. The result is a good deal of what might be called the quacking quality in the voices of adults of the present generation.

There were, indeed, a great many good readers in the log cabin days. The teachers had got, somehow, better training in this all-important branch of learning than university women and men take into their high school teaching now. As reading was the most important of the "three R's," it had the most attention.

When I recall the people and voices of the country neighborhood where I spent my childhood, it is with a sense of the pervasive tranquillity of unhurried living.

6

Manners and Customs

Household manners and customs in the forties and fifties were necessarily simple. As the furnishings of the settlers' cabin and the later log house were determined beforehand by necessity, there was little reason for formality and elaboration. When the mistress of the house had finished preparing the meal, she called the family, took off her apron, sat at the head of the table, and poured the tea, coffee, or milk. The master of the house took his place opposite. Everything that was to be eaten at that meal was on the table. The plate of bread stood at the master's right hand, the pie or pies stood on the other corners of the table. Meat, vegetables, preserves, butter, and apple butter occupied the middle of the table. One plate, upside down, one knife and fork (two-tined) had been put down for each person.

Tea and coffee were poured from the cup into the saucer to drink, the cup was set on a little cup-plate, in the better-ordered families, to prevent rings of stain on the homespun linen. Pie was usually a part of every meal and was of course eaten from the same plate as the rest of the dinner. Napkins were not in use. This omission, however, was not so barbarous as it may sound, as table rules about dropping things on the floor or on the tablecloth were very severe, both for grown people and for children. There was no exception to these customs in the neighborhood. It was not until the middle fifties that the cup-plate wholly disappeared and everybody drank tea and coffee from cups with handles. Somewhat later than this the small sauce-plate began to appear. The men were called from the field at half-past eleven by a long tin dinner-horn, and the dinner was served promptly at twelve o' clock.

All the cooking and other work requiring fire was done at the fireplace, except such larger operations as had to be done out of doors in the iron or copper kettles, until my fifth or sixth year, when my father and mother bought a stove, which was put into the lean-to at the nearer end. There were but two other stoves in the neighborhood then, I believe—one at my grandmother's, and one at Mr. Bremerman's. Our meals had heretofore all been cooked by the open fire, in a three-legged bake-oven (elsewhere called a Dutch-oven), in three-legged skillets, and in iron pots which hung on hooks from a bar put across inside the chimney.

Bread was baked in the three-legged oven set on coals before the fire, and covered with coals which were kept in place by the flange around the iron lid. Yeast bread, salt-rising, corn pone, biscuits, flat cake, griddle cakes, corn dodger, corn bread, pumpkin bread, and snow bread in its season, crackling bread, cakes and pies, rusks and gingerbread—all came in turn out of the three-legged oven. As I never knew of snow bread in use anywhere excepting in our family and my grandmother's and as I never find anyone now who ever heard of it, it seems worthwhile to tell what it was and how it was made. It was a bread of corn meal made with snow after the following directions: To a quart of fresh corn meal salted to taste, add two quarts of fine drifting snow; take the meal out of doors in a cold pan, stir in the dry mealy snow thoroughly, then pour the mixture at once into a large buttered dripping pan, sizzling hot, in the oven; spread level with a spoon and bake in a quick oven about as long as ordinary corn bread; if successful, you will have a crisp, sweet, delicate bread, delicious eaten with new milk for supper. This bread can be made only in very cold weather, when the snow is dry, and drifting about. We children used to beg for it whenever we saw that the snow was right.

There was no stint of food anywhere in the settlement. Everybody had a generous table: the very best home-cured meats, raised on their own farms by the farmers themselves on the table three times a day, with changes of fresh-killed meats, fowls, eggs, vegetables and fruits, maple sugar and syrup made in February and March from their own sugar trees, dried apples and peaches in winter with all manner of sugar-preserved fruits, berries, pears, with loads of apples from the orchards—all these furnished the tables with an abundance I have since seen nowhere else.

The cooking in pioneer homes of this time was generally excellent, though here and there was a family in which the yeast bread and biscuit were never good. Meats were fried or boiled, seldom wasted, and never broiled. Fowls were often wasted, however, after the introduction of the cooking stove. Soups were not a regular part of the diet, and appeared only occasionally in wintertime and seldom other than bean soup or beef broth with cabbage or turnips.

Pies were the universal dessert, and were made of a great variety of materials. The housewife's ingenuity was taxed in some seasons of scarcity to find pie stuffs. When it is remembered that the only way of preserving fruits then known was by drying, or making into preserves with an equal weight of sugar, it will be seen that much of the year pie stuffs would be wanting. Molasses pie, vinegar pie, potato pie, and sweet-potato pie had to find favor with the chronic pie appetite. I knew one housekeeper who used the common field sorrel, known as sheep sorrel, to make pies of in the spring, before berries or even currants came. Rhubarb was, at this time, unknown in our part of the country. Pies made of cooked dried pumpkin, or apple butter and milk were not to be despised either. Pies of some kind there must ever be.

The simple manner of serving in families in which every part of the work was done by its members made all easy enough in comparison with the elaborate artificiality of more modern eating. With sewing, weaving, spinning, dyeing of wool and flax—when all is said, women had more time to live than they find now. Clothing was simply made, but with the greatest pride in the handwork of the stitching, hemming, and gathering. Men's best shirts were marvels of beautiful sewing, counted threads in the gathers, and stitched fronts. Women's gowns were sewed together at the waist with thread-counted stitches.

The usual custom of early to bed and early to rise prevailed in the neighborhood. Breakfast was commonly eaten by candlelight in the wintertime, and at night the fire was covered and the lights were out often by eight o'clock. Unless somebody was sewing or reading, the fireplace furnished the only light for the evening circle. A single candle or the lard lamp was the only other light in use even to the early fifties. Tallow and wax candles were made in my own home, often with my help in putting the wicks into the molds ready for the tallow or wax. As we never bleached the beeswax, our wax candles were usually dark in color.

The dye stuffs used by the various families were lump indigo, cud-bear, copperas, log-wood, cochineal, madder, and anatto.* These were of course bought of the druggist. Saffron from the garden, black-and-white walnut barks, yellow poplar bark, willow bark, mosses, and lichens from the woods were some of the natural vegetable dyes available, though generally not in favor. Skeins of varicolored yarns drying on our yard fence, and often at our neighbors, were familiar sights to me as a child.

Although matches had been invented, they were not in use in our neighborhood in the forties and early fifties. I do not remember seeing matches, though there must have been some in our house before the end of this decade, as I do remember having, and seeing other children have, the little wooden cylinder boxes in which matches first came. These little boxes, as indeed any small box, were a rare and precious plaything to us children. The candle or lamp was lighted with a burning stick from the fire. People who smoked searched round on the hearth for a coal of suitable size to be taken up in the bowl. If in the warm days of spring the fire was allowed to go out, someone went with a shovel to the neighbors to bring back live coals to relight the fire. In summertime, fire was kept on the hearth by covering with ashes.

As there were no postage stamps and no envelopes in those days, letters were folded in squares without a covering and sealed with wafers. Letters were prepaid or not, as the writer chose. And it sometimes happened that an inconveniently large postage fee was demanded before one could have his letter.

Carpets, even rag carpets, did not come into general use until about 1850. In the hewn log houses which succeeded the settlers' cabins, there was generally a "big room" which might have a rag carpet, or on the more enterprising farms, a "girthing" carpet, which was a home-woven fabric, made of brightly colored home-dyed woolen yarns, used as very closely laid warp which covered the woof or filling of coarse yarn. The reds, greens, and yellows were usually graded in arrangement from dark to light, and made very

---

*The word cud-bear is a corruption of cuthbert from the name of Dr. Cuthbert Gordon, its discoverer. Botanically it is a lichen, *Lecanora tartarea*. It makes a rich purple color. Anatto, a yellow dye made from berries of a semi-tropical tree, used for coloring cloth only, not for butter.

bright stripes lengthwise of the web. It was called girthing because it was woven like saddle-girthing. The first I saw of this kind was at the house of a neighbor named Gardner, about 1847. It was a piece of news to tell when this or that neighbor had finished her piece of girthing carpet and was going to lay it on her big room floor. It was like walking on rainbows to enter such a room. A little later, one or two families bought what was called a Turkey carpet, a finely woven two- or three-ply fabric, invariably of brilliant red and green figures in a ground of the same color.

The larger operations of household economy such as soap-making, washing, apple-butter making, dyeing, before the advent of stoves, were done in large iron or copper kettles, hung over the fire out of doors. A stout pole was laid across two firmly fixed forked posts about eight feet apart. On this, two or three kettles hung by the iron bails so that the fire could be built directly under. Extra water for scrubbing the floor, or scouring the wooden covers of the milk crocks, or preparing the lye for lye-homing was heated out of doors. A necessary addition to this outdoor fireplace was the ash-hopper for the making of lye out of ashes. Sometimes the hopper was made of small logs laid on a slant platform, but generally of four-foot clapboards set up in the shape of an inverted truncated pyramid on a slant floor. The ashes were put into this on a thick layer of straw which served as a filter to the lye running off into a wooden trough.

If lye of greater strength was wanted, the already leached ashes were taken out and thrown aside, new ashes put in, and the lye from the trough poured in once more. The strength of the lye was tested by seeing whether it would bear up an egg. In some families, as in our own, I remember, a fine starch was made by the women by stirring and soaking wheat bran in a tub of water, until the whole fermented, the starch sank to the bottom, the bran was poured off with the superfluous water, and the cake of starch at the bottom taken out and dried on plates. This was used for starching the finer linens. Common flour starch served for ordinary use.

Up to the end of my tenth year (July, 1851) my life had been that of a child in a semi-pioneer settlement; for the township in which I lived was just beginning to emerge from the farm-clearing, log-cabin days, and the simple manner of living of those times still prevailed. Our clothes were handwoven and homemade; we raised our own wool and flax, and prepared these for the loom; the wool, by washing, picking, and carding, and afterwards spinning and dyeing; the flax, by pulling and rotting in the fields, breaking, scutching, hackling, and then by spinning and weaving into linen cloth for all household purposes and for summer clothes. We made all our sugar from the maple trees. Of all these things I was a part, and took my part, to the extent of learning the processes by sight, and some by practice.

I learned to spin wool and flax, though of course I did little of it at so early an age. I "handed-in threads" in the operation of "putting in a piece" of cloth, I "filled the quills" for the shuttles by turning the little quill wheel and winding blades. Not until all the quills had been filled in the mornings was I free to go with my sister to the woods to play. Usually my mother gave me three skeins from the spun wool or linen hanging in the "loft" to use for filling the quills. I looked them over, took the most tangled one first—I had learned this myself because it was my experience already that the nearer the time came to go out to play, the harder it was to wait to untangle yarn, that the time seemed to come more quickly when I could turn my wheel fastest with the smooth last skein.

"Handing-in threads" was a tedious process: I sat behind the heddles, between them and the warp beam, passing to my mother on the front side of these "gears," as they were generally called, each thread, one by one in its warped order, with nothing to see or to hear, but "one-thread-at-a-time-with-attention." If by chance one thread was omitted and the next put into its place undiscovered for some time, then all must be taken out and done over; and it was warm and close and stupid. My mother could easily have lightened my task by stories, but if she had tried to do so she could not have given her attention to "a thread at a time just so," and mistakes would have crept in. Sometimes my Grandmother Ryan came in and relieved me by taking my place behind the heddles.

It should be explained perhaps that the "quills" were made of branches of elder by cutting them into about four-inch lengths and pushing out the pith; these were used as bobbins on which to run the thread for the shuttle.

I have said elsewhere that almost everything used by the

farmers at this time was made at home. This included many of the farming utensils and conveniences for carrying on the varied kinds of farm and household work. There was no money to spend, for example, for buckets to be used in sugar camps, so that vessels for collecting the maple sap had to be made by hand. These were usually troughs dug out with chisel and mallet from a split section of a log, two or three feet long. At the end of the sugar season the troughs were either gathered up and stacked in the camp shed or, what was more common, each was turned up on end against a tree.

Hardships of some kinds were so common that they became the source of certain habits, which were afterwards followed by preference, for example, the habit of going barefoot. No child would willingly have worn shoes in the spring and summer, nor put them on until the winter snow fell. As all the farmers made their own shoes and those of all their family, there was no waste of such necessary work. Usually, the calfskin too was of their own manufacture. The shoe-bench and kit of tools was as necessary a part of the house furnishing as the wheel and loom. Grown men and women, however, seldom went barefoot; that was regarded as shiftlessness. My first pair of shoes, made by my father, served me until I was four, so far as I now remember. The shoes were always made on straight lasts, and the children were required to change them from left to right as did the grown people. Very often the lasts were whittled out at home; thread and pegs were prepared there also. The sewing was done by means of an awl and a thread with a pig bristle twisted into the waxed end.

The day I was taken to the new schoolhouse in Dooley's district—five or six, I must have been—was in October. We started early, while the frost was still on the ground. I was barefoot, for the day promised to be sunny and so far warm, and besides, I had no shoes, and it was too early to begin wearing them if I had had any. The road was dry and dusty, but frosty most of the way. I drove up some cows, still lying in the road waiting to be milked, and warmed my feet in the spots which they left. This was a trick I had more than once enjoyed, when there was no particular need as on this long cold walk.

As almost everything that was eaten on farms was produced there, few excuses for borrowing ever came; sometimes a cup of green coffee-beans, or a little saleratus, or any such small matter.

Every family seemed sufficient to its own immediate needs. But there was always a good deal of friendly exchange of commodities. "Don't you folks want some currants? We have more than enough, come over and help yourselves." Or, "Our early apples are ripe, and yours are not in yet. Send over and get some." Or maybe, "Mother sent over these turnips, ours are earlier this year." "Why, much obliged surely, and I'll just put some of these spareribs and a mess of sausage into your basket." The compliments of the season went back and forth between neighbors all the year round; if there were kinds of fruits or vegetables that one's neighbor had not in his garden and orchard, then it was a privilege to send them to him. "Come over and help us" was not often said, because those who could help anticipated the cry.

The hard things in pioneer life were offset by such real compensations. And yet how simple, uneventful, and slow it looked—and looks now to those who see from without! I hardly think our neighborhood was any better or any worse than the neighborhoods that pieced on all around. True we had few shiftless, few very poor, and few unthrifty among us. All were at least trying to live decent, self-respecting lives. I do not remember more than one family—and they disappeared while I was still very young—whose house was dirty and whose women and children wore dirty clothes. They were subjects of comment so often that one who listened even to what she did not understand could not forget—and could not on after occasions fail to observe.

Shelling corn for the mill was an evening occupation which came whenever fresh corn meal was needed for bread. The best ears of white corn were chosen, brought in after supper in the bushel basket, and set by the fire. At home my father, helped by the two children who were old enough, shelled, while my mother sat sewing or knitting by the candle or the lard-oil lamp, or perhaps by firelight. When enough cobs had been stripped of grain, my sister and I built cob houses, which we begged to have set on the coals between the andirons—"to see the house burn." But every grain must have been taken off; it was wicked to burn corn. If corn shelling took place at my grandfather's when I stayed all night there, the scene was much the same, except that more took a hand at it, there were no cob houses, and the next morning someone, usually the youngest, who

[67]

was I, had to get down on the hearth and pick all the grains out of the cracks of the flagstone hearth before sweeping was done. For it was wicked to burn anything that any creature would eat, and although there was abundance of grain and other food for all the fowls, at their command as it were, this rule was so rigidly observed that none of my grandfather's children would have broken it, for two reasons—fear of punishment by my grandfather, and "because it was wicked." What grandfather said was wicked was doubly so, because nobody thought him a religious man.

I have heard my father say that he had gone into the corn field in October to get ears of ripened corn to grate on the kitchen grater to make meal for bread for breakfast. "But," added he, "that was not uncommon in the wilderness times in Kentucky in my father's early family life. He lived thirty miles from a mill, and my oldest brother had to go on horseback that distance with a bag of shelled corn behind him to bring back meal for bread." In our part of the country there had been Bruce's Mill since 1812, so that going to mill was a simple matter. In my childhood grating corn for meal was never merely on account of need; but the old necessity of doing it had left a taste in the mouths of the farmer folks for a supper of mush-and-milk made from the freshly grated and sifted meal of the first frost-ripened field corn; and for the new corn bread next morning of the same sweet handmade meal.

When a bag of corn was taken to mill one waited until it had been ground. It was then returned to the bag unbolted, that is, with the bran still mixed with it. The sifting was done by hand at home as the meal was used. When a farmer took a sack of wheat to mill he took home with him the bolted flour, the middlings or shorts, and the bran. In each case his grist was less the miller's toll, which varied, I believe, with the quoted prices of grain.

An apple bee, or apple cutting, as it was called in the Middle West, was a common entertainment in the fall among the farmers. After the summer's work was laid by, in the lull of the year, the apple orchards were scenes of jollity and abundance. The early fall apples and what were left over from the late summer trees were gathered in heaps in the orchards among their own trees, some for the cider mill and apple-butter making, and some for drying. For both of these processes large quantitites of apples peeled, cored, and quartered were necessary, as every family made at least a half barrel of apple butter, or never less than one big copper kettle full. Dried apples were greatly depended upon also, as fruit canning was then not known. Preserving meant jellies, sugar preserves, thick and rich, and made so strong as to require no sealing.

Usually invitations were sent about by word of mouth a few days before the apple cutting was to come off. Tubs, baskets, large kettles, all sorts of receptacles came into use to hold the apples brought into the house for the workers. Usually the "married folks" came and worked all day or afternoon, peeling by hand and with peelers, coring and quartering, and spreading out on improvised scaffolds in the sun to dry. At noon or later a dinner, such as Washington Irving describes in "The Legend of Sleepy Hollow," was served. Some of the visiting women helped the hostess to make ready what was necessarily left to be done—coffee, hot biscuit, and vegetables.

Before the neighbors left there was a clean-up after the work and more apples were brought in for the young folks who were to come to work after dusk. More baking of pies, cakes and biscuit, and supper for the family alone, while the old folks went home to send the young ones for their share of work and fun. Then work, with jokes, tricks, counting apple seeds to be named—"One I love, Two I love, Three I love I say, Four he loves, Five she loves," etc., throwing a long peeling around the head to see what letter it would make. (How did it always happen to make the right one?) Jokes about Ben's slow peeling, or Nancy's slow quartering, or Mary Ann's poor coring, "Leaves half the core-eyes in," "And you leave a ring 'o peelin' on both ends of every apple, and that's why I can't keep up corin' for peelin' after you—huh!"

Then came supper, apple and pumpkin pies, cider, doughnuts, cakes, cold chicken and turkey; after which games, "Forfeits," "Building a Bridge," "Snatchability," even "Blind Man's Buff" and "Pussy Wants a Corner," then going home in the moonlight. All these customs I knew of before I was ten years old, by having been present at an apple cutting in my own home, and one at my grandmother's. Quiltings and wood choppings were other forms of neighborhood helpings in common. There were no hired people in those days in that community, so that when a man or woman had too much of any one thing to be done by one person, everybody lent a hand and made good times and quick work out of it all; always, of course, with much good eating and plenty of simple and wholesome fun. Husking, sheepshearing, wool picking, carpet-rag cuttings, geese plucking, corn planting, house-raising, logrolling, sewings furnished times and occasions for festivities. With most of these forms of amusement I had become familiar before my father moved his family to Eaton, where there was seldom need of neighborhood civilities of this kind.

The custom of serving a drink of whisky to the men in the harvest field and at house-raisings was going out of favor in the middle forties, as was that of offering toddy to casual callers. I have a dim recollection of hearing an argument by someone with my father because he had said he did not intend to offer drink to the men at his hay harvest. "Then the men will not come." "Well, they can stay away then," answered my father. This seemed to be about the time of the last struggle for existence of this custom, as I never saw or heard of any further use of it.

I never heard of any custom of this kind in my Grandfather Hardy's family who, though Kentuckians, were decided total abstainers.

Whenever a neighbor came to spend the day on a visit to my mother, a part of the entertainment consisted, as a matter of course, in showing her patchwork quilts, finished or in process of making, a piece of cloth in the loom, or lately woven, and any new garment made or in the making. In the same way, every quilt pieced and quilted in the neighborhood was known and spoken of in other houses. For the most part the quilts were pieced of scraps of calico or gingham left from the few dresses of those materials owned by the maker and added to by the friendly exchange with neighbors, each woman generally brought back from a visit a little roll of quilt pieces, and every woman could tell, in showing her quilt, of whose dress or apron or bonnet each square was a piece. Before I was eight years old, I used, while still in bed in the mornings, to say, "This is a piece of mother's dress, and this one of grandmother's, and this of Mrs. Arrasmith's, and this of Aunt Margaret's," and "Mother, whose is this?" These "nine patches," as they usually were, often contained a good deal of family history. A little later in this decade, young women made quilts of bright-colored calicoes, bought for the purpose and cut into various intricate designs, which were sewed down, or applied on white cotton cloth. Months of work were often sewed into the closely wrought and elaborately quilted designs. Such quilts were much admired and usually put upon the best beds on great occasions. The designs often had fanciful names, as "Mary's Dream," "Morning Star," "Rose of Sharon." My mother never made any of these elaborate bedcovers, as she did not admire them very much.

Another part of a visitor's entertainment, if it was winter or spring, was the bringing out of the seed bag and dividing up of the kitchen garden and flower seeds. Very often these seeds were named from the neighbor who had given the start of the plants. I remember hearing my mother say, as she gave some large white beans with pink specks on them to a neighbor, "These are Maria Crane beans." Each kind of seed was tied up in a piece of cloth in a little round bunch.

One spring Sunday morning (in 1846, I have since learned) I was at my grandmother's in the living room, with some of my younger aunts about, when in came Uncle John Obed and his bride, Mary Bremerman. They had just been married at the bride's home on a farm a mile away, and had walked over to the groom's home for a wedding trip. One of my aunts went to the bride, took off her bonnet, and laid it on the bed; she then untied her cap strings and said laughingly, "You shan't have this thing on," took it off, and laid it with the bonnet. I stared at the lovely pink cheeks and blue eyes of my new aunt without understanding anything of what it all meant. I only knew that this pretty lady was another aunt somehow. The simple ceremony at the house, the bridal cap, the walk to the husband's home, were all characteristic of the time. A few days later the newly married couple went to their new home in Howard County, Indiana. Sometimes in the more well-to-do families, especially if the couple had the approval of everybody concerned, there was what was called an "Infair," a great dinner to which the relatives of both families, with other neighborhood guests, were bidden.

[71]

7

What the Woods Taught Me

I do not remember when I learned the names and looks, smells and tastes of the trees, shrubs, flowers, and weeds in our fields and woods. But I lived so much among them, winter and summer, and was so curious about everything, that this delightful knowledge came early and easily, especially since my father, though no trained botanist, knew everything about the woods practically. But for the most part the children of my age in the neighborhood did know these things at an early age. Like Indians, we ate of everything edible in the woods—roots, buds, barks, young shoots, leaves, sprouting seeds and nuts, and the sprouts of wild fruits. We very early learned to avoid the poisonous plants and their fruits, as we were told by our parents and other elders, so that there was really no danger to us. We never on any account tasted a plant or fruit found for the first time, but took it home to ask about.

My father was often with us in the wood and answered many questions about what was around us. Among my earliest recollections are frequent memories of him returning from a walk through the woods—a shortcut road home from town, maybe, with some "simple," root and all, in his hand, or some rare plant new to him, or beautiful wild flowers. The common wood and field "simples" were used much as medicinal remedies; every family gathered mints, heal-all, pennyroyal, boneset, snakeroot, sarsaparilla, catnip, bittersweet, and other roots and herbs for the winter ailments. Spicewood, which we sometimes used, as we did sassafras-root bark, instead of tea, and which made in maple sap, as we thought, a very delightful drink, was also put away to be used in winter for colds.

In whooping-cough time too we had swamp-cabbage root, a not delightful powdered remedy served hourly, mixed with honey, for much coughing. Spikenard and elecampane, yellow poplar bark and slippery-elm, and tonic yarrow were also in store, as well as rue and saffron, camomile and anise from the garden. Tincture of camphor was also kept in every house and given in drop doses for summer complaints of all kinds; it was also used for dressing cuts and other wounds. No doctor was asked to come unless something very serious seemed the matter. Strong medicines, mostly calomel in heroic doses, castor-oil, vermifuge, tincture of iron, and lobelia were their remedies.

In spite of these, the patient survived heavy attacks of fever and the like, on account of soundness of constitution inherited from sound parents who had lived a simple, open-air life in well-ventilated houses—log, with open chinks and great chimneys. Ordinary attacks of illness were treated by the grandmothers or the family mother with teas from the herb stores.

Further in relation to my wood lore: I was acquainted with the common names of the birds, small animals, and the more conspicuous insects. I often played with the "Bess-bug," a large, shiny black beetle with corrugated wing cases (belonging to the genus *Lucanus*, I think) and having a delightful habit of squeaking when touched on the back. Another insect playfellow was a large spring-beetle "snapping-bug" (afterwards known as the Eyed Elater), which made me, whenever I found one, the envy of my playmates. In those woodland years I saw almost every sort of insect wonder, some of which few people see, even students of insects, as I found in my college work long afterwards.

Among these was that curious caterpillar parasite which grows from the insect's head in the shape of a plant. I have never heard of any other person who has seen one in Ohio. I was eight or nine years old playing in the wood and found one lying by an old mossy log; so strange it seemed I would not touch it, and did not mention it at home because I did not know how to say what it was like. The Chinese, I have since read, use it for medicine. Gibson's *Sharp Eyes** has a picture of one, and of a bunch of dried ones, as preserved by the Chinese. The green cicada with his ominous *W* on his back was an object of wonder and of some fear, at least to touch,

---

*As an example of one of the kinds of books Miss Hardy enjoyed, the full citation is William Hamilton Gibson, *Sharp Eyes; A Rambler's Calendar of Fifty-two Weeks among Insects, Buds, and Flowers* (New York, 1892). [Ed. note]

as he was reputed to have a sting; about the only mistake, I think, that I afterwards recognized in what my father had told me about insects, or any other wood thing.

My eldest sister and I were great climbers; no tree in the forest was much beyond our skill, unless of a very large trunk with no branches near the ground. We climbed beeches, which were the friendliest sort, because of their frequent small branches, smooth trunks, and low branches near enough to be reached and dragged down to climb up by. Many a time we climbed high up and sat swinging our bare feet in an ecstasy of joy or content, disputed only by the birds who would fly down and peck us sharply on the head— sometimes a jay whose nest was near us. When we were in the woods with playmates, usually "Frank and Elly," our talk was of the trees or wood in this fashion:

"You can't guess what kind o' wood this chip is, now."

"Ho, that's just red-oak. I know; smell it."

"Well, you don't know what this fence rail is."

"That's hickory—huh!"

"Well, then you don't guess this little stick."

"Ho, ho! That's off the yellow poplar (magnolia); look, where the leaf fell off. Now, then, you tell me this: what's that dead tree across the field?"

"Anybody'd know that by the way the limbs go. It's white oak; sides, I've had acorns from it. Tain't so long dead; father deadened it last summer. You can see the ring from here."

"Well, what's that little tree in the field with shaky leaves?"

"Baby'd know what; what is it, Baby?"

"It's a quakin' asp, that's what it is."

"And that with the bees, buzzin' in it here, Addie, what's it?"

"Linn, I know."

"Now, here's a hollow stump, all round inside, and all dead out- side. It's a red gum. Father says it's the only one about here. Our well curb is made of its trunk, cut across."

Botany, through the senses of taste and smell, came easily to children who spent three-fourths of their waking hours in the woods. There was little in the woods even among common weeds that we had not acquaintance with and a name for. And yet we never seemed to exhaust the supply of new things; surprises, nature seemed to have for us all through the year. The woods could never be twice alike even in the same spots; there was a perpetual joy in the presence of trees, and what they could do for us at any season of the year. We knew them from base to crown, and our childish fingers fumbled at their secrets as they fumbled about their boles to find ways of climbing into their arms.

Violets, wild violets, in the spring! I wish I could set down the sensation that these flowers in the wild woods of Washington Township aroused in me, a helpless, wordless little child, when I saw them in groups in the angle of tree roots and all around under the trees in the woods. I know that it is said that the first sensation, or anything quite like it, cannot a second time be experienced. I believe I must differ. Last year some roots of violets came to me by mail from Ohio. I planted them near a pile of rocks and stumps. Last spring (1905) they were full of leaves and flowers, the counterpart of those I had seen in my own home grounds and woods fifty-five years ago and more. The same leap of the heart, the same intense joy!

The "Little Woods" was a small piece of beech woodland, seven or eight acres perhaps, opposite our house across the road, surrounded as all fields and woodlands were by rail fences. It was free from underbrush and covered with grass and flowers in the spring and summer. In the further end was a wet-weather pond from which a brook ran most of the year. The northwestern corner rose by a gentle slope from the pond and had on its highest part a deep and wide well, usually covered with boards. Around in the fence corners near the well grew elder bushes, which showed white through the woods in blossoming time. This small bit of wood had been left at clearing-time by my grandfather, as if for a play place for his children and grandchildren, but mainly, I suppose, as a convenience for sheep and cattle, though they were seldom put there, except a few sheep sometimes in the spring. The pond was a source of great delight to me and my sister, and Frank and Elly, both in the winter and summer. Sometimes in the winter it was frozen over for many days, when suddenly on a day the middle would fall in, leaving a slant of ice very fine for "sliding."

Its clear water in summer, the white-rooted cresses growing in the shallows, the green-jacketed frogs, mossy logs on the brim, from which we dangled bare feet into its clear waters, made it a perpetual delight. Beechnuts in both seasons, sprouting and sweet in spring, dry and nutty in the autumn, black acorns, a fine echo in one end to be had by climbing a stump and "hollering" at the shell-bark hickory, the wind-blown tulips that fell from the big magnolia ("yellow poplar") in the wet spring winds, the clumps of spring-beauties and bunches of Johnny-jump-ups, the spotted lilies, wild peanuts, "crow-toes," moss-house building, and numberless other delights made this the best schooling place that any child could have. It was surpassed, in some ways only, by the Big Woods, which lay just behind our house and seemed to have no end to itself or to the things to be found in it.

In the autumns of my sixth, seventh, and eighth years, our part of the country was visited by enormous numbers of passenger pigeons, coming for the beechmast. In one of those years, which I cannot tell, the branches of the beech trees were weighed down with a quantity of nuts. Flocks of pigeons, like great clouds, flew over our house not far above the trees. We could hear the rush and see the silvery flicker of their innumerable wings above us. The people on the various farms made coop-like traps and caught them by hundreds.

One day about this time my mother took us to visit at the house of Horatio Gardner a mile away, where we saw hundreds of these captured birds in a large coop. The beautiful creatures with their silver and tan and purple, and their long shafted tail feathers, clung to the sides of the coop so close that we could have touched them. Their unhappiness in being thus trapped touched me with some kind of a pang that I could not put into words. Which thing I suppose has kept the birds in my memory. I am told by an ornithologist that this beautiful creature is now almost extinct.

Once after a visit to an uncle in Indiana (Uncle Curtis Hardy, my father's eldest brother), we found a big black snake in the woods not far from the house. Indeed, I had stepped on its tail as the animal lay gorged and stretched at length near a favorite log of ours, on one side of which grew a pig-nut tree, where we were looking for nuts. I ran to the house at once to ask mother if we couldn't have him for a pet kept at the barn to eat rats, as Uncle Curtis kept his big fellow, Major, of the same species, to clear his barn of rats. I had seen "Major" carried down to a brook nearby, on a forked stick, for water and a sunbath. But my mother feared so large a snake near since the baby was often out on the ground sitting about when we were playing in the yard, so that the poor animal had to be killed.

I have said elsewhere that the winter's cold did not bar us from the pleasures of the woods and fields. Our way to school in winter lay partly along the roads and partly across fields and woods. On frosty mornings after a cold rain, when the roadside pools were frozen, we often stopped long enough to break with our feet the thin ice which showed by its whiteness that the water had sunk away underneath; then stooping down, we looked under the broken bridge of ice, and saw such lovely things as I would not undertake to describe here, for the reason that it has been done a thousand times better than anybody else can do it by James Russell Lowell in the prelude to the second part of that wonderful poem, *The Vision of Sir Launfal.*

Anybody who has thus looked under such broken ice will have the picture. The sharp metallic sound of the little white circlets of ice frozen over the horse tracks in the muddy road gave some of that pleasure which little children take in the noise of smashing and breaking. It was a sort of music to us, and one or the other would fall behind the group to trample around on these thin layers of white ice and then would have to run to catch up. Warmly dressed in flannels, mittens, and shawls, we played in the woods on days when the snow lay deep and the ice on the ponds glistened and reflected the trees in the patches left clear by the winds. Often the air was cold enough to freeze, although the sun was bright enough to make pictures of the naked branches singing in the wind above us. In and out among the trees we followed the paths we had known in the summer: we found tracks of the squirrel and the rabbit and manifold other marks made by dropping twigs, fallen icicles of the day before, a chance belated nut now and then, and other precious little sights.

8

Fields and Gardens

The cornfields as play places were second only in interest to the woods. They were, indeed, to little folks a kind of pleasant green forest, full of the rustling of leaves, the good smells of the corn and things to play with, corn silk to make doll's beds of, corn husks to make the dolls themselves, ground cherries, and in some places, pumpkin vines or melon vines, rough bean leaves to dress yourself in by sticking them over your flannel dresses, the soft pulverized earth for your bare feet, and above all the nice feeling of being hid away where nobody could find you. Later in the season the cornfield gave us other pleasures: fiddles made of the corn stalks, little animals made of the pith, red-speckled beans gathered from the vines along the edges of the field.

I have not mentioned the better known pleasures of stealing and roasting green ears, or of seeking out the melon patch in the middle of the field, for these belong to children of a larger growth who have lost the capacity to enjoy the real presence of the cornfield spirit. I do not forget the winter pleasures of creeping under the "shocks," which were made by cutting the ripe stalks in the autumn, setting them on end, and tying them together at the top, like wigwam poles; nor of imagining, as we looked from the window at the shocks in their different positions, that they were living persons, usually women, some spreading their skirts out, some making bows, some throwing their hands out and shrieking, some looking back at their fluttering ribbons.

Working in the field a little in summertime at haying, corn planting, in wheat harvest, and even in corn-gathering time was not in my youth labor which women scorned. On the contrary, helping a little then was a sort of gala-day pleasure which was gone into with zest as a change from ordinary indoor business of a backwoods

[78]

farmhouse. Young as I was, I helped at haying, raking hay into windrows, getting up on the stack to place the hay as it was thrown from the wagon, or going out with "the ten o'clock piece" to the field with my mother.

As the men were in the field by daylight in the summer, something to eat in the middle of the forenoon was indispensable. Baskets of bread and butter, cold meats, pies, cake and jugs of milk, or ginger water (maple syrup and water with a little vinegar, and a sprinkle of ginger) were sent out from the house to the shade of a tree at one side of the hay field, and men, women, and children ate through a good half-hour in the hay-scented shade. Jokes and merry talk and the very joy of living made such days memorable to me. In wheat harvest I was allowed to go to help carry the hand-bound sheaves, a dozen to each place to be shocked; much my feeble strength could not do, but to be able to carry or drag a big tall sheaf and lay it down with the others, by the sweat of my small brow, was a sweet responsibility, for wasn't I helping?

Corn planting was a simpler matter, for it meant, as I have earlier described, dropping four grains of corn from your apron into each hollow, afterwards to be made into a hill by the coverer who came behind, with his hoe. The furrows clear across the field were long, and the days were sometimes very warm, but maybe the season was late and everybody that could do anything was needed. No men were to be hired; it was as in the days when (Isaiah XLI.6) "They helped every one his neighbor, so the carpenter encouraged the goldsmith and he that smootheth with the hammer, him that smote the anvil." And the whole of it was good fun and good work— at least to the children, and always to me.

As soon as the clearing of the settler's fields was far enough advanced, his first care was the planting of an apple orchard. This would have been evident to any traveller through the western counties of Ohio, as early as 1840, for in my own memory every farm had its orchard of trees already large and in full bearing. The soil was rich, the growth rapid, and insect pests and blights were unknown. Every spring brought a world of blossoms, and every summer and fall an abundance of apples.

My Grandfather Ryan's farm had three such orchards, two near the house, and one on the further side of the fields. His orchards, like those of all the neighbors, were for the most part of what was called natural fruit, that is, seedling fruit, as they had all been planted from seeds brought in from eastern orchards or, as some say, from apples taken from the earlier planted, isolated trees found here and there through the country and said to have been planted by Johnny Appleseed, an eccentric travelling preacher who had frequented these regions years before in the early part of the century. I have myself seen two or three of these trees whose story my father told me.

The fruit of these orchards was of very fine quality and great variety. Many kinds took names to themselves and were reproduced in the various orchards of the neighborhood in the middle forties by grafting, which was then new, and usually done by a travelling grafter. Two or three trees in my grandfather's orchard were thus treated, one, successfully. It bore a branch of long, dark-red sweet apples, called Sheep Noses, another of Striped Sweets, a third of a dark-red apple unnamed. The best apples in the orchard, however, were also nameless, excepting that they were the Big Sweet Apples, luscious, golden, crisp, and sugar sweet, ripening in August. There were two trees of these, one in the near, and one in the further orchard, as there were also a small, white, dry-grained, very sweet apple called by us children Sunday Sweets, probably Sunny Sweets, apples of marvelous fragrance, as they sweetened all their end of the orchard. Winter apples there were in abundance, the Russets, the White Belleflowers, the Rambo, Milam, Vandiver, Greening, Greasy Pippin, and Grindstone. In some of our neighbors' orchards, other varieties had their reputation: the Black Apple, a late-winter variety, whose presence in the house in February or April you could not conceal from people who had the sense of smell, which might cause you to be set down as stingy if you did not offer some. Another delightful variety was a juicy summer apple, called by the children Half-sweet-and-Half-sour; quite as well known was the Spice Apple of another orchard.

These old orchards were the sources of an important part of the pioneer's food supply. Large quantities of the fruit were eaten raw, most of the year round. The surplus summer and fall apples were dried or made into cider and cider apple-butter. The cooked fruit made its appearance in one form or another on the tables every day.

[80]

Some of the farmers kept their orchards planted to corn, oats, and such field crops, others planted them to orchard grass, after they had begun to bear. Whatever may be said about the lack of cultivated beauty in this rural pioneer life, no child could ever have grown up in it without a vision of beauty, beyond any work of man's conception, in the yearly blossoming of the orchards.

Grandmother's garden was a place of delights to me from the earliest days of my knowledge of it, at perhaps four years of age, until the last time I saw it in 1876. Yet it was nothing more than the old-fashioned farm garden like those of the early settlers' days, mainly for vegetables, but incidentally for flowers as well. It was a rectangular oblong, fenced with handmade palings on the sides and inside end, and with a board fence next the road. It made place as well for small fruits, and two large Marillo cherry-trees next the outside fence. Under these and across that and the opposite end was a hedge of currant bushes, and along the fieldward side some yellow raspberries. The gate was near the east end of the house and was flanked by two lilac trees interwoven with thickets of thousand-leaf roses, whose odor there is none other like out of paradise.

Beyond the gate toward the smokehouse was a leaning peach tree which had late freestones much desired by the young folks of the family as they ripened in the fall after all the other peaches had gone. Inside on either side of the gate extending to the ends was a narrow bed for flowers, sweet old perennials that cared mostly for their own welfare with the help of the favoring summer rains and winter snows, and met our expectations year after year with abundant gifts of flowers. Nearest the road at one end of this bed was a snow-ball bush, the very essence of early spring, bloomed out winterly, and full of little showers after the rains that would beat off some of its flakes. Next it toward the fence was a bunch of asparagus, pardon me, spare-grass, used only as an ornament when full grown and covered with red berries between its feathers. A pitcher full on the bureau in the big room and other vessels filled with it in the fireplace were some of the things that had to be in grandmother's house every summer.

Toward the gate from these were two clumps of columbine, a

deep purple and a whity lavender—always there every year to be looked at, not to be picked; behind these two, which stood near the boarded edge of the bed, was a plant called "Lovage," which I think must have been a sort of celery, for so its odor follows me now. We were allowed to break bits of its tall stems to chew sometimes. On this plant I saw, all the summers in succession, the cross-striped naked caterpillars of black, green, and orange which long after I knew to be the creatures that grew into the swallowtail butterfly (*Asterius*), and there I learned that poking with a straw made these fellows stick out of their heads with a startling suddenness two orange-yellow, strap-like horns, at the same time diffusing about a pungent smell, enough to frighten away hungry birds.

Along the edges of the bed was a border of May pinks. Then came Sweet Williams, hollyhocks against the fence, "tree moss," live-forever, and Johnny-jump-ups and a big clump of red peonies (affectionately called pineys). These last looked across the narrow walk to the onion beds bordered by more little all-alike pansies with two purple petals and three yellow or white, with tiny stripes. An onion bed without a Johnny-jump-up border was never quite right to my mind. At the end of the straight-rowed onions toward the road was a green, green bed of camomile, sweet to touch and smell but bitter to drink in bowls of tea when one had a cold or other ailment—much prettier with its vivid mossy green, without its little single-daisylike flowers, than with them. Here and there in the onion beds, most summers there flaunted a poppy plant or two which had escaped weeding time until it had begun to bud, and was then left to grow "just to see what color it would be," some said. But I had a notion, confirmed after by some of my own tricks, that nobody had the heart to destroy such a thing after it had gone so far in life and done so well for itself.

Somewhere in this bed was a row of garden simples—sage, summer savory, thyme, coriander, sweet anise, saffron, and rue. Another path on the further side of the onion beds separated them from potatoes, turnips, cabbages and squashes, beets and parsnips, all of which except the squashes were "holed up" for winter on the very spot where they had grown, and showed in winter under the snows, along with the apple "holes," a range of snow-covered mountains of various heights and sizes. What delight I have known among these same mountains, when I was allowed to go out to hold the lantern at night sometimes when I stayed at grandmother's, while an aunt or uncle went with a pail to open the hole in one side then in use, and stuffed with straw to keep out the cold. As one stretched down a long arm to pull out the apples, I looked to see what kind came—white Bellflower, Vandiver, Milam, Pippin, Russet—what?

The two Marillo cherry-trees full of buzzing bees in flowertime (and if there is anything more beautiful than such a tree in spring—O except an apple tree!—I have yet to see it) and full of juicy black cherries late in summer, for the Marillo is a late ripener—were a part of our riches. We climbed at will with vials into which to squeeze the juice as we picked from some crotch in the tree, held our vials closed with thumb and finger, then compared and enjoyed the redness of the juice—sour, to tell the truth, for tasting.

Of all the odors reminiscent, none serves me as that of the currant bushes full of red bunches and slightly changing leaves toward the end of currant time. In the afternoon, when the sun was on the garden, a scent so subtle (all my own, for nobody ever noticed it but me) made me perfectly happy, without my knowing why. Something, not earthly, nor not heavenly that I know, but something of the spirit and not of the senses, it was. The nearest thing to it is the breath of the oak tree, which I find that people generally never breathed—the more poverty theirs!

9

Certain People

In our neighborhood, nearer to Bailey's Schoolhouse, lived Mrs. Julia Gentle, or "Aunt Juley" as she was familiarly called. Her husband had died before my recollection. She had in my time an adopted son named Jerry, who was one of the big boys in Bailey's School when I went in the wintertime of my fifth or sixth and seventh year to school to my father. "Aunt Juley" was a tall, large-boned woman with marked features, particularly the nose, gray-blue eyes, and a large jocular, grunting laugh. She generally wore a black lace cap with green or blue ribbons, and brass-bowed spectacles. She was always kindly, and always interested in the neighborhood gossip in an amiable way. My mother told me that she had rescued the child she adopted from death by smothering: his temporarily insane mother had sewed him up in a coverlet folded four times. He was always called Jerry Gentle, until as a man, he called himself Jeremiah Gentle Parker. My mother said also that Aunt Juley was considered by some of the neighbors to have some occult power. Once when mother was at Mrs. "Dordie" Crane's, her hostess, who was churning, could not "bring the butter"; after some hours of work and no butter, she remarked that the milk was bewitched and that she would "fix" the witch. Whereupon she heated a horseshoe red-hot and threw it into the churn. In a few minutes the butter came. ("Extra heat, of course," said my mother.) But close upon that came Aunt Juley Gentle who displayed her ankles, covered with bloody scratches (she wore low shoes without stockings on that warm day), saying that she had jumped into some blackberry bushes as she climbed over the field fence, coming cross-lots. "Didn't I tell you?" was Mrs. Crane's comment afterward to my mother. At the time too she conveyed the same by a significant glance, when Aunt Juley showed her bleeding ankles.

I afterward saw Mrs. Gentle often, as she moved to Eaton where we had gone in 1851. My mother lent her our old loom, with which she earned a livelihood, by weaving rag carpets. I used often to take her fruit and vegetables, or a loaf of bread, or some butter sent by my mother as presents. She sometimes brought us things from her own little garden. I always loved her, and liked to go to her house and have her come to us.

On the farm adjoining my early home lived an old widow and two daughters, by the name of Snodgrass. The mother soon disappeared from my recollection, but the maiden daughters were still living in the old hewn log house when we moved to Eaton. Soon after they came to the south end of town and lived in a little two-room cottage. They were quaint, old-fashioned, guileless women, who lived what seemed a very narrow but placid life. One of them, Sally Ann, was blue-eyed and had curly red hair; the other, long-faced, large-eyed, with dark hair already turning gray, which she wore in a single curl on either side of her face. Their voices were low and plaintive, especially when they called each other by name, one "Sair," with a rising inflection, the other, "Harriet" (*a* as in "far"). They had a very small income which supplied their needs. My mother used to send me with gifts of butter and vegetables from our town garden. They used to come sometimes to spend the day at my mother's invitation, always wearing black lawn slat sun-bonnets and straight-skirted calico gowns. They belonged as we did to the Christian Church, where they went every Sunday until the church acquired a reed organ of which they disapproved. After two or three years, however, they returned to the church, their conservatism having given way to modern innovations.

In later years, when I was teaching in the South Building in Eaton, I often stopped to see them. Their little cottage, always spotlessly clean with its bare front-room floor, its high-piled best bed with its tufted white counterpane, its one or two chairs and old-fashioned bureau, all as I had known them in my childhood. While these two sisters showed no special marks of affection toward each other, they were so closely knit that they seemed to think and feel alike, though so different in looks. After I left home for college, Harriet died, and Sally went to live with a sister, but died of grief a few months after.

These good women made more impression on my childhood and early womanhood than most other people of the neighborhood—

[85]

not for what they said, because that was very little but more for their very quiet, simple lives, which seemed to have a strong spiritual expression, unconscious both to themselves and, at the time, to those whom it affected. Yet whatever religious life they lived was without any expression in words. There was something about them which commanded the respect even of the lightminded, who might otherwise have been disposed to ridicule their quaint figures and old-fashioned manners.

Uncle McD. was another person whose face, manner, and idiosyncrasy made a permanent place for him in my memory. I saw him often on his slow, heavy-bodied horse, in his ancient light-wool hat, under which gleamed a pair of little black eyes, and his straggling, very black hair about a swarthy face; oftener so than near enough to see him unhatted and hear him speak. Once or twice this happened however: once at my Aunt Margaret's on a summer day he lay flat on his back on the porch in his shirt-sleeves, his hat off and his black elf-locks hanging around his face. The joy of his life seemed then to consist in teasing my cousin Rachel about "her beau": "Now, tuk cyah, Rachel, tuk' cyah. Don't say what you cyan't bide by. I judge he'll be comin' long 'bout tonight."

His strong point, however, was prophecy, and "argyin' scripter." He could not read a word, but what of that? The queer thing about it was that he was a sort of neighborhood oracle where he lived, on Lower Paint. He knew beforehand about every occurrence in the neighborhood, and always came forward with a tale to show that he did. Was there a fire? Had a neighbor's horse fallen into a pit? He foreknew it all—at least that something had happened or would happen. But it never came about that he knew in time to avert the disasters. But this did not affect his reputation as prophet.

Another interesting man of our neighborhood was John Bailey from whom our schoolhouse and school district took their name. He was a deacon in our church, and my father's friend; a good, plain man, with little learning and great common sense. His figure was short and slightly bent. His hair was thick and bushy, and dark, not in the least gray, although he must have been past sixty as I remember him. One of the shortcut ways to the Bailey School from our house lay across his fields and by his house and barn. I used to see him there about his work. He never talked much but had a kind of dry humor which frequently met my father's dry humor of another kind, in conversations which I now know to have been epigrammatic. At such times his gray eyes under their bushy eyebrows twinkled brightly, although no smile lighted his strongly marked features. He was, as he and my father believed, heir to the great estate of Bally Castle, Ireland. His great-grandfather, a younger brother of the heir of that time had come to America and settled in Virginia. The older line had become extinct, and the Virginia line had carelessly lost records, although there still existed in John Bailey's boyhood a paper of some value, in his father's possession. But indifference to the claim and lack of means to prosecute it left him undisturbed in the obscurity of an American farmer's life. The truth was he seldom gave it a thought.

I saw him not infrequently, and visited at his house with my mother sometimes, after we had left the neighborhood. His house was about halfway from our country home to the suburbs of the town to which we had moved. He was always in his place on Sunday in the old Public Church, on a bench near the pulpit. And his strong face there is one of my permanent recollections of the meetings in that historic building.

On the road near a little orchard on one end of John Bailey's farm, still stood in 1846 and 1847 the original pioneer cabin, with the usual clumps of neglected thousand-leaf roses about it. In this old house in those years lived Granny Ghaut whom my mother sometimes went to see. I went with her once, and often saw Granny standing in the door in her old-fashioned ruffled white-cotton cap, a feeble but stout figure, framed in the doorway as I went by to school. Although she had relatives living in the neighborhood, she was dependent on the kindness of John and Mary Bailey for her support and other care. The kindly responsibility which they quietly took upon themselves as a sort of matter of course, because she lived on their land, shows the large and generous spirit characteristic of John Bailey. My memory of Mrs. Jane Ghaut's words is confined to a single saying of hers repeated by my mother once after a visit to her. It was evidently out of some talk about names, in which she showed a contempt for her own: "Jane ain't no name, Ann ain't no name."

[87]

Solomon C. was a man whose wrecked life made an impression on my childish heart. He used to be seen about the neighborhood woods at times with a very strange-looking woman who was his wife, they said. They slept in the woods on beds of leaves by a great log and were seen about bareheaded, he redfaced, she often with black bruises on her face. They never spoke to us if we met them, and our shy and fearful looks and hastening steps would not have encouraged them to do so. We never knew what they ate, nor where they usually spent the winters. In later years I used to see him in town, sometimes at church, sometimes on the street.

After the first election of Lincoln, a celebration at night with fireworks, illuminations, guns, and bonfires took place in the streets and everybody, even those as fearful of noise and gunpowder as I was, thronged the blazing streets. Some ill-conditioned persons had given Solomon enough whiskey to make him funny and had got him to going up and down shouting "Hurray for Jackson!" I saw his red, masque-like face in the blaze of the gun firing and his thick-bodied, short-legged form go up and down in the hurly-burly.

The last time I saw the poor fellow, he offered himself for membership in the New Light Church, whose pastor, the Rev. J. D. Lauer, asked for converts. Our hearts stood still when the poor drunkard, who had been converted so many times, at the Methodist Church and a time or two before in this church, rose to go forward again. This time he advanced up the aisle slowly and timidly with his eyes fixed on the pastor's face. His strange form, now clothed neatly in a poor plain suit, looked as on a man from another land— which indeed it was, an alien land of sorrow and weakness. Mr. Lauer's fine face was moved as he stepped down and took the poor fellow's hand with, "Thank God!" on his lips.

Granny Stroh was an interesting figure appearing twice a year in our neighborhood. She came and went with the seasons, a somewhat small, spare, but erect old woman who lived by going from door to door, though she was not a beggar. She would sit by our fire, take a coal for her pipe and smoke. Silent, watching everything with bright black eyes, staying to a meal if you asked her, or for a week or all night if invited, but moving on to the next house if hospitality was not offered. Truth to say it was so offered at some places because there was a half-accepted belief that she was a witch and could do harm. However that may be, she was always treated with courtesy. I have often seen her passing the main road. We knew her at once by her faded tunnel sun-bonnet, faded short calico gown, and her bundle on a stick carried across the shoulder. I never spoke to her, and suppose I must have stared curiously at her at such times as she stopped at our house. My sister Laurinda and I were once much troubled for fear her inopportune call would hinder our starting on a visit ten miles away to my aunt's at New West-ville. We children were all dressed in our best, mother was ready, father had gone to put the horses to the covered wagon, when in came Granny Stroh. Mother gave her a chair, helped her to a coal, and went on with her preparations putting away the dishes after a hasty meal and setting things to order. We did not dare ask questions, but Laurinda and I were voluble in looks to each other. Evidently, however, her manners were equal to the occasion as she rose and went out with a "Good day!" when she had done smoking. She generally spent a week at my grandmother's on each round. The last I saw of her was once on my return from my grandmother's, as I neared town—the same faded figure in faded clean cotton, silhouetted against the green field opposite. She did not turn to look at us but moved on at the same pace I had observed years before.

I was well grown up then. She was still living when I was eighteen. It was then I recognized a granddaughter of hers among the children in my backwoods school in Lanier Township—a Margaret Wertz. There were the same restless black eyes, swarthy skin, and undershot lower jaw. Granny Stroh died some years after in the County Hospital where she spent the winters of her last years, although she had children and grandchildren who would have taken care of her if she could have endured to live with them. She was said to be one hundred and five years old. I never knew the extent of her wanderings, but heard of her having taken the northwestern and southeastern townships of the county into her regular itinerary.

Podgauger was an old, wool-hatted, tan-coated man whose deliberate over-to-that-side and back-to-this-side motion in the saddle expressed all the time there was, as he rode by on his fat, round horse. Listening from my perch on the rail fence to the suction sound of his horse's feet as they lifted from the road mud was one of my unconscious pleasures, never missed if I saw his stout figure turning up the road that led by our house. I came to know in time

10

Neighborhood
Religion and Other Matters

In the forties and fifties, there still existed in our part of the country, both in rural churches and in the towns, certain forms of religious expression which, for the most part, were disappearing. One of these very common in the Methodist churches and as I have been told, in the Christian Church, though I never heard it there but once was what was called "Shouting." Not only at revivals, but at the ordinary Sunday meetings, some old-fashioned people when they got, as they said, very "happy," would walk up and down the aisles of the church waving their arms and shouting in a half-breathless voice "Glory!" (or "Praise the Lord!" or "Hallelujah!"). Sometimes merely incoherent shouts, "Eigh-o-o-o-o, eigh-o!" I have seen and heard a certain good lady, Peggy B. by name, do this several times, getting up in the middle of a sermon when anything was said that moved her feelings. This seemed not to disturb the preacher and congregation, nor to interrupt the proceedings in any way. I believe that she continued this practice so long as she lived. I heard my mother speak with disapproval of those who sometimes were thus excited at meetings of the Christian Church; she thought it unseemly and out of place in a house of public worship.

The preachers of the country churches known to me between 1841 and 1851 were mostly plain men of comparatively little education. Their language was simple and direct; their subjects generally practical and fundamental to life. I am able to say these things of them because I heard most of them preach after I was twenty. Two or three of them had the "pulpit voice" and manner. Of these I remember that I listened, as a child, to two of them who had the habit of beginning the sermon or the prayer in a familiar, conversational tone, then as they warmed up to their subject, they gradually increased in pitch and volume until they had reached what seemed to me the upper end of a high inclined plane, when suddenly they would drop the voice to the original level, from which they would again climb to heights and again drop, repeating the process to the end of the sermon.

At this point the speaker with red and streaming face, swollen neck veins, and hoarse voice drew upon my childish sympathies, although I felt it a great relief that the crack and roar of his voice had ceased and I could unclasp my tightly clenched little fists. Doubtless the exercise of such nerve-straining piety was of little value as a part of my religious education. I had my choices among these ministers, although I never expressed them. I then liked best among them a man who used to talk in the pulpit as he did when he came to our house.

My knowledge of and my acquaintance with a preacher of entirely different type and education began when I was an infant of six or seven. I went home from school one evening to find sitting by the hearth, opposite my mother, behind whose chair I took refuge, a dark young man with very black hair, a strange-looking stranger. Wonder was added to my staring eyes when I heard him speak. It was the first time I had heard an accent unlike our own. He was a young Welshman but recently come to America. He became afterwards one of the ablest and best known preachers of the Christian denomination. Not long after his arrival in our neighborhood, he opened a private high school in the little Berea Chapel not far from my home. Young men and young women of the neighborhood studied with him through the winter. He was often at our house and became a lifelong friend of my father and mother. His name was Evan W. Humphreys.

A few years later, after we had moved to Eaton, Mr. Humphreys, who was pastor of the Christian Church there, always brought visiting ministers to see us, some of whom sometimes called of their own accord. Among these latter was a revivalist whose aggressive way of breaking through people's personal reserve had been hitherto unknown to me. Before leaving our house after a call, he prayed with the family as was customary, but he prayed so long and so loud that I heard nothing that he said, for fear that neighbors across the creek would hear and think desperate things. He seemed greatly wrought up in his feelings, but had no more effect on mine, other than that of relief when he had finished. He shocked me more when a day or two afterwards he asked me at the church door, before my mother, if I didn't want to be saved. It seemed as if he were trying to break down the walls of a place that belonged to me alone.

There was as I remember, however, little verbal expression of religious thought or feeling in our neighborhood. It was the custom to go to meeting whether one belonged to the church or not. It was the general opinion that it was the right and decorous thing to do; besides there was the pleasure of meeting one's neighbors and friends. Sunday was strictly observed so far as work was concerned, but visiting and being visited were not frowned upon. Everybody dressed for Sunday, even though he stayed at home. I remember but one exception to Sunday observance, in a well-to-do family who were secretly looked down upon because they sometimes worked in the field on Sunday, never went to church, and made no other difference in the day.

A common custom in the churches of the Christian denomination, from its beginning in 1801 after the great Kentucky Revival and lasting, in my memory, through the fifties, was that of "exhorting." This seems to have descended directly from the Presbyterian Church, which licensed those known as "exhorters." In the Christian Church, however, any deacon or any young man preparing for the ministry might, when he felt like it, rise at the end of the sermon, come forward and stand below the pulpit and speak to the congregation exhorting sinners to regard the words they had just heard; sometimes he added warnings of his own in Old Testament phraseology. These exhortations usually lasted but a few minutes. They were not always liked, as they sometimes pointed a moral too definitely, especially if the exhorter were old and severe and criticized the doings of the young men of the neighborhood. But usually their remarks were confined to exhortation of the people in general.

The custom of "lining out" hymns was still common in the forties and had not wholly gone out in the early fifties. Very few people had hymnbooks, and although the most of them knew many familiar hymns by heart, the minister after reading the hymn through would go back and read again the first two lines which the congregation would sing and then wait for the reading of the next two, and so on with every two lines throughout the hymn. Usually someone with a ready voice would start the hymn to some well-known tune; failing which, the minister himself would lead. This goodly custom had the effect of teaching many of the good old hymns to the people. As I remember it the effect was one of dignity and solemnity.

Baptism in the Christian (New Light) Church was always administered by immersion. It was not, as with the Disciples (Campbellite Christians), necessary for admission to church membership. In the early history of the church it was, however, customary to conform to it as soon after joining the church as opportunity was offered. This ceremony was always performed in some stream. The fact that the water might be frozen at the appointed time did not postpone the baptism as the ice was cut for the occasion. I never heard that any ill effects resulted. In the later history of the church, baptism was not insisted upon, at least in some churches of which I knew.

As Paint Creek Christian Church was the only religious organization in the near neighborhood, it was the center of whatever religious expression there was, excepting that a number of families living nearer to Eaton were connected with the Christian Church there. This organization was the first religious body which took form in Eaton after the settlement of that town in 1808. It still had its meetings in the Public Church there as late as 1855, I think, after which it moved its place to a hired building on Barron Street, and later to its own new building which it still occupies.

Paint Creek Church was named from Paint Creek which was so called because of a yellow earth on its banks, once used by the Indians for paint. It was built of brick in 1840 and was in its prime of usefulness in my childhood. It was an oblong building without spire, typical of that time and region, with windows on the sides and a door at either end, where at first men and women came in separately and sat on either side apart. Even with families of small children the parents did not sit together. The pulpit was a high paneled structure furnished with oil lamps, and stood in the middle of the west side of the room. Here my Grandfather Ryan sometimes went to meeting—his family usually, if they went at all. I often went with my parents while we still lived in the house built on a part of my grandfather's farm and later but less frequently from our town home.

Among my early recollections of this church stands out one of hearing a preacher then very young, slender, blue-eyed, with yellow curling hair. My memory of him at that church recalls him as kneeling in prayer in the middle of the floor in front of the pulpit, dressed entirely, and for that time, exquisitely, in snow-white summer clothes. The farm of my Grandfather Hardy was separated from the plot of ground on which the church stood, by the Concord Road, so that my father was brought up almost within a stone's throw of the pioneer church built of logs, in which his father had preached. Here too I heard in my childhood many of those plain pioneer preachers who were so much a part of the religious influences of the time.

This church was the nearest place of worship until after a secession of some sort, and the building of Berea Chapel, in the Bailey District nearer to my home. Here I went to church and Sunday school between the ages of eight and ten; often also to a singing school led by my father, with his clear tenor voice and ability to read "round notes," as well as the "buckwheat notes." I easily read the buckwheat notes myself then and sang with the best of them—all grown-up people. I often went with my parents or aunts to Paint Church, however, even after we had left the neighborhood. The last time I was present there was once when I walked from our home in Eaton one Sunday morning with my father. It was the year—about 1854 or 1855—when wide-brimmed straw hats (called "flats") had come into fashion in that region. I, arrayed in one of these and a pink-sprigged muslin, feeling very properly dressed, went happily along the road, holding my hat in place by the ribbon "bridle" fastened to the ribbon band in front to keep the hat on in a breeze.

At church we heard then for the first time the new instrumental choir made up of two or three Dooleys, fathers and son and others, with violins and cello. They sat in the middle of the church around one of the wooden pillars which supported the roof and played to the singing of the congregation, which not long before had sung without hymnbooks, to lined-out hymns read by the minister. On this day too, I heard the voice of Hester May singing "counter," and soaring above all the voices of the congregation and the sounds of the orchestra. I looked at her shining black hair, her red cheeks, her stylish bonnet, silk crepe shawl, and silk dress with great admiration. She was the daughter of a wealthy farmer and considered with a good deal of interest by all the young women of the neighborhood. I think it was James Neal who preached that day—a good man without much education, a good deal of zeal and courage, and marvelous patience under afflicting family circumstances. His preaching was, of course, extemporaneous—honest, simple, concrete.

Superstitions of various gentle and obsolescent kinds were common among the grown people of our neighborhood, as well as among the children. Ghosts and haunted houses were commonly believed in. Most people had "seen" ghosts. My mother early in our childhood told us stories to dispossess, or anticipate, any such beliefs, which she knew we could not be entirely shielded from. As it was the custom to take all one's children along to any gathering of women for sewing, quilting, or wool picking, there was a great deal of opportunity to hear all kinds of talk. Though much of it passed harmlessly over childish heads, here and there a bit would stick in the memory with some wonder connected with it. My mother divined this, as she also knew that my young aunts were more than likely to tell us eye-opening tales of ghosts and haunted houses. Not infrequently too my grandmother told us ghost tales around the evening fireside when sometimes in the winter I stayed there all night after I was ten.

One of my mother's stories is pertinent here as showing the condition of living then and there and something of my mother's naturally fearless mind even in her childhood. She was the eldest of fourteen children, and at the time of my grandfather's emigration to Ohio was twelve years old. The farms which grandfather chopped out of the woods lay three and a half miles from Eaton, then a mere village, but so much of a county town as there was. Little money was in circulation, little was needed, but that little had to come from the sale of farm products of the smaller sort—butter, eggs, dressed chickens, maple-sugar loaves. These things had to be marketed in town by some member of the family. So then, my mother, being the most available, and old enough and not afraid, was sent to town on horseback, starting at three or four in the morning, with whatever could be spared from the family larder. A road still more or less beset with stumps, and brush, woods on either side, a sky still with its night aspect at that early hour, nobody but herself on the road—there was a chance to see things, and this was her story:

"I was going to market one misty morning with butter and some dressed chickens, and had got as far along as where Plummer's house now stands, near what we now call Bruce's Hill, when I saw in front of me in the road a great white thing. I should have to pass it close—and what could it be? I stopped and looked. Black Bess paid no attention to it, why should I be afraid; nothing could hurt me. There were no such things as ghosts. Go on, Bess. We'll see. And what do you think? A big white cow got up on her knees, rose, and stalked away as I came close. She had looked as large as a haystack, and that, children, was the only ghost I ever saw."

"But Mother—Aunt Juley says there's a ghost in the Talbert house. You know____." "That ghost is real live people standing at the window different times in a white gown, and with a lighted candle. I know." So always ended my inquiries about ghosts, if I went to my mother. Somewhat later than the time of the cow ghost it was that my mother saw the great shower of meteors in 1833. She was again on her way to town on horseback, but, though awed, felt no fright and went on slowly looking at what she supposed to be falling stars. However, I often heard my father's sister Laurinda say that many people spent the night on their knees praying, as they thought the end of the world had come.

Other objects of superstition were often the merely unexplainable, or the weird and unusual. Living in the woods where many strange and unaccountable sounds were of common occurrence, it was natural that some of them should be thought ominous, or portentous. The long shriek of a wind-moved branch of a tree down in the woods, as it scraped against another tree, what did that portend, but the passing of a soul? On still winter nights I heard that sound from my grandmother's porch, and can yet feel the chill and thrill of it, as a young aunt by my side would say, "Somebody's going to die." All the time I knew it was just what it was, but how could I know that it did not foretell? Certainly it did not make me afraid, for there was my mother at home, who would explain. Then besides, I had been too often in the woods and heard just such noises and with face upturned had hunted up the very limbs that made them. But in the night with stars and someone beside you to suggest fearsome thoughts it was hard to disbelieve.

If you were running hard after others who were running and you got a sharp pain in your side, it would stop, if you would pause long enough to turn over a chip, or a bone or a stone on your way. And it did! If you found a pin point toward you, it was good luck if you picked it up. You could go round to the other end before you took it up, if it was head toward you. If you put your apron on wrong side out, it was good luck too, if you wore it so all day. If a cock came to the door and crowed at you or if a bumblebee flew in at the door and out again, you might as well get ready for dinner, for company was coming. If a bird flew against the window pane at night, someone of your friends was ill, or would die.

If you dropped a knife, a woman was coming, if a fork, a man—and alas, if a spoon, a fool! If you should drop a dishcloth that was dirty, a slatternly housekeeper would visit you. You must not kill your pigs for winter meat in the wane of the moon; the meat would all frizzle up in the cooking. And your beans must be planted in the sign of the Twins; and you must not build your rail fence in the dark of the moon, or the lower rail would sink into the ground. If your butter did not come, it might be that someone had bewitched it, but this was held by few and hardly countenanced as a respectable opinion—indeed, it had general discredit, though it had some life on the tongues of the neighborhood.

But dreams meant a great deal, and their interpretation was a matter of individual notions; though dreambooks were to be seen on the shelves of the neighbor families, their hold on opinion was very slight. Muddy water and clear water, a wedding or a funeral in dreams meant good or bad according to whether you took them by contraries or as they were.

I myself have been haunted by the bad portent of a certain dream or two. To dream of a falling tooth or of carrying a sick child—ah, well, I can not get away from the feeling to this day that something evil is imminent. Reason cannot down the thing. Charlotte Brontë had a similar obsession about the sick-child dream. I suppose most people take shame to themselves for similar unreasoning prepossessions—one cannot call them beliefs. I once heard a youngish woman, an Oakland teacher, say that if she had one inch of superstitious flesh on her body she would cut if off. Even she would not turn her apron, if she happened to put it on wrong side out—'twould bring bad luck.

Two or three haunted houses there were in our region, the Talbert house near my grandmother's and the log cabin from which my father moved to our own hewn-log house. The first was altogether the best house in that part of the country—white frame with green blinds and a good porch in front.

Of ghost stories, the permanent one still alive there, I think, (1905) was one we became familiar with after our removal to Eaton. It was connected with the scene of St. Clair's defeat near Fort St. Clair, the site of which is still traceable southwest of Eaton a mile or so. But the tale must have been imported from New York, by some Dutch emigrant. A headless horseman, followed by a dog, and walking beside his horse was often seen, they said, climbing the hill. I had heard the story recited often and read Judge Abner Haines's version of the legend; and I had opportunities enough to see the apparition on my way home on Friday evenings in winter. But the moon reflected in the waters of the Garrison Branch, the black shadows of the willows on both sides of the road, the graveyard on the hill on one side, and a dark wood on the other—the ghost had a chance at me, but never took it.

The language of our neighborhood between '41 and '51 was somewhat dialectical, but mainly in the matter of grammatical forms as, for example, some of the people used the past participle of irregular verbs as "seen" and "gone" for past tenses and objective forms of pronouns for nominatives, and the reverse. There were some curious words whose sources I never knew: among them, was the word *cevendáble*, meaning *first rate* or very *good* or *excellent*, "I made some real cevendáble bread yesterday." This word so far as I know came from Kentucky. *Slompy* meant *slatternly*, *tizza-rizzen* "I have a tizza-rizzen in my head," which meant a feeling like the beginning of a sick headache; *Wamus*,* a garment generally made of

*Supposed by those who used it to be from the words, *warm us*, but really from wamus or wammus German wams from M.H.G. wambeis, a garment worn under armor from, O.H.G. and Goth. wamba, body.

red flannel worn as a blouse by farmers—the corners were usually tied in a knot in front of the waistline.

Cope was used to call horses: as "Cope Dinah." *Doncy* meant something very like softly sentimental or weak; it was sometimes used to mean tired and feeble—with perhaps a sprinkle of laziness. To be called *doncy* was very uncomplimentary. *Riley* was used to mean muddy—of course from *roil. Strubly*, which I heard much later, meant disorderly, and was of Pennsylvania origin. On the whole, the English of that region was very good considering opportunities. If children grew up to speak ungrammatically it was because as elsewhere they heard such language at home. In my own home correct language was the rule.

Now and then as elsewhere some person would show a genius for the descriptive, in making compounds for himself, which he would use as briefly describing a stranger recently met: he was probably *dish-faced*, or *squirrel-jawed*, or perhaps *slab-sided.* The words *traipse* and *traipsing* were in common use, but always with a sense of criticism of the act or actor, or of conditions, as for example, "I shall not *traipse* to church in such mud as this," or "She goes *traipsing* over the neighborhood gossiping about her betters," or, "I have *traipsed* all over the place and can't find an egg."

I was much surprised as a child when I heard my Aunt Eliza talking about *currants* to find that she meant what I had heard called *kurns* by the people of the neighborhood. Even now the word *currant* brings up the good smell and taste of green *kurn* pie.

Children were taught to say "Yes ma'am," "No ma'am," "Yes sir," "No sir," to their elders and "Ma'am?" and "Sir?" instead of "I beg your pardon" or "Excuse me" when they would ask over what they did not hear. Phrases used in the neighborhood as I now remember bore traces of Kentucky or Virginia origin. *Passel* for *parcel* was one of these. It was used in the sense of a *great many* or a *great deal*; as a "*passel* of chips," "a *passel* of greens for dinner," or a "*passel* of pigs in the garden." This word was made to do several kinds of service.

It was common in the neighborhood to speak of people who came from Kentucky as "Tuckahoes," which without doubt came from the use of the word *tuck* for *took*: I "*tuck* a hoe and went to the cornfield."

[100]

Donnick was used as the name of a small cobblestone that one might pick up on the road or in the field. "Throw a *donnick* at that pig and drive him out," "That apple is as hard as a *donnick.*" I am told that a similar word, *darnic,* with the same meaning was used further west. *Kiver* for *cover,* both as a verb and a noun, *kiverlid* for *coverlet,* *cowcumber* for *cucumber,* were occasionally heard from the older people in the neighborhood. I heard *cowcumber* in Eaton as late as 1855. *Arrant* for *errand,* *beholden* for under *obligation* were often heard. *Lappin's* as in the sentence, "She never gave me as much as the *lappin's* of my finger," was an expressive way of complaining of stinginess. This may have either of two meanings, *wrappings* or *lappings* with the tongue.

The Christmas Saint, though not very well known in our neighborhood, was spoken of as Kriss Kringle to the children, but his name was not very often heard, and he was of a far more hazy personality than Santa Claus. He was believed by some children to be so good as to put candy into your shoes if you should place them on the steps at night, even in summertime, but he never treated me so.

Between 1840 and 1850 there was no singing in the schools, and so far as I know there were no songbooks. I have spoken elsewhere of the singing schools which began to be in the middle of the decade, but the books used contained sacred music only. Ballads and songs were handed about by written copies and by singing. Some of these must have come down by word of mouth, as I never heard or saw them elsewhere, afterward. Later, but before my tenth year, I remember hearing a young uncle sing some sentimental songs from a pamphlet ballad book. One which he very much favored was "Meet Me by Moonlight Alone." Two of perhaps a little later time were: "I'd Offer Thee This Hand of Mine," and "Thou Hast Learned to Love Another." I heard my younger aunts and other girls of their age say to each other, "Will you write me the ballad of that?" or "She promised me the ballad of_____." Some of the songs I heard then were stories which I did not understand and therefore cannot recall. Very much later in life I heard one of these old songs called "Peter Sweet," of twenty-seven verses, of which I remember nothing except a comically pathetic situation.

In my eleventh year a new girl sang for us:

> So buy me the tally wooly eye-sy.
> So buy me the tally, wooly, thribble, double, dilly, wiley, Sukey dukey right green gown.

and so following with:

> Will you wear the red?
> I won't it's the color of my head.
> So buy me etc., etc.
> Will you wear the white?
> It's a color I don't like.
> Will you wear the black?
> It's the color of my hat.

till it comes at last to:

> O will you wear the green, O narrow, narrow?
> I will wear the green,
> Cause it's the color I do mean.
> So buy etc., etc.

As I said elsewhere, there were no singing books in the old schoolhouse, nor, so far as I know, was there any singing until after 1850. I think my father was among the first, if not the first, to introduce singing into the country schools. This he did by setting some of the poems contained in the readers to easy tunes which he taught his school to sing. Among these sung by him were: "He Never Smiled Again," beginning, "The bark that held the Prince went down"; "Come to the Festal Board To-night," "Alone I Walked the Ocean Strand." As late as 1867 I used this device of singing from the readers, in a school where I had no singing books.

I had been in a class in Kirkham's *Grammar* but happily knew no technical grammar. I could spell Webster's *Spelling Book* through and some of McGuffey's. I could sing a little and even read the buckwheat notes, as I have said. I had never been taught to draw. Making pictures on a slate in school was a misdemeanor.

My knowledge of the outer world around me as to form, color, taste, name, general appearance was as full as observation and inquiry and a real delight in external forms could make it. My knowledge of people was limited by the boundaries of the neighbor-

hood and such moving about in it for me and for other people as
was then customary.

Our removal from the conditions and surroundings thus far
described to Eaton took place in the summer of 1851, at the end of
my tenth year. The simple life of the log cabin, the influences of
quiet neighborhood annals, as well as those of the level fields and
woodlands, now gave place to much that was similar in effect
though greatly different in some of its details. Very little that is
definite concerning the removal itself has place in my memory, but
I can still see the look of the empty house, I can still hear the
peeping of a lost chicken which we could not find and the loud
pot-rack, pot-rack of the guinea fowls which flew to the tops of the
beeches and had to be left behind.

Halfway to town our old white cat jumped from the wagon and
ran back home, much to our childish grief as we thought her lost
forever. But my father brought her to our new home a few days
after, from which she immediately disappeared. Again she was
brought from the old home, after which she went about the new
house looking at everything, smelling the furniture in all the rooms
until she seemed to understand what had happened and after
that was satisfied to stay. Thus without other conscious observation of mine ended the first ten years of my life history. The old
clock on the wall with its quaint Arabic figures on the dial, its
insistent shorthand pointing to the hours, and its emphatic long
hand pointing to twelve as in confirmation, its bell with the
mysterious strike above, and its equally mysterious weights to be
wound up nightly—the old clock was now to mark off the hours of
my days in other surroundings.

Strange people would sit around our fireplace and sleep in the
room where our beds had been, and their hands would draw water
from our well to drink at the curb. The story of the woods and
fields would go on, with songs of birds, the opening of buds, the
falling of leaves, and the blowing of winter winds. And we should
not be there to know or care. Strange as it may seem, no such
thoughts as these disturbed me then, but with the eager onlooking
of a child I went away out of these places and times without a
thought of grief, carrying with me none but trivial memories to
mark that day which was an epoch in my life.

I was never again in the old house as we did not know the people who took possession of it, but I always looked at it across the field and road as I passed on my way to visit my grandmother. I saw it for the last time in 1876, when it looked much the same as when we had left it. The Big Woods had been slain and were then a desolate-looking cornfield with charred stumps and dead naked trunks of a few of the trees I had so loved and lived under. But my memory, refusing to dwell on this picture, still rejoices in the living woods it once knew so intimately. The Little Woods at that time showed no changes, but in its March aspect looked as I had always known it at that season. I wandered about under all the trees where I had played, and stayed so long after sunset enjoying the good companionship of the trees that my little grandmother whom I was visiting grew uneasy. When I came back to the house with a handful of brown beech leaves and a piece of green moss, she said, "What do you want with those things, child?" I could not have told her and only said, "Oh, I like them."

YOUTH AND
YOUNG WOMANHOOD

1

Eaton

The beginning of my second decade of life at our new home in Eaton is as unmarked by definite recollections as the close of the first. Some impressions still remain, however, that free themselves from the innumerable others of wonder and interest in the new things that crowded, all at once, into the plane of my observation. The large rooms in the house, their ash floors, the staircase with a door letting out, halfway up, into the backyard on the hill, the smaller fireplaces, and the white-plastered walls are all that I am able to differentiate from the general mass of impressions. All else seems entirely overlaid by later definite experiences which have their place in the records that follow.

Eaton, the chief town of Preble County, was laid out by William Bruce on his own land in 1806.* It was named by its founder for General William Eaton, one of the heroes of the war with Algiers then in progress. Several of its streets, Barron, Decatur, Israel, Somers, and Wadsworth, celebrate other heroes of the same war, as does also the name of the county. All of these local names not only show William Bruce's patriotic interest in the struggle, but point to the general feeling of the people of that region. The town site was on the slight elevation of the east bank of St. Clair Creek, and its main street east and west was afterward a part of the great National Road, a macadamized thoroughfare built in Jackson's administration. Barron Street crossed Main at right angles, and divided the town plot equally. The first house in the place was of logs and built

*For further details, see *History of Preble County*, p. 98 ff., and *Directory of Preble County, Ohio for 1875:Historical Sketches and Biographies of Eminent Pioneers. . . .* (Eaton, 1875), p. 153 ff.; hereafter, *Directory of Preble County*. [Ed. note]

in 1806 on the corner of Main and Beech, the street next west of
Barron, on the spot afterwards occupied by the house of Felix
Marsh.

The first religious service in Eaton was held by Elder Smith,
a preacher of the New Light Christian denomination in 1807, in
which year that church was organized. But as the settlement was
yet too small to have a church building, religious meetings were
held in turn in the various settlers' cabins. Of the three denominations represented in the settlement the Methodists were the first to
own a church building, which they put up on the corner of Decatur
and Maple Streets in 1829.

Previous to this, however, the united community had built what
was known as the Public Church near St. Clair Creek on the west
end of Wadsworth Street. Here these two denominations and the
Presbyterians had held their meetings in harmony until, one by one,
they grew strong enough to build separate tabernacles. But the
Old Public Church was still the church home of the Christians for
some years after the other denominations had gone to their new
places of worship uptown.

Here I went to church and Sunday school in the early fifties.
Later, in 1858, when the last of these religious societies had found
a more convenient place of worship, I went again to the old church
as teacher of the little children who gathered in one corner of it as
a public school. The old building was still standing in 1894, a
monument to the tolerance and brotherhood of the early settlers.
Owing to the fact that the town records were destroyed by fire in
1859, the date of its erection has been lost. But by consulting an
old history of Preble County I find that the Public Church was built
soon after the organization of the Christian Church in 1807. This is
the church of which John Hardy was pastor at the time of his death
in 1819.

The history referred to also records that this organization flour-
ished for the first fifteen years of its life and counted in its membership a large number of pioneer families, among which were such
names as Banta, Bailey, Bloomfield, Brubaker, Bruce, Crawford,
Duggins, Fleming, Hardy, Sellers, and Van Ausdal.

But in 1823 the doctrines of Alexander Campbell began to make
headway among the churches of Ohio. The church at Eaton, like
many others, was so affected by the doctrinal test of Immersion,

that a large number withdrew to the rural organizations, and the church at Eaton was discontinued. It was reorganized in 1841 with most of the old membership and continues to this day a strong working force in the town of Eaton.

In the summer of 1851 when we took up our residence near Eaton, that town was a place of 1,500 or 2,000 inhabitants. Its streets were, for the most part, macadamized, and many of its wide sidewalks were covered with flagstones. The greater part of the dwelling houses on the two principal streets were built sheer with the sidewalk. Some of them were so low in foundation that one could step from the front door directly to the ground. This would mean, of course, that there were few front yards and no flowers to be seen on the streets. At various irregular intervals maples or locusts had been planted, but it was not until later years that tree planting became general, and gave to the streets that beauty which now characterizes the town. The new courthouse was not completed till the next year, when its great Ionic columns became objects of admiration to me. The railroad was opened for travel in the same year by a free excursion to Hamilton.

Our home at Eaton was "St. Clair Cottage," a house which had been built some years before by my uncle, S.S. Young, and taken by my father in exchange for some wild land and a lot nearby on which we had intended to build our new house. "St. Clair Cottage" stood on a hill opposite the town, on the west, and beyond St. Clair Creek, overlooking the mill dam and the west end of town. It was a two-story structure of stone walls two-feet thick below, and a second story of wood frame, the whole finished with plaster inside and out. Built on a side hill, it allowed us to walk out of the second-floor doors to the shade of the great apple trees above and at the back. It had open fireplaces and ash floors and staircase. At the south end was my aunt's greenhouse, built of brick and full of wonderful plants which I had never seen anywhere else, the "grape-geranium" (pink begonia), lemon verbena, an orange tree, tea roses, and various species of cactus with gorgeous flowers with their throats full of thread-like stamens. But the greenhouse was soon built up into an addition to the main house, and my aunt and uncle moved to their own new house on the place where my father had intended to build.

Our grounds were spacious and shady with fruit trees, vines

and ornamental shrubs, grapes, roses, and honeysuckle. Behind and above the house were seven very large apple trees, beyond which was the gate into the carriage road leading to the highway. In front was a level terrace covered with grass and edged with a row of red cedars, which gradually descended on the right and left to meet level walks below, leading off to the ends of the garden. Directly in the middle of the terrace in front was a staircase of wooden steps, giving on a broad, grassy path to the gate at some distance below. The gate opened out to a footpath leading by the millrace and milldam, and very near to the former, so that in times of very high water in the spring there was now and then no room to pass between the fence and the water.

Our life was happy and full of interest in these days; for we had these beautiful grounds, a barn at the northwest corner, the orchards nearby (Van Doren's orchard was open to the public, at least nobody seemed to care who went there for fruit or play), the creek and millrace, walks with father, the quarry where I found trilobites for father to dig out from the blocks of stone, and the hundred and one things to be seen and learned in these places, between school times. In winter we sat in the deep windows on cold days and looked at the skaters on the dam; at night their fires shone into our rooms as we went to bed. I have shivered with apprehension as I have seen some skillful skater whiz by the crowd toward the edge of the dam as if he were intent on skating over to kill himself, turn suddenly and come back as if nothing had happened. I have laughed at the awkward, fish-like flopping of a skater whose red hands seemed a mile out of his sleeves, and whose skating was more like the movement of a jumping-jack than like anything else—all this between pages as I sat in the deep window reading Scott or Cooper.

Bruce's milldam, which lay between us and the west side of town, furnished a large part of our outdoor interests. We never looked out of the windows, upstairs or down, without seeing whatever was going on near or just beyond it. Its banks and the dam itself with the millrace and its high headgate all formed a part of our playground, summer and winter. Although we never played about it without leave, we spent a good deal of time on its banks and climbing about looking curiously among its piles of rocks, its great rock-filled log buttress and its bright-bottomed shallows when the stream was low.

At the end of the dyke which filled the space between the dam and the millrace was a thicket of wild roses and every year a clump of wild touch-me-nots. From both of these we exacted our toll of pleasure: from the one, sweet-smelling roses through the summer, and bunches of red rose hips to string for bracelets in the autumn; from the other, little pitcher-shaped flowers with velvety brown throats and little bombardment of seeds when we touched the ripe seed vessels. The picture of this delightful spot would hardly be complete without the image of a certain lone kingfisher that used to sit on the high, vertical bar of the headgate, beautiful and motionless until disturbed, when he flew to cover in the secret places of the rose thicket.

Down through these grassy stretches of common to the water's edge came the west end of Somers Street, and led many a thirsty horse to drink, standing shoulder deep in the cool waters of the dam. Here too came congregations of people, usually from the Christian and Disciple Churches, to administer the sacrament of baptism. I recall the cautious movements of the black-gowned pastor as he went first down into the water feeling his way with a cane to the right depth. Returning, he took the black-gowned candidate by the hand, and while the congregation sang a verse of a hymn, went slowly down into the water. After a short prayer, the low tones of which I could faintly hear from the terrace, and the immersion, they went slowly back while the congregation sang another verse of the same hymn. These religious services were never made the occasion for the gathering of curious spectators, as but few people besides those directly concerned came to look on.

Sometimes, too, the milldam was a source of exciting interest: at the time of heavy rains which brought down huge logs and plunged them over the dam with a great roar; or the ice gorge which came crashing down from above, and covered not only the whole dam itself but the shores on either side with heaps of broken ice. In very cold weather, when the ice was thick on the dam, groups of men and boys with wagons and saws cutting ice to fill the icehouses made another winter picture.

[111]

Many a night have I sat at my bedroom window, looking out between the tops of the dark cedars at the moonlight glittering on the clear waters or gleaming on the ice, and often have I been waked in the middle of the night by the long, steely musical sound which I knew to be the sinking and cracking of the ice on the milldam, accompanied by the steady roar of the falling water. Often, too, have my sisters and I dared to cross on the sometimes uncertain ice which cracked behind us as we ran. Thereby we saved a quarter of a mile, perhaps, of the way to school, and had the fearful pleasure of feeling that we had escaped a danger. It was our habit also in the summertime to save this same quarter of a mile by crossing below the dam on the out-cropping stratum of limestone which stood above the low water far enough to make a dry footway. It was at these times that we saw black water snakes lying in great tangled piles sunning themselves on the rocks at the creek end of the dyke. But we passed them without fear, for they never moved as we went by.

Our removal from a farming country of level fields and woods to St. Clair Cottage among the low hills west of Eaton made a far greater change in our surroundings than so short a distance would seem to suggest. The cottage itself on a terraced hill, surrounded by shrubberies and orchards, overlooking the milldam, a wide expanse of water; the dam itself with its fall of twelve or fifteen feet or more, these things and others made upon my unconscious mind impressions which became important elements in my growth and development.

Bruce's Mill I had seen two or three times before we moved to St. Clair Cottage, when I had ridden in with my father in my new calico dress and Leghorn bonnet to visit my Aunt Eliza at St. Clair Cottage, while he waited for the grist. The mill was then, and always afterward, a place of great interest to me, with its forebay, its great slow-turning wheels, its red-cheeked, blue-eyed miller in his white-powdered clothes. My father still took his own hand-shelled corn, and his own sacks of wheat to this mill, even after we had moved to St. Clair Cottage. We children often stopped to look in as we went down the creek, or to Bruce's Woods.

The beginning of this mill was made in 1808 by William Bruce, before which time the people had to go long distances for their flour and meal—thirty miles, I have heard it said. In 1832 the mill was completed as I knew it and milling was carried on by Charles Bruce and afterwards by his son William until 1886. Even as late as the seventies the farmers depended largely on this mill for their breadstuffs; although after the building of the railroad, in the early fifties, flour from other mills could be bought in town by the barrel.*

Connected with the memories of these places are recollections of short excursions taken on sunny Saturdays with my father and sisters, usually with the intention of collecting geological specimens. We often went to a place called Lower Leas's, where were some high limestone cliffs; a little below these but further from the creek was a bed of chain coral which I could find now if I should go looking for it. On the opposite side of the creek we found a spring whose water made petrifactions; and there once I saw a little gray newt hovering about a nest of transparent eggs. As the entire region about Eaton was rich in fossils, our eyes soon became keen for specimens and our happiness was complete if we found anything which father thought worth keeping. All through my life and to this day these delights return to me in dreams. I seem to myself to be walking on the bank of a sunny creek, or climbing a rocky hillside which, as soon as I see, sets me to searching for a specimen. I look down as I walk, and presently find some thing in some little crevice of the rocks, brilliant in color and beautiful in shape. I take it in my hand and look at it with delight, thinking that I will carry it to father. I put it into my pocket, and go on with my walk and search, but soon stop suddenly with the question, "Did I really find that or was it a dream? No, it is real, it is there!" I look at it again and go on with my dream-walk.

My first term in the Eaton schools in September after my tenth birthday introduced me to many new and confusing ways and manners. Dress, shoes, desk arrangement, large classes, a sort of graded system, a good deal of stir and far more lax discipline— all tended at once to make my little, quiet country soul look about itself with considerable interest and curiosity. "Delaine" and calico dresses must be worn, I found, when the cold weather came on, just

*For Charles Bruce, see *History of Preble County*, pp. 140–41. [Ed. note]

as in summer. But my mother was afraid to turn us out in such thin clothing, and put our flannel and linsey dresses on with a calico overdress. Our home-knit stockings were not quite right, to my mind, but they did not give much trouble.

I suppose my habit of looking steadily at anyone I was interested in must have been much in the nature of staring, as I sometimes had rebukes for it from other children. Behind me in that first term sat an older girl named "Tud" L. (Elizabeth Tudor L.), who had brilliant coloring and was probably pretty. I was once sitting squarely around in my seat absorbed in looking at her pink cheeks, black hair, and blue eyes, when she suddenly stopped talking to her seatmate and said, "What are you looking at me for?" Abashed, I turned away without answering. There was at the same time a boy named John M. who had the same pretty coloring and was much admired by all the little girls, myself included, though we never any of us had a chance to speak to him, as the boys sat on one side and we on the other, and the play yards were separate. Various slate games, "Puzzle," "Tit-tat-tow," "Guess the Name," were played with impunity in school time, a thing that would have brought punishment in the district school. Indeed the men who had the "Third Room," until my father had it, could not contrive to keep any sort of quiet for study.

The town of Eaton at that time was peopled mostly by old settlers and their immediate descendants, so that everybody knew everybody else. The schools were all in one building of four rooms, a square brick house of two stories, white-washed inside and out, with plastered ceilings, brick walls, and yellow poplar floors. There was a narrow hall from which a steep, straight staircase led up to a similar hall in the second story where was a place for hooks or nails for hanging hats and shawls. A big stove, with drum over it, in each room furnished heat; it stood in the middle of the room and was "accommodated" to the chimney at the end by a long pipe swung by wires to the ceiling. Which manner of heating illustrated very well all the zones of temperature on the face of the earth. On the walls were then no blackboards except one of wood at the teacher's end of the room. But in my time plaster boards were put upon the unobstructed longer side opposite the windows. Our desks were of varnished walnut and individual, which was also an innovation; but they were arranged in pairs with a partition between, in rows lengthwise of the room.

I began to *learn* arithmetic in my eleventh year and got on so well that my promotion to the Fourth Room came by the middle of the next year. In my second term I was a very popular person at the grammar recitation hour, and in the rush for a seat made by the whole class, there were sometimes quarrels among three or four girls as to who should sit by me, as I always knew my lesson and there was no law against prompting. We had Timotheus S. Pinneo's *Grammar*, then new, and a step forward (it was thought) from Kirkham's, upon which I had been fed from my eighth to my tenth year in Dooley's school. There I learned in a way and by littles the rules on the big folded sheet in the front of the book; also that *to* and *for* were prepositions, perhaps to know nouns when I saw them, certainly not much more. But now my time had come to understand grammar, as it was given to me at eleven (though of course much too early in the natural order) and therefore I began to learn it. It was so with arithmetic—I was growing old enough to understand some things in it, and therefore learned it with no difficulty.

Here, too, I began the study of mathematical and descriptive geography. Not until then did the place of the map and the position of my seat affect my notion of direction. The map of the United States (which was cut off with a wide waste of red paint beyond the Mississippi marked "Great American Desert") was hung on the south wall between two windows. Our seats faced east, and from that day to this I have always to turn the map of North America (which soon replaced the old United States one) around in my mind so as to "think" the east coast in the right place, and right end northward.

My first teacher there was Samuel McClure. He had a refined face and was a good scholar, I have been told, but was an unpopular teacher. I never knew him very well, as he moved away from Eaton with his family as soon as his connection with the public schools ceased. My next teacher was Gamaliel Jaqua, a tall, black-haired man with a kindly face and manner. He was a good teacher and disciplinarian. Under him I wrote my first compositions—not under compulsion, but under the general invitation "to have something for Friday afternoon; write a composition or speak a piece."

I was the only child who responded to the composition invitation—where I had got a notion what a composition was, I do not know. But I had lately read about (save the mark!) "Whales" and "The Ocean," and so stood up and read what I had written from memory on one of these subjects, following it on the next Friday by the other, both much embellished with watercolor paints on the fold of the outside, with my name written in the middle.

I was the first of three prize-winners in spelling in Gamaliel Jaqua's class, whereby I was made the happy possessor of a large lithograph of a beautiful lady, "Augusta," in golden curls and a pink gown, holding between two very long-fingered hands a wreath of roses so that every rose could be counted. The second prize was taken by a nice, long-haired girl named Pamelia Riggs and was a similar picture of "Susan" in black curls and red gown, not half so pretty. The third prize was a picture of George Washington on horseback, and was taken by a boy named John Sloan. These were the days when lithographs of this kind were about all the examples of art accessible to western village people. But the steel engraving began to be known and admired about this time through *Godey's Lady's Book*.

Another recollection of some importance connects itself with this room. One day a man came in with some new books and told us that we were to bring next day twenty-two cents each, and that then he would give us one of these beautiful, clean, new readers for the money and our old, shabby books. We told this at home with some excitement, which was speedily toned down by the doubts about giving up our McGuffey's *Readers*; but as the exchange had been sanctioned in all good faith by the school board no further objections were made. Next day we all rejoiced in a copy of Mandeville's *Fourth Reader*, a new book which promised much. It was the first advent of the book agent, and a very unfortunate experience for this school, as it proved. For the lessons were very poorly selected and arranged, besides being printed in a huddled and uninteresting way. Added to that the books were so badly sewed and bound that they fell to pieces in a few weeks, even with careful handling. No second copy was ever bought and McGuffey's *Reader* took its place again.

The large number of new impressions necessarily experienced in a room crowded with strange boys and girls under a discipline so different naturally superimposed one on another, and thus made no clear record of themselves. There was a good deal of confusion and stir, no rule was enforced against talking and such play as could go on with one's desk neighbors. The most important intellectual lesson that I learned in the first few weeks was how to add, and this I learned from a girl named Annie Stanton, who sat next to me in class. We were having questions in the addition table, and as I saw her counting on her fingers with her slate pencil, it suddenly dawned on me that I could thus add, so that to her and not to any teacher I owe my first mathematical lesson. In a few months I was able to help my classmates when they asked me how to do examples in written arithmetic.

Annie Stanton had been absent from school some weeks when we heard that she was dead. As was the custom in those days, groups of children went to see her, I among them. It was the first time I had ever seen the face of the dead. She lay in the parlor on an old-fashioned sofa as if asleep. I can still see how her long lashes lay on her lovely waxen cheeks, which looked much as when she was alive. One of the larger girls in the crowd that stood around her suddenly said, "Poor Annie!" as if to herself, and then we all went out.

I may say, in this connection, that it was a common custom for children and others to go to see the dead even though they were strangers. One other time I stopped with a crowd of children to see a little girl who was a sister of one of my classmates. She had died of scarlet fever, which fact did not deter visitors. The day after the funeral of this child, her two sisters spent the afternoon playing with us, with at least no ill effects in our family. My mother, however, forbade me to go to any stranger's house again on such an occasion. Why epidemics were not common under such circumstances it would be difficult to say.

After Samuel McClure I had, in turn, three other teachers before entering the high school: my father, Gamaliel Jaqua, and a Miss_____. It was still the custom in these schools, as in those of the country districts, to have less expensive teachers in the spring and summer. Usually teachers were employed by the term and not by the year.

A second epidemic of cholera in Eaton in 1854, brought from Cincinnati by a stranger, renewed the terror of that disease in the minds of the people in the whole country around. Recollections of the former epidemic in 1849 were still vivid among all classes and all ages. I remember that in my grandfather's family at their home on the farm, a sort of sickening dread took possession of the household. Work and business of all kinds in the town ceased. My father and mother decided to move, temporarily, back to the old neighborhood. The only available house was Berea Chapel, then and for some time before, unused as a church. Having had leave to go into this refuge, we moved beds, a cooking stove, a few strips of carpet and other necessary articles into the one big room, with its high pulpit at one end and its movable benches on either side. Two of these benches placed seat to seat made a very good bedstead for our straw and feather beds.

The three weeks of our stay passed tranquilly by. One Sunday the Rev. Peter Banta, our former neighbor and friend, preached to a small congregation of the neighbors sitting around among our furniture on the unoccupied benches. The preacher stayed with us to dinner and visited afterwards in a friendly reminiscent talk. This seemed particularly pleasant; for, on account of a feeling of uncertainty and dread, people did not visit back and forth during the summer, and we had been much alone. Among other things we had for dinner that day were some sliced cucumbers and ripe tomatoes. We all ate moderately of these, except my father, who had a dread of cholera too heavy upon him, for he shared the common belief that these things were a cause of the disease. Mother and I had brought the vegetables from our town garden, to which we had gone on horseback the day before. We had found the garden full of ripe fruit of various kinds which was untouched, although the place was unguarded. At other times, even when we were there, we had had some difficulty in keeping the village boys from helping themselves. While we were in the garden, we saw two short funeral processions cross the bridge from the town, on their way to the cemetery.

The epidemic proved less serious than that of '49 and there were comparatively few deaths: eleven, as the record tells.

Mound Hill Cemetery at Eaton, Ohio, was, as early as I knew it, a much crowded place of burial, a half-mile west of town. It contained an Indian mound of perfectly hemispherical proportions made by the aborigines who had once lived in the woods of that region. A hollow cup in the field nearby exactly corresponded to the size and shape of the mound as if it had been scooped out by some enormous hand and set down flat-side down without breaking, in the place occupied by the cemetery and near the rim of a hill which sloped down to the bed of the Garrison Branch. On this mound had been set up by the young men of the town a tall shaft of marble "To the memory of Lieutenant Lowery, and thirteen others," who fell in battle at Ludlow's Spring, seven miles from Fort St. Clair, in 1793. A Latin inscription, *"Dulce et de corum pro patria mori,"* was translated to me when I was a little child by my father, and I used regularly to go up and read it whenever I went to the cemetery.

One or two other monuments among the crowded groups of stone I often went to see. One was a gray slab some eight feet or so high, by two and a half or three broad. It had been carved by Shobel Vail Clevenger who afterward made some name for himself in Italy as my father told me.* There were others more elaborate in design and more costly in construction, but none of them seemed really beautiful but this. The inscription was cut in an oval around which was a semi-wreath of oak leaves and acorns. In each of the upper corners of the square in which the oval was drawn was a cherub in high relief, very well done, as I knew after I had grown up. Whose memorial it was I did not remember until after lately rereading about the cemetery in an old history of Ohio, in which we are told that it was a piece of the earliest work of Clevenger and in memory of Fergus Holderman. But those stone babies, oak leaves and acorns I still know as a beautiful part of the furniture of my memory. My Grandfather Ryan's monument stood under the lone sugar maple tree on the east side of the cemetery. It was a wide white slab carved with the conventional short, thickset, melancholy woman leaning stiffly on a monument under an impossible willow. A long extract in blank verse beginning "Of the omnipotent" was cut under it with age, name, etc. I used often to go there while I lived at Eaton. The quaint old slab was replaced some years ago by a modern composition of some kind.

---

*And in America, where he executed busts of Henry Clay, Edward Everett, and Daniel Webster, among others. [Ed. note]

[119]

I was one evening sent out for the cows which had strayed away; I took the road to the cemetery and went beyond the Garrison Crossing. Coming back, although it was after sunset, I decided to take this chance to see a new monument which had just been put up at the grave of Sevier Hawkins, a lawyer of local fame who had recently died. Tales of the very splendid and costly stone had made me curious to see it. Climbing the fence to the west end, I ran across to the place where I knew the grave was, and saw the tall broken shaft with fluted column rise above the highly ornate base on which was carved the inscription. Roses and other flowers wreathed this and the shaft, and the semblance of a full-blown rose lay carved on the edge of the base. It was very wonderful, but later I liked it less than the gray slab with the oak leaves and the cherubs, and a plain gray shaft, without decoration, in the same row with the broken shafted one. When I turned to run back to the road, the red light had well nigh faded, and I grew breathless with something that was very like fear as I heard the rustling of Something, I knew not what, in the tufts of dry grass at the heads of the graves I passed.

In the northeast corner of the cemetery not far from the old stile where we used to enter was a slender shaft of white stone "To the memory of_____ Woodworth, a young stranger who died in Eaton in_____. Erected by the young men of Eaton." I often went to look at the grave and wonder about the young man who died among strangers. I used to know the spot where every person in it was buried, but that was learned on our walks there, as we were not permitted as many children were, to go to funerals.

2

Men of Local Prominence

Among persons who attracted my attention as a child, between the years '51 and '61, were several men of local distinction in the town of Eaton. I had come in '51 from a country life which had sharpened my wits and my powers of observation till in some respects these were like those of an Indian. I saw and learned faces thoroughly and very rapidly, and soon knew almost everybody in town by face as well as by name. In a little while I knew who were the most important men in town: General Felix Marsh, General George D. Hendricks (militia generals), Judge Abner Haines, Judge William Gilmore, Jacob Chambers, Jefferson Larsh, Louis B. Ogden, and Cornelius Van Ausdal.

I used to pass the house of General Marsh on my way to school, and often saw his erect military figure on the street. I once heard him say, at a meeting of the old Washingtonian Temperance Society, which had a revival that winter, "I have not tasted intoxicating liquors for thirty years, but I should be in the gutter tomorrow if I tasted wine at the communion table." He was a strenuous advocate of total abstinence to the end of his life, and the weight of his influence was felt by many young men of his time. Felix Marsh was a man of scholarly tastes and especially interested in education. I heard my father say that he always bought every new grammar that came out, and read it at once. My father's first examination for a teacher's certificate was given him by General Marsh.

George D. Hendricks was a member of the school board for many years. He used to visit the high school when I was a student there, and generally made a speech. His spare, thin face, with keen eyes behind gleaming glasses, his straggling black hair in elf-like locks on his forehead, in a certain way emphasized his sharp, laconic sentences, full of homely wisdom and a kind of backwoods humor which never for a moment brought a smile to his own face.*

Abner Haines was a locally eminent lawyer noted for his eloquence. He used to speak at the Fourth of July celebrations. One in particular I remember, held on the site of old Fort St. Clair, a mile distant from town. I had long before begun to notice the difference in the manner of speech of public speakers, and though I could have explained nothing of the effect that their language had on me, I felt the difference very keenly. When I heard Judge Haines, a larger vision of what language could do came to me. I remember nothing of what he said, excepting in a dim way that he spoke of the three dead soldiers in the graves at the edge of the wood. The single word "reminiscences," heard for the first time, is the only definite recollection of any of his speeches.**

Judge Gilmore's personality, in the greatest contrast to that of Judge Haines, made an impression on my noticing mind far different from that of any other public man of those days. His distinguished dress and manner, his refined speech and aristocratic bearing acquainted me with a type of man hitherto unknown to my experience. He visited my school in Eaton, in my thirtieth year, and I had no occasion to revise or change that impression.

Jacob Chambers was a man of very different type. He was the only jeweler at that time, and his windows were usually attractive to children. I used to see him through the large window at work over watches or jewelry. After I grew older and went into the shop on business I began to admire the man, at first, perhaps, for his elegant manners and somewhat ornate manner. He used very dignified and formal language which always seemed to me to appertain to the business of working in gold. He was a rather small, slender man, with dark eyes and skin, and hair just beginning to turn gray, brushed up high on his head. He always wore black broadcloth and a white waistcoat. He always talked to me as if I were a person of

*George Dixon Hendricks was the son of David E. Hendricks and was born in 1805, the first white male child in Preble County. He was a colonel under Sam Houston in the Mexican War. For a sketch of his life, see *History of Preble County*, pp. 143-44, and *Directory of Preble County*, pp. 107-8. [Ed. note] ıote]

**Directory of Preble County* includes two historical sketches by Haines, "Site of Fort St. Clair," p. 21, and "Military History," pp. 103 ff. [Ed. note]

some consequence, and I have no doubt that he lifted my estimate of my own powers somewhat each time I saw him. After my first contribution of verse to the county paper, he never ceased urging me to write more, and said that I should be ashamed to "hide my light under a bushel." I think that it is likely that I did write much more than I otherwise should have done, because of his frequent notice of what I wrote, although I was then working very hard in a large school.

Thomas Jefferson Larsh was a very large, tall, well-built man, Indianesque in looks. I knew him and his family when I was between the ages of thirteen and seventeen. He was much interested in public education, was generally present at the yearly sessions of summer school, and was ready to join in the discussions of the hour, whatever they might be. A part of one speech of his followed me for many years and aroused in me curious speculations. It was to the effect that "perhaps it is true, as I have often thought, that every word we say goes on echoing off into space forever and ever, widening in effect as do the waves round a pebble thrown into the water, and that we may hear those words again and so be condemned by them."

Another man whom I observed with great interest at this time was a merchant named Louis B. Ogden. He was a newcomer into the town some time after our own arrival there. The impression that Mr. Ogden made upon my mind was that of his personality rather than from anything that he ever said to me or in my presence. His wife had been a Miss Isabel Hardy and had looked up our family and made out some relationship with us as soon as they came to Eaton. Thus began a friendly intimacy which continued for me until I went to college.

Mr. Ogden had a face marked by great refinement of features and habit of expression, his black hair and very dark complexion seeming somehow to emphasize this refinement, perhaps because they were so unusual among the people that I knew. He talked very little and although I was often at the Ogden home I never heard any continuous conversation except the little I heard at the table and with the children, and this, both on his part and that of Mrs. Ogden, was always in low, even tones which especially affected me as something unattainable by ordinary people. Mr. Ogden's smile was rare and very beautiful. After the beginning of the Civil War

[123]

the Ogdens went to Washington where Mr. Ogden held some office under President Lincoln, with whom, not many years before, he had been intimately associated. The fact that he was Lincoln's friend seemed to harmonize with the character of the man, and somehow to account for the impression that his personality made on me, although I had known nothing about their friendship.

Not many months after our removal to Eaton I began to be entrusted with errands to Van Ausdal's store. This was the general merchandise house with which my father and mother and many of our neighbors had done their "trading" for years. At this time, in the fifties, all the ordinary needs of the household could be supplied by this one store. I often saw there Cornelius Van Ausdal, the founder of the firm, who was then a somewhat feeble old man, though still much alive to what was going on, and full of talk to the friends who came in to see him or to do business. Such scraps of talk as I now remember related to political questions, or sometimes were merely reminiscent. He never spoke to me and I stood in awe of him without knowing why, excepting that he was the owner of the big house and all it contained, in its store and handsomely furnished rooms for living.

Among the clerks at Van Ausdal's was a James Nelson, a young man who afterwards became a member of the firm. He had been brought to Mr. Van Ausdal's notice by his heroic conduct during the epidemic of cholera in 1849, when he was but sixteen years old. He had come to Eaton a little before that time to ply his trade as carpenter and at the breaking out of the epidemic had devoted himself to visiting and caring for the sick and dying, had helped to bury the dead and even to dig some of the graves, for so many had fled the plague in terror that there were few left to perform the last offices and to attend the small number of those who recovered. As a child I remember meeting this youth on the street often on my way to and from school, and later as a young woman when I was teaching. His quick, firm step, his preoccupied air with his gaze directed straight in front of him recur to me now as very characteristic of the man.

Soon after our removal to Eaton we became acquainted with a German family named Bringman. They spoke English with a strong foreign accent and quaintly turned idioms, all of which made them interesting to me. When in the next year they moved into the town, out of our immediate neighborhood, I sometimes went to see them in their own new home on High Street. I noticed with childish curiosity the manners and customs of their household, so different from those of my own home. More particularly, I noticed the solemn, unsmiling manner of Jacob Bringman himself, which contrasted so strongly with the pleasant, cherry habits of his wife. At the table the grace before meat said in German by the father with his face bowed on his right hand, and his "Gott sei dank!" after the meal, struck me with a sort of awe. Jacob Bringman was the sexton of the Presbyterian Church, of which he was a devout member. It was he who rang the bell which tolled off the years of one who had just died. Later he was the sexton of the cemetery, and it was his tall, thin, slightly stooping figure we saw going up the West Road toward the cemetery. He wore, as did most men of the time, whatever their occupation, a high hat, and, as I remember, turned his head neither to the right nor to the left as he went up the hill, usually carrying in his right hand a rod or a rope. He was not without humor in spite of his solemn visage, for I have often heard my father report some odd saying of his.

One of the most clearcut memories connected with my church going, after the removal to the Campbellite church, is that of seeing Uncle Johnny Goldsmith, as he was called, walk up the north aisle and take his seat, always in the same place, near the front on the left. His silky, snow-white hair flowing over his shoulders, and his long brown overcoat gave him a venerable and dignified appearance, which was heightened by the quiet expression on his smooth-shaven face framed in the white hair falling evenly on both sides. Long afterwards a picture of John Milton in his old age recalled this face. I never heard John Goldsmith speak, but I saw him at church often in his last years. He lived with his wife on a farm west of the town in one of the early pioneer log houses. Polly Goldsmith always came in at the church door with him and walking sedately up the south side, sat down on the woman's side halfway between the door and the pulpit. It was this good lady who used sometimes to practice "the exercise of shouting" which I have earlier described.

As I recall the figures of these men in their places of business or on the street, there come to me also the images of less familiar personages, who were held to be people of distinction. Thus, I have a very dim recollection of Francis Cunningham, his name connected with those of two Mexican boys named Louis and John Leroux, sons of a Mexican Grandee who had put them into Mr. Cunningham's care for two years to learn English in the public schools. My father taught these young men with the *Primer, Spelling-book, First* and *Second Readers* to read in a very short time.

The daily history in which I lived between my tenth and twentieth years made its impress as a whole by registering on my manners, mind, and morals certain general conclusions. One of these was further strengthened and made into almost positive knowledge by facts forced upon me in the schoolrooms where I taught from the age of sixteen to twenty. The young people with whom I had been associated in the high school, and the children whom I taught in the primary and grammar grades were, for the most part, descendants of the contemporaries of my grandfathers and grandmothers. Their family histories were known to my father and mother. Their qualities and characteristics came directly under my own observation.

In some of the earlier terms of my school teaching in Eaton I knew most of the children entering a class on the first day, by the family resemblances. Thus I had before me, in some cases, examples of excellent inheritance of body and mind, which I could trace back to grandmothers and great-grandmothers. Others there were whose history went back a little way to periodic habits of drinking, originating, perhaps, in the common social custom of toddy drinking and good-fellowship dram drinking on farms in harvest time and at raising-bees. Briefly, I may say that I have thus known families whose history, after this kind, ended, or was ending, in my own young womanhood. In later years I have sometimes been thought to be fanatical on the subject of the drink and tobacco habits, and the choice, in ill-sorted marriages, which takes no account of family history.

3

Real Books

After the age of ten I had access to more books, as we then lived near Aunt Eliza (Mrs. S. S. Young). She had a library and took Nathaniel P. Willis's paper, *The Home Journal*, a weekly literary paper which I read for years. Then my father was one of the charter subscribers to a little library which was bought by some enterprising young lawyers, Gideon McNutt, the Gilmores, and others. So I came to Scott and Cooper, most of whose prose works I read, and many repeatedly. Other books that I read from this library were *The Chronicles of the Bastille*, Abbott's *Histories*, some of Irving, and Lossing's *Life of Napoleon*. I could not read Dickens then; I did not understand him as I first met him in chapters of *Bleak House* in current numbers of *Harper's Magazine*. The Chancery court was too much for me. Nor would I read Bulwer. My father had read all the old novelists, knew Scott and Bulwer besides, but read Dickens and Thackeray much later. He did not direct or interfere with my reading in any way.

During a long illness after scarlet fever in my thirteenth year I read, in the times in which I was able to be up, Elisha Kent Kane's *Arctic Explorations*, Frémont's *Report of the Exploring Expedition to the Rocky Mountains*, Irving's *Astoria*, and *Bonneville's Adventures*, Austin Layard's *Ninevah*, and a volume or two of Humboldt's *Cosmos*. After I was able to go back to school again I read Bayard Taylor's *Travels*; with great enjoyment I followed him through *Views Afoot* and with my imagination made vivid by his travelling style followed him through many hundreds of miles in the Desert of Sahara, Egypt, Palestine, and India. The accurate map-geography in which I was drilled at school about this time became something more than bits of countries, rivers, and mountains, through the magic of Taylor's leading. I went with him, too, through California. Later knowledge of that country has not effaced the pictures which the great traveller showed me from his horseback trips along the valleys and among the foothills of that state.

I gradually grew to a taste for other books Aunt Eliza could lend me. She was always very ready to encourage my greedy book appetite, and helped me to many things to which I could not otherwise have had access. There was no other person in the town at this time who had such a taste as hers for the purely literary. Her judgment and temperament were of a distinctly artistic type. She had not intimates outside of her own family and no acquaintances who could have ministered much to her aesthetic enjoyment. Her books, her garden, and her rare flowers were more to her than anything that the life of the town afforded. I often tried to read books of her selection, some of which I found to be on a level with my taste and state of development and others for which I had not yet understanding. But for the most part I contrived to forage successfully for myself, and by this time, too, we had acquired a small library of our own, a miscellaneous collection, it is true, but all worthy to be on any library shelves. Among these I remember, *Essays of Elia*, a small *Biographical Dictionary*, and others.

My uncle-in-law, Samuel S. Young, had very little influence on my reading, though indirectly he taught me some things by casual conversation. He was away from home a great deal on business connected with inventions of his; a small contrivance called an Adding Rule, which was much in use in the 50's in banks and counting houses, and an Interest Rule, made a little later after much the same plan. He had been a teacher in his youth, and was a man of more than usual education. I remember his language as being distinguished from that of others by the use of the Italian *a* instead of the flat, middle-west *a*. He was a clever mathematician and said that there was no example in arithmetic that he could not do by a process called "Double Position." "Besides," he always added, "if I can't do it at the first trial, I leave it alone till the next day and always dream it out in my sleep."

He knew the eighteenth-century poets very well, and frequently quoted Pope; but his favorite poem was Butler's *Hudibras*, which, for him, had apt phrases for almost any occasion. My father did not

[128]

share my uncle's admiration for this poem nor agree with him that Wordsworth couldn't write poetry. Uncle Young also had a contemptuous opinion of Mrs. Browning's poetry, some of which he had read later. He was an expert chess player and had once played with Paul Morphy at New Orleans. When I asked him how this game came out he said, as he balanced his cane on his finger, "Oh, he beat me, of course." I once hinted to my uncle, when I was about fifteen, that I should like to learn chess, but he said that he had not the patience to bother with beginners. Just so when I wished that he would teach me the guitar, which he played a little. He and my father had frequent intellectual tilts of various kinds, and often worked together on mechanical inventions, which they never completed.

One of the first evident results of my early reading came out in the desire to tell stories of what I had read. Before I was ten, while I was still in the country, I was accounted by my playmates a good storyteller; at least it must have been so, as I remember very well that I was in great demand for telling stories when we were so tired of play in the woods that we were willing to sit down and listen. My best story was "Hop-o'-My-Thumb," which I told repeatedly to appreciative listeners. But later I ceased to exercise my gift, perhaps from shyness, as there were others who told more stories than I had to tell. Besides, I spent more time reading.

An aunt of mine, a pretty young woman, once brought me a paper-covered book, which she said was a good story. I was to read it without letting anybody see it. As I had never had anything forbidden to me, this did not mean much, and I did not stop to ask why. I suppose my aunt had been told that reading novels was wicked, and thought that it would not be permitted to me. However, I read it, *The Black Avenger of the Spanish Main*, a prize story, whose author I do not remember, with nothing wrong about it; some sort of ingenuity in the plot I believe it had. I told this story a few times to schoolmates and my sister Laura with evident enjoyment and wonder on their part. My recollection of it now is entirely lost, except that there was a black dwarf in it whose business was to guard a lone prisoner in a mysterious and lonely castle on some inaccessible seacoast cliff.

4

Schooling under Isaac S. Morris

Somewhere soon after my eleventh year I was examined in arithmetic in simple operations in whole numbers, decimals, common fractions, and U.S. money by the high school teacher who also the principal of all the schools. The result of this examination transferred me to the "Fourth Room," or high school, where one could study whatever he was ready for from further advance in grammar school studies to Latin, algebra, physiology, geometry, and trigonometry. Reading, spelling, and defining went on for everybody, and every day. It was at this time that I came under the instruction and influence of Isaac S. Morris, a teacher and one man among a thousand.

He was of Quaker parentage and home training, had a college education, perfect health, the most cheery of spirits, and endless patience and wisdom in dealing with the young. He was a born teacher and inspirer; not so much a "disciplinarian" in the usual sense, but a controller and leader of those who wanted to GO ON. It was in more than one sense a liberal education to have him for a teacher as I had for five years. There was then no set curriculum for the "Fourth Room" but one began where he was and took up advanced studies as he was able, and went on with them until he had pretty thoroughly mastered them. I entered classes in the various studies and stayed as long as it seemed wise to the teacher. I had no classmate in astronomy and recited alone from Elijah H. Burritt's *Celestial Geography*,* traced the constellations alone or with my father, and now and then Mr. Morris; I recited daily

*Its actual title was *Geography of the Heavens*, which appeared in many editions. Burritt was the brother of the more famous "Learned Blacksmith," Elihu Burritt. [Ed. note]

in my desk, he sitting in the next one, while the school went on about us, more or less alive.

The most attractive parts of the book to me were the mythical tales connected with the descriptions of the groups of stars, and lessons about the planets. I did not take up Latin because I did not think of it, I suppose; although my Cousin Claribel who sat near me recited in *Caesar* every day. Reading was a daily pleasure, and a time of real enthusiasm. It was there and then the young men and young women of the school were, without their knowledge, "introduced" to prose and poetry, by reading for us and with us and leading us to read rightly, appreciatively, the poems and prose extracts in McGuffey's (old) *Fifth Reader*, all or most from classical English sources. It was there and then we came to know Shakespeare, Milton, Scott, and some of our own countrymen who had said things, and most of all, the man who daily led us by their thoughts to see into his mind, and to know, dimly as we did, the sources of his knowledge and inspiration.

There was no rule against whispering in any of the classes at the time of my entrance to the Eaton schools. We turned around in our seats, we talked to our neighbors, but we were not supposed to leave our seats without permission except to go to the waterpail in the corner of the room for a drink from the tin dipper. But two or three years later than this the self-reporting system came into use, and every child in the building reported at evening roll call the number of times he had spoken to anyone without leave in school hours. The result on the discipline of the rooms was evident at once in the greater quiet and better order generally. The conduct of each pupil in the Fourth Room was reported weekly to the parents by means of a little book in which the daily reports were recorded. Many discussions arose among teachers at their various meetings as to whether the system was a safe one or not. As it came into general favor and continued to be used more or less throughout the whole country in one form or another at least as late as 1880, it is not my purpose to discuss its merits or its defects, for in this, as in every other question affecting school arrangement, the vital element is the character and power of the teacher. Certain it is that in Mr. Morris's hands the plan worked out well.

[131]

I remember one instance of his questioning a pupil's report. David B., a gay, careless lad answered "two" when his name was called. Mr. Morris quickly said,

"Why, haven't I seen you talking more than once today?"

"No, sir, I began as soon as I came in and haven't stopped till now," he answered laughingly.

Mr. Morris smiled gravely and doubtless made an entry to suit the facts in the case.

Our textbooks in this school were McGuffey's *Fifth Reader* and speller, Ray's *Arithmetic*, Stoddard's *Mental Arithmetic*, Ray's *Algebra*, Davies's *Algebra* and *Geometry*, Mitchell's *Geography* and *Atlas*, Burritt's Astronomy and Celestial Atlas, Cutter's *Physiology*, Pinneo's *Grammar*, Bullion's *Latin Grammar*, Wright's *Orthography*, and Goodrich's *History of the United States*. We also had a little school singing book, *The American School Song Book*, of which we made a good deal of use at least twice a day, always led by Mr. Morris, who had a rather strong, loud voice and a correct ear. The exercises given us in the lessons in Wright's *Orthography* were of great value as they trained us in enunciation and the knowledge of how each sound of the language was formed by the organs of speech. Composition writing and declamation were not obligatory until the later years of Mr. Morris's rule.

There was great enthusiasm shown by the school in the study of mental arithmetic, geography, and reading. Mr. Morris had a form of drill in quick calculation which I have seen used nowhere else excepting afterwards by his own pupils in their schools. We became adepts in multiplying mentally to 25 x 25; in squaring numbers ending in five to 115; in the instantaneous multiplication of such numbers as 47 $\times$ 43, 74 $\times$ 76, 88 $\times$ 82, and the like. I recall many a lively skirmish over crabbed questions in Stoddard's *Mental Arithmetic*, when a younger classmate of mine, Maria B., and I attacked single-handed the "Wolf and the Bear" question, or the problems of hour and minute hands of the clock, and mental questions in the Double Rule of Three.

In geography we grew excited and interested over trips around the world made to order by anyone called on in the class. Such impromptu recitations included some account of what was to be seen and bought at each stopping place. I remember admiring the cleverness of one girl, Hester Balentine, who stopped at the Azores for oranges, and at the Canary Islands for canary birds, which latter she recited laughingly.

It was found necessary, in the fall of 1854 when the school was very greatly crowded, to have an assistant. In the early fifties, it will be remembered, there were few women teachers and these had all been educated in "Female Seminaries" which gave a more or less formal, "polite" education along harmless lines of study. One of these teachers was brought from a distance to take some of the classes in our school. As I remember her she was of a distinct "Female Seminary" type, tall and precise, with large, prominent eyes and two long iron-gray curls on either side of an oval face. She taught our history class in a way entirely new to me then. After every recitation she sat down in turn by each member of the small class and marked out in the text the single sentences which were answers to the questions in the back of the book. Naturally, when we studied the lessons we looked only at those bracketed sentences, omitting everything else. Of course very little remained in the memory of this term's work in historical catechism.

For some reason this teacher thought it important that the young women and girls should have a more ladylike book than McGuffey's *Fifth Reader* so that we were required to buy Hemans's *Young Ladies' Reader*, which omitted the speeches of Daniel Webster and Patrick Henry, scenes from Shakespeare's plays, and extracts from Milton, Grey, Cowper, and others substituting liberally poems from Mrs. Hemans, Eliza Cook, and other prettinesses of the kind, and various pale prose articles, probably from *Ladies' Annuals*. I remember nothing about the prose definite enough to be sure of this. Toward the end of the first term an exhibition of the school was to be given in the public hall. Among other things there was to be a "Colloquy" taken part in by a large number of girls and young women. These were to impersonate the various Abstract Virtues, who made speeches about themselves in heroic verse in a lesson of the Hemans's *Reader*. We were to dress in white and wear a blue sash across the breast on which was the name of the virtue to be represented, in large gilt letters.

For two reasons I chose a speech of four lines called "Content";

[133]

first, because it was the shortest, and I had extreme difficulty then in committing poetry to memory; the second reason, as I now remember with a curious feeling of never before having expressed it, was caused by something in the back of my mind which made me think of the expense it might be to have many big gold letters on my sash. Of course I had never heard of gilt paper. What was my perplexity when the teacher said, "Yes, you may have that, but you will have to call it Contentment." But as I was taken ill a few days afterwards, I missed my only chance of an appearance on the stage. A too-early return to school after scarlet fever was paid for by months of illness.

At the age of sixteen I went away to teach, and when I came back, between the first school and the next which I began in the following April, I went again for two months to the old school. But in this time an assistant, a Mr. James Wilson, had been added and Mr. Morris had more the office of superintendent of the town schools, which had so increased as to require other rooms, and I saw little of him in the schoolroom. But he was then and always, so long as we lived in that part of the country, a loved and intimate friend of my father, and both families often saw each other at one or the other house and home. Soon after, I went permanently to teaching in the town, first in the old Public Church in one corner of its big room, and had no more direct schooling until I went to college at the age of twenty. Mr. Morris soon after left the profession and became editor of the *Eaton Register*.

The time for me to be influenced very much by other women than my mother did not come till after I went to college. My friendships among Eaton girls, at least those amounting to intimacy, were few and without definite effect. All the girls of the school were on good and friendly terms, but the whole tone of girl relations was unmarked by the violent admirations which often characterize girl friendships of the present time. We talked together at school, we took short excursions to the woods, or up and down the creek, we visited each other in our homes, and thus moved around in a pleasant world of unrealized privileges.

The recollections of two or three girls of that time recurs to me with distinct memories of their looks and qualities. One of them, named Julia D., comes before me now because of her kindness at all times, under all circumstances, to all sorts of people. She belonged to one of the most aristocratic families in the town, but her kindness was distinctly democratic. The goodness and well-poised mind and soul of Hester B. gave me lessons also. I greatly admired her intellect and always had a sort of sub-conscious wish to be as clever as she was.

Near the end of my high school life I had a friend named Rosalind Blythe, a small brunette with blue eyes and long black hair. She had a keen sense of humor and a gentle volubility which sometimes expended itself in telling entertaining or curious stories. She was often at my home and I at hers. I was very fond of her and I think that the stimulus of her friendship toward me was mainly intellectual, as we read the same books and talked about them.

Lucy S. was full of laughter and ready to laugh at her friends as well as at other people when amused by any trifle of dress, or speech, or circumstance. It sometimes happened that her girl friends were hurt or offended by her ridicule, which never had, I think, any sting of ill-feeling in it. Once when we were about thirteen years old, I myself was the object of this kind of humor. In a sudden flash of anger I turned toward her and said: "Lucy S., I will not speak to you for a year." Which foolish threat I kept too literally, because I thought I must keep my word, although longing many a time to be friends again, as Lucy vainly tried to induce me to be. She was a girl of deeply religious nature and of clever insight. It was from her that I heard the story of an extraordinary name given to a girl who went to school to her brother, Thomas S. The name, which he used sometimes to call out in full, was as follows: Clemintina, Monta Rose, Josephine, Fannie Farmer, Folding Green, Rebecca, Ann Maria Welding, Brower. This is in no sense fiction, but actual fact.

The one other girl who belongs to this period of the high school was my cousin, Claribel Young, who had practically finished her school life with the class which had gone before, but who came in for an hour every day for Latin. She was a girl of great dignity. In a certain sense I stood in awe of her fine manners and her ladylike behavior. (I was a mere country tomboy yet.) Although she was only three years older than I in age, she was much older in experience. Being the only child of my father's sister Eliza, she had been

[135]

5

The Teachers' Institute

An important part of my ante-college education was what came to
me through my attendance at the Teachers' Institute of our county,
held in Eaton. When I began, at thirteen, the sessions were only a
week long; but they were soon lenghtened to a month—usually
August. First they were conducted entirely on the lecture plan, by
some distinguished educator of the state or of Indiana. Such
institutes were gathering places for the teachers near the towns in
which they were held, and were attended generally by all in the
county. The teachers of district schools in the forties, in Preble
County, were men for the winter schools, and generally even for the
spring schools, if the householders thought best to have any more
than the winter months. The only women teachers in the early
forties were a few elderly spinsters who taught the child too young
to be of any use at home for a few months in the summer.

These conditions, as I have said, held until the beginning of the
fifties, when a few women, better educated and of more natural
ability, began to take the spring schools. It may be asked where
and how the men teachers got their schooling. Many of them were
self-taught by their own firesides, except those Irish schoolmasters
who had emigrated from the states east. Some, as was the case with
my father, got private tutoring in various branches by walking
miles at night to the house of some man who knew more than they
did. My earliest recollections include evenings at home alone with
my mother and the baby, because my father had gone two or three
miles across the woods to the West Road to get lessons in arithmetic of George Hendricks. This private tutoring, in my father's
case, continued until I was ten years old. Other teachers, perhaps,
studied in the same way. A little later a few, I think, had a year or

two at Miami University, Oxford, Ohio, a college in operation as early as 1824.

My father was every year appointed to teach one or another of the common branches at the sessions of the Institute, and occasionally to lecture on history. By consulting the catalogue of the Teachers' Institute at Eaton in 1854, I find that there were twice as many men teachers of the county registered as women; and that many of the latter were preparing, but had not yet taught. Among those who had taught was Mercy Larsh, whom I remember very well as a keen woman with strong sense of humor of whom I was very fond, and who permitted me to tag about after her. I did not then understand why I was allowed or encouraged to go with my father to these institutes. No other girl so young as I went when I began. But I afterwards knew that my father was looking to the time when I should be able to take a certificate and teach so that I might later go to college.

Among the lecturers and teachers of those summer school days whose scholarship left some mark on my training was Dr. Joseph Ray (of the *Arithmetics*). From Dr. Asa D. Lord, Josiah Hurty, and others we had a good deal of the "Theory and Practice of Teaching"; from Dr. Ray some astonishing things in calculation and mathematical memorizing; from Dr. Samuel K. Hoshour we had many interesting things about unusual words, particularly long words of Greek or Latin origin such as were likely to make the unlearned stare. He had written a quaint pamphlet in which he had expressed himself wholly in such words. I do not remember the purpose of the book, but I do remember the enthusiasms of the old man, half droll and half serious, as he expounded his ideas. He gave us also a startling lecture on "Female Education and the Position and Rights of Women."

From William H. Venable, who had even then made himself known as a writer of some local distinction, we had lectures on some subject relating to literary culture in the schools, but I have less distinct recollection of them than of his face and general appearance. He was a slender and delicate though well-built youth of some age in the twenties. His features were refined and expressive and dominated by the forehead of a peculiarly handsome head covered with loose, dark hair. His eyes were gray blue and long lashed. In short, his head and face were those of an idealist and a poet, yet of a man who was not without an unusually high grade of common sense. When I saw Edward Rowland Sill years later, I was reminded of Mr. Venable.*

As the longer sessions of the institute were conducted as school classes with distinguished lecturers and professors from colleges as teachers, it soon came about that Preble County had teachers among the best in Ohio. With the coming of Horace Mann, the first president of Antioch College in 1853, began an awakening of educational activities throughout the state. I saw and heard Mr. Mann lecture twice at one of these summer institutes, and also heard him talk on "Reading," which he illustrated by reciting from memory Leigh Hunt's "Abou Ben Adhem." In one of his informal talks, in a session of the next day, he described a recitation in geography which he had recently seen in a school in Germany. This was so vividly explained that we seemed to see the teacher drawing at the board, every touch of his chalk as he moved it, recited from by the class, while the map grew like magic under his hand. A few years later in this same room my own classes and those of other teachers were able to do similar work.

Horace Mann, as I then saw him, was to me like a being from another world. His tall, straight figure, immaculately clothed in black broadcloth, his speckless linen and shining shoes, all of themselves unusual in their quality and in his manner of wearing them, were enough to have attracted my attention; but his grave and wonderful face, his high brow, over which fell on either side snow-white hair, and his dignified manners impressed me greatly. Such clothes I had seen, but such a man *and* such clothes, never; broadcloth and speckless linen and shining shoes were not at all uncommon sights, but everything about this distinguished man seemed to take distinction from him. His speech was in every way as distinguished by being, as it seemed to me, a part of the perfect man.

*William Henry Venable became a distinguished Ohio author and editor. One of his notable works was *Footprints of the Pioneers in the Ohio Valley* (1888). [Ed. note]

Another lecturer known in Europe for his scholarship by his scientific writings for English and German magazines, but comparatively little known then in America, was Daniel Vaughan. He was an astronomer, linguist, geologist, botanist, chemist, and physicist. Besides all these he was a classical scholar and thoroughly acquainted with the humanities generally. Dr. Vaughan came about this time to lecture every summer for a number of years from Cincinnati where he lived. He became my father's friend, and we saw a good deal of him then and long after in the summers, for he was invited to come to the institutes at a good salary for one or two of the four weeks each summer for ten or twelve years. His scientific lectures were wonderful for enlightenment of those who heard; his learning was prodigious, his nature simple and shy as a child. I owe much to him as an inspirer in the study of such branches of natural history as I then and after followed, and in such general scholarship as I afterward attained.

Daniel Vaughan was Irish, a Dublin University man, who came while young to America. He was connected with the University of Cincinnati when we first knew him, as a lecturer or professor of chemistry. His first summers at the institute at Eaton were as lecturer on chemistry, physical geography, and astronomy. His lectures on chemistry he illustrated by apparatus made by himself after he came. He was also a graduate M.D. After my father's family moved into the country, to his old home district, I usually boarded in the summers at Mr. Morris's in town during the session. Whenever Dr. Vaughan came to lecture Mr. and Mrs. Morris entertained him at their house, so that I saw a good deal of him from one year to another. In 1858 after a summer session at Eaton, I went for a day to the institute at Richmond, Indiana, where I again met Dr. Vaughan, who was lecturing there on chemistry. He saw me there and came to my seat after the lecture, showed me some specimens of various kinds of crystals which he had just been using in his lecture, and talked for some time.

When I started from the schoolhouse to the train and had gone a block or two, I heard rapid steps behind me; it was Dr. Vaughan, who, with old-world courtesy, begged my pardon and said that as I seemed interested in shells he would send me a work on conchology, and added a message to my father with a promise to write to me after he returned to Cincinnati. Thus began a long and rather curious friendship, continued through my subsequent years of teaching at Eaton, my college years, and on until after my coming to California. I still have his letters written during the Civil War, and showing all his heartfelt interest in the outcome of that time. He was still my father's friend to the end of his life, but owing to his failing health and occupation with scientific work, absorbing of its kind, they lost track of each other in his later years. I was in California, and he was never communicative about his situation. He died in the Catholic Hospital of the Good Samaritan, Cincinnati, in 1879.

A bronze bust was made and put in the Cincinnati Public Library in memory of Dr. Vaughan. He was elected to the director-ship of the Cincinnati Observatory a day or two before he died— a post which he had long wanted because of its opportunities for continuance of studies which he wished to pursue—a post in which he would have been comfortable and able financially to take better care of himself, and in which he would have made Cincinnati cele-brated as a center of discovery. But jealousy and schemes of various kinds prevented the election of a non-political man for some years; and at the end, when it was too late, the post was given to him, and Cincinnati thought well of herself for thus caring for her one scien-tific man, who had made the bare name of the town known in Europe by his scientific writing. As a friend of his bitterly wrote me, "He asked for bread and they gave him a stone."

Dr. Vaughan was an honored member of a number of scientific societies of various European countries. He was very greatly inter-ested in the study of earthquakes, and published an exposition of his theory regarding them, which, if I remember rightly, has not been superseded by later discoveries. His studies of the constitution of the sun attracted wide attention. Personally he was a slender, delicately built man with finely cut features, blue eyes which had the look of overuse, and generally wore his thick hair in a sort of shock around his head. His manners were exceedingly shy and quiet. Children were very fond of him and hung about him for the quaint tales which he was always ready to tell them. At Mr. Morris's table he was full of anecdote and stories of personal experience. Among strangers he was silent.

At the sessions of the summer school he usually sat at one of the desks between his lecture hours and listened to whatever was going on. Very often in the discussions which arose at the time of the critic's reports he was appealed to as an authority on questions of language in dispute. I have seen him at such times looking as if his mind were entirely absorbed in his own thoughts until someone would say, "Perhaps Dr. Vaughan will give us his opinion on this subject"; then he would answer in a way which showed that he had heard every word of the discussion. On one occasion the matter in question was about the use of a certain form of a verb. Dr. Vaughan answered by quoting three or four lines from Pope and another passage from Milton which contained the word, and then added what he had observed with respect to current usage.

I once had the good fortune to be present in Mr. Morris's house when he introduced to Dr. Vaughan Dr. Edward Orton, president of Antioch College and afterward president of Ohio State University, who had come to deliver a course of lectures at the summer school. The two men had never met, though I think Dr. Vaughan at least had known of Dr. Orton. Dr. Orton had a way of asking questions which would drain an ordinary mind in a few minutes of everything there was in it which he wanted. Soon after his introduction to Dr. Vaughan he asked him if the health of the town was good at that time, evidently taking him for a local M.D. Dr. Vaughan answered quietly that he believed it was. The next question let in but little light, but piqued curiosity. Then followed a fusilade of questions, the answers to which left Dr. Orton a greatly astonished man. Meantime Mr. Morris and I were enjoying the situation to the full. "Why," said Dr. Orton afterward, "I never met such a man, where has he lived that I have never known of him?" The two men were together the remainder of Dr. Orton's stay. It was delightful to see how skillfully Dr. Orton's impetuous leading questions were met by the simplicity and penetration of the other man. And no one would have supposed from his manner that he was enjoying the tilt.

Among other interesting men who taught us at the summer school in 1857 and later was Charles S. Royce. He often talked with groups of us at the recesses, at which time he told us some of his own personal history. He had served several years before the mast on a whaling vessel, and had left the sea on account of his mother's wishes. That life and subsequent training in Dr. Lewis's School for Gymnastics had made his body a splendid example of systematic development. He was at that time about fifty years of age, but his thick brown hair and beard, his bright observant eyes, and his suppleness and alertness gave him the look of a much younger man.

He trained us in connection with our elocution lessons in light gymnastics, which many of the teachers afterwards introduced into their own schools. Mr. Royce's instruction in reading was also reflected in the schools of the county, through the teachers who had been enlightened by his reading of lessons familiar to them in the reading books. Of him also we took lessons in shorthand, which was then new to the country towns. Benn Pitman of Cincinnati had given, about this time, lectures illustrating the usefulness of this art. We were also introduced by Mr. Royce to the study of phonetics. To him we owed, besides, many commonsense ideas about school management and ways of teaching grammar and other subjects.

The summer school, as a body largely composed of men, as I have said, gave back no uncertain sound on moral questions. At every yearly meeting there was some emphatic expression on the subject of manners and morals as related to teachers. In the catalogue for 1856 this consensus is thus set down: "Resolved—That in the light of morality and Christianity, the members of this Institute look upon the use of *ardent spirits*, the use of *profane language*, and the use of *tobacco*, as practices inconsistent with the *true* and *enlightened* Teacher." Later catalogues record similar action. I recall but one example of a school teacher who used tobacco, and I remember that in some districts such use would have prevented the employment of an applicant. In fact, I may say that a tobacco-using teacher was seldom met in the schools of Preble County during my connection with them which ceased in 1871.

Perhaps one of the most pleasant features of these summer sessions was the custom of taking walks after the early supper until the time for the evening lecture in one of the churches. We gathered at the schoolhouse and walked in a body, the women bare-headed and in light summer dresses, out to Aukerman's

6

Interludes

Fifty-two years ago on this very date, April 1, 1910, at this very hour, making due allowance for difference in longitude, I was standing in the big room at my grandmother's as first bridesmaid to my pretty, young Aunt Sarah. On my left stood my youngest aunt Eleanor and my cousin Elizabeth. On the right of the groom stood the three groomsmen, the only persons not belonging to the family present at the wedding.

The bride wore dotted Swiss muslin, cut low and with short sleeves and a white-ribbon sash. The bridesmaids wore gowns of the same material and of the same fashion, excepting that they had sashes of color. The groom was dressed in dark blue broadcloth with brass buttons. Who performed the ceremony or what was said, I do not remember as I was so occupied with my part in the ceremony and fears that I should blunder. A memory of the faces of my father, mother, and baby brother, of my grandmother and several of my aunts and uncles is all that remains of the picture,

After the ceremony we went out to a luncheon on the big back porch. As it was a cold drizzling April day, we ladies in low-necked muslins did not greatly enjoy the feast. We had no flowers on the table excepting a single little blossom of what we had always known as wild peanut, which Aunt Ella and I had found in the woods. My aunts were much amused at my insistence that it should have such a place of honor.

After luncheon we changed our gowns, about which I remember nothing excepting that my own was of dark green merino. A bonnet of mingled dove-colored satin and black velvet trimmed with a spray of red roses and leaves, and a half-length black cloak completed my costume.

As we started on the wedding journey, the first groomsman and I were in a buggy in front, followed by the bride and groom, who in their turn were followed by the other two couples in separate vehicles. We were to drive to Dayton, about thirty miles east on the National Road, and were expecting to dine at Johnsville, a post village halfway. There we found that the people had just moved into the only hotel in the place, and although they could feed our horses they could give us nothing to eat. While we women waited alone in the dining room, the bride went to the tall cupboard and, opening the doors, brought out a dish of cold baked potatoes, the only edible there. She passed them around to us. So we four stood in the empty but clean dining room eating our wedding dinner. The men did not fare so well, for they got nothing but the fun out of ours. The whole day was drizzly and gloomy. When we reached our hotel in Dayton, we found that the people had just moved in there but they gave us a good supper.

The next morning was bright and sunny. We drove out to the farm of the bride's brother, my uncle, in West Dayton where we were to have the "infare dinner." After a walk about the farm and garden, a row across the Miami River, and my aunt's bountiful dinner, we started home. On account of my extreme shyness and my having had no acquaintance with my escort, I had had a very dull, stupid ride the day before, knowing very little how to talk or how to be talked to. The ride home was much pleasanter on account of the better weather and better acquaintance, though I suspect that my somewhat mature cavalier found as much relief at parting from his two day's companion as I did in saying farewell to him.

I have gone thus minutely into this account because the details are essentially characteristic of the time. Such wedding processions as our four carriages were not uncommon. People would say as these parties passed by on the road: "Oh, there go some weddiners!"

In the 50's and 60's, in country places in Preble County, the friendly custom of speaking to everybody you met on the roads was still a matter of course. The driver of any kind of a vehicle hailed anybody overtaken on foot with an invitation to ride, which was always accepted. I was once walking from Eaton out the Brookville Road to spend the night with my grandmother. Hardly a mile from town I was overtaken by a strange old-fashioned two-horse carriage, so quaint it seemed to have driven out of an old English book. Huge, long-bodied, high, and well-preserved, the thing looked formidable to mount. The single occupant had stopped on overtaking me and invited me politely to ride "as it was a warm afternoon." He was as ancient as his carriage—looked eighty at least and habited in very old-fashioned clothes from his hat to the shoes. He began to talk at once as soon as I was seated beside him, and found out who I was by guessing I was, "one of Jimmy Ryan's granddaughters I reckoned as soon as I seen you." "Going to visit your grandmother, eh?" That settled, he began at once to tell me all about his farm, where it was, how big and fine it was, how many cattle and horses he had, &c, &c, &c, adding that he had a good house and "was well-fixed," also that he was alone, as his wife had died some time before—eight or nine months, I gathered— and that all his children were married and settled.

"Any woman would be well off to get into a home like mine," added he with a ghastly grin. "Ye don't know any woman, do ye that 'ud be willin'?" No, I didn't.

A dimly formed resolution in the back of my mind never to accept the invitations of unknown octogenarians who might overtake me in my rural walks registered itself, as I climbed down from the high seat across the fore-wheel of the venerable howdah. Kindness, I reflected, isn't always free from selfish motives, even when offered by the ancients. The vexatious thing about it was that I had lost the enjoyment of the pleasant walk, the sight of the fields and woods, of the well-known old neighbor's gardens and yards, the wayside path along the worm fences, with their shrubbery and vines; the quiet and the kind of loneliness in which I walked along singing to myself because the sky was so blue, the grass so green, and everything so cheering. But I suppose the fun afforded those who listened to the recital of the ride was a little in the way of balance.

I sometimes went to woods meetings, as they were called, in the neighborhood of Paint Church. One in particular I remember for several reasons. I went with one of my younger aunts to a meeting held by the Universalist Church of Friendship, in Dooley's

Woods. It was on a summer Sunday when the woods were in full leaf. A rude pulpit and rough benches had been prepared for the congregation the week before. A reed organ was brought in an open wagon, which served as a choir center near the pulpit; some stringed instruments, violins and 'cello, gave interest to the musical part of the service. The preacher was Rev. Mr. Nye from Cincinnati, a man with a most astonishing vocabulary and flow of words. I do not remember anything that he said, or why and how he was a "Universalist"—with a capital U, though I did afterwards learn that. After the sermon the people gathered into groups around the luncheon spread on tablecloths on the ground and had a good social time before going home.

On one of my not infrequent visits to my Aunt Margaret Jones, who lived on Lower Paint Creek, seven miles from Saint Clair cottage, I stopped at my grandmother's about three miles on the way, as agreed upon, for my young uncle, Francis, who was to go with me. The walk of seven miles in the sharp spring air of March was made without fatigue, which fact I felt a peculiar pride in, as it seemed to boast of my good health. This, I remember, was more robust than it had been for a number of years. I was not yet seventeen and had grown much taller in the preceding six months, so that I was then very near my adult height of five feet eight and three quarter inches, which was about that of my Aunt Margaret. This I mention because an almost tragic incident fixed it in my memory.

My aunt and two cousins and a young visitor who was the accepted lover of my cousin Elizabeth, were standing about in the dining room talking while waiting for dinner, about to be served. The visitor, seeing a gun lying on the top of the low cupboard, took it up to examine it. Much amused at the quaint old-fashioned flint lock, he was handling it rather carelessly when Cousin William, its owner, said "Be careful, boy, it's loaded." But he, thinking this a joke, lifted the gun, pointing it directly at me, and was about to pull the trigger when William cried, "Be careful I tell you, it's loaded!" Suddenly turning white to the lips, the youth dropped the gun from its aim saying "It isn't possible." William took the gun, showed him how he had tinkered with it until it would work, for the fun of it. Had the boy fired he would have struck me in the throat and my aunt, who stood just behind me near the fire, exactly in the same place, as we were the same height. A perceptible shadow disturbed the minds of us all so that Elizabeth's good dinner gave less cheer than it might have done. The young marksman scarcely tasted food and did not regain his natural color for some hours. The owner of the gun, a mere boy, took the lesson to heart as well.

On a later visit to my aunt, I went with my cousins, William and Rachel, one evening in early September, to visit some neighbors a mile or so distant. The road lay partly through a piece of thick woodland, a mere foot pathway to which we kept by the light of a lantern. In the middle of the wood stood the cabins, pulpit, and benches of a deserted camp-meeting ground, where I once, at the age of five or six, had been with my parents to a Methodist camp meeting. The light from a great burning log nearby showed us the weird shapes and shadows of the deserted scene of so many religious gatherings. We passed through the shadows by the burning log, on through the wood to the edge of the cornfield, and up the hill to the house. Friendly lights from a summer kitchen door streamed across our upward path. We found the women of the household ironing in the kitchen, where they greeted us volubly and whence they presently took us into the main house. There they regaled us in the large house-kitchen with innumerable melons of various kinds, while all talked in jolly fashion. Later they took us into their parlor, a large, low-ceiled, whitewashed room with a rag carpet, white muslin curtains, and old-fashioned wooden furniture. On one side stood a bureau with glass knobs on which was a large number of plaster images of cats and dogs and flower baskets, fruit baskets, and other images. But the pride of the collection was a white horse about eighteen inches high and of beautiful proportions. One of the young men took it up and showed it to us with evident delight. On one of the walls was an old-fashioned clock and near it a family record in a wooden frame.

But the most vivid recollection of this visit centers about the old camp-meeting ground and the burning log which again showed it to us as we went homeward.

When I consider the years of this decade of my life as a whole, I seem to see it as a mass, varied by incidents of differing importance and also by many unrelated trifles which push themselves up into the plane of my consciousness with little relevancy.

One of these memories is of going with a violent toothache to the little office of our old family physician, Dr. Sturr, to have a tooth drawn. There were no dentists in our town at that time, and the family physician was expected to perform all such operations. As I entered, the doctor stood near a very old lady who had come to be bled as was her custom every spring. Her outstretched left hand grasped the head of a cane. The doctor motioned me to a seat in the corner, where I sat, all eyes, having forgotten my own trouble while I looked at the spurting blood and the horrid basin. Meanwhile the two talked as unconcernedly as people do about the weather. By this time my tooth had stopped aching and I decided to keep it, the doctor being not at all insistent.

The other doctors in town at this time, contemporary with Dr. Sturr, were Dr. Parramore and Dr. Pliny M. Crume. Dr. Parramore was a very stout, old-fashioned man much older than the other two, born I think many years back in the eighteenth century. He had travelled up and down the country roads for many years, winter and summer, in all kinds of weather, when called to care for the farmer folks. I had been much afraid of him when I was a little child, and used to crawl under my mother's spinning wheel to get out of his reach. He had a way of putting a very fat forefinger on my tongue when he asked to see it, which, followed by an ugly dose of medicine, greatly increased my dread of him.

The winding of the town clock in the courthouse steeple came to be of interest to me through hearing my father tell about it. He sometimes helped to wind up the great weights which were made by filling two wooden boxes with stones. The man who had this great responsibility upon him called in anybody who happened to be passing.

Funeral cards were in use in Eaton as long as I lived there. It was the custom to print an announcement of the death with the accompanying dates and an invitation to attend the funeral at a given time and place. These cards were delivered at the door of every house in town by the carrier of the weekly paper. Funerals were always largely attended. The long procession sometimes extended from the west end of Main Street across the Red Bridge to the cemetery gates. Usually a church bell was tolled until the procession was out of town. The bell was tolled also immediately after the death, with strokes that numbered the years of the departed.

Little Johnny M., a bright infant of three or four years of age, had been told by his mother after an attack of illness from eating green gooseberries that if he ate any more she would have to punish him. When the temptation had proved too much for him a second time, she took him into the cool, darkened sitting room, shut the door, and said, "Now, John, you remember that mother told you that she would have to whip you if you ate gooseberries again." Whereupon the infant began to beg off, to promise solemnly that he would never do it again. But his mother was unrelenting. At last, when the child had exhausted every argument to save himself in vain, he remembered that everything else ceased at family prayers and suddenly dropping on his knees before a chair said, "Let us pray." "Of course I was vanquished" said his mother as she told me.

Among the things that children used to take to school to eat in school time or at recess was parched field corn which was liked much better than popcorn. I have often parched a skillet-full on the stove and filled my pocket to take to school to eat and to distribute among my fellows. This was a common practice even in the high school among the well grown-up children, and no one hesitated to ask of another who was eating, "Oh, give me some corn." Cracked hickory nuts served a similar purpose.

The county fair began to be an important educational factor in the farming districts in western Ohio at least as early as 1853. It was held at the county towns in grounds set aside for that purpose, usually near or in a piece of woodland at a convenient distance from the town. Some months before the exhibition the list of premiums offered for exhibits was published in the county papers. The farmers generally took a good deal of interest in the fairs for other reasons besides the possibility of taking premiums on their products.

Fair time was a sort of holiday which gave them an opportunity of exchanging ideas, of comparing their cattle, horses, pigs, sheep, and poultry with those of their neighbors and other farmers in different parts of the county. They met old friends and took time to talk over their own and their neighbors' affairs. The farmers' wives brought their quilts, coverlets, webs of flannel and linen, rag carpets, their best handmade garments, knitted stockings and laces, linen thread, butter, cheese, preserves, pickles, corn pone and other breads, and various other things not called for by the advertised list. As it seemed worthwhile to the officers of the county fair to encourage new handicrafts, they gave premiums for any expression of originality or ingenuity in manufacture and even in attempts toward artistic expression, so that there were examples of bead work, embroidery, wax flowers and fruits, even oil paintings and pen drawings. Specimens of handwriting also received attention, and I remember that my father's writing took premiums several years in succession. My mother offered her fine linen thread spun by herself with similar approval.

The exhibits were shown in three large open halls or sheds. The domestic manufactures, occupying the first hall, were displayed on a long table running from end to end or hung above the table where they could be seen to advantage. A wide passage on either side permitted visitors to examine whatever interested them. In the horticultural hall were placed the grains, fruits, vegetables, and flowers. Domestic and agricultural machines were shown in the machinery hall. Sheds and pens were provided for the exhibit of animals on one side of the grounds. In front of these was a covered stand adorned with flags, for the judges before whom the various animals were brought out in their turn to be examined and passed upon in their several classes. The winners of the premiums were led back to their places wearing the blue or red ribbons indicating their success. The same stand was sometimes occupied by Lockwood's Brass Band.

There were no race horses shown, there was no gambling or betting. The only horseback contest was for the silver cup offered for the best horseback riding by women. Even this contest was discontinued after the first few years. There were no drinking saloons, no restaurants, and no side shows. People brought lunches and picnicked in the woods and visited with each other, inviting any chance friend who happened to pass by while they were eating around their tablecloth spread upon the ground.

In later years many of the features which I have mentioned were modified or changed by the gradual evolution of things. Some new things were added from year to year. I saw, for example, in 1873, the last time I went to the county fair, a cooking contest, in which young women under twenty competed for the premium of a cooking stove. This prize was to be given for the best dinner "from the stump" prepared in the shortest time. "From the stump," it may be explained, implied that every dish must be cooked then and there from the beginning, hot bread and pie included. A row of open sheds, each with a stove and other conveniences, provided the place for cooking and serving and also gave the public a chance to observe the process.

7

First Teaching Experiences

I began to teach in the primary room in the old North Building of the Eaton Public Schools. When I was about fourteen Mr. Morris used to send me downstairs to the primary room to help Mrs. Hutchinson, or to take the class entirely on days when she was ill and absent. I do not know why I was chosen, as there were older girls in the high school, possibly because I was tall and serious-minded and my father was a teacher. I usually made out somehow, but it was a formidable undertaking for one so young and so much of a child as I was in matters of judgment. The experience was of little value, as I was not old enough to profit by it, nor was the usual discipline of the school class, nor the teaching, of a kind to enlighten me. The room was overcrowded with children of ages from four to ten—ABC's to *Second Reader.* I had already a teacher's certificate but made no further use of it, and it lapsed before I took a school.

In 1857 in August or early in September, I, being then sixteen years old and a month or more, went to Richmond, Indiana, sixteen miles by rail, to take an examination before the City Board, preliminary to applying for a position to teach. I stayed at my Aunt Laura's, and was escorted next morning to the high school building by my Uncle James.

William D. Henkle (of Henkle's *Algebra*) was then superintendent, and conducted the examination with a Mr. Wilson of the high school and a third person I do not remember. I was a green, overgrown girl, in my first long dress. I had never been away from home alone, or scarcely at all. The examination was entirely oral except in spelling, in which I missed *champain*, spelling it thus, the heraldic term, instead of *champaign*; *campaign* and *champagne* were also in the list. The result of the examination brought me out

[154]

with 91%, the highest in the class getting but 92%. All the others were mature women, one of them old. But my recent high school training had made me confident in the subjects. All were fresh in my mind, except United States history in which I had had no instruction excepting the catechetical lessons to which I have referred.

While I stood waiting at the board for more work I "fooled" a little with algebraic formulas. "Do you know algebra?" asked Mr. Henkle, and gave me some problems in theorems. Much astonished at my glibness with chalk, he remarked in an aside, which I overheard, "Can any good thing come out of Nazareth?" From which it may be perceived that the town I hailed from was not in good repute at that time in Quaker Richmond.

The result of the examination was reported to the Board of Directors, and I was elected at once, without having been seen, I may remark, by any one of them; which thing shows that their judgment was as defective as my own, but not from the same cause—extreme youth. I served for three purgatorial weeks as a substitute in a class in the high school for which there yet lacked a teacher. This lasted until the little secondary school, to which I had been elected, could be arranged for. At the end of that time I was transferred to my own class in the old Public Square building, with a Miss Fulghum in the only other room. The most that I remember of those first three weeks of substituting is that I had not the least notion about organization, or discipline, although I had had theories enough for some years in the summer institute lectures; also that my mind was still an immature child's without judgment or ability to organize my knowledge for immediate use. Many of the students were several years older than I. It was a cruel experience. Nothing remains, I say, but the memory of a few blunders, and a short list of names, *Madeline Doloff, Seth Smith Griffith, Joseph Iliff, Emma Fulghum*; the first two because they were odd names, the third because it belonged to a troublesome boy, and the last because it was the name of a very pretty, very naughty and impertinent girl, who stared at me like an image of steel with brilliant blue eyes.

The second grade class was better, and there I did some good work, despite the mistakes natural to so young a teacher. I taught the term (four months) out and went home at the end. There was no more public school that year, because, as my father said, "An ignorant Democratic legislature, elected that year, had cut down the public school session to that time, throughout the state." The remainder of the year was "pay school" everywhere. My experience was a hard one, which hardness I kept to myself from my family and from everybody else. I was terribly homesick and a good deal of the time sick from the bad water and other unwholesome conditions. My life at my aunt's was pretty busy though I paid my board, as there was much to do and only one pair of hands to do it. I went to teachers' meetings on Monday nights, to one concert, to a lecture or two, to see two or three of my pupils, and to church a few times. At the concert I heard for the first time a public singer, a Miss Louise Rosenkiewicz, of Cincinnati. She was a tall, beautiful woman, and sang ballads, among which I remember for the first time "Annie Laurie," and "Down the Burn, Davy Love." A little later than this I heard James Murdock, a Cincinnati actor-elocutionist, lecture and recite. Among the readings he gave, I remember only Willis's "Parrhasius," and Poe's "Bells" and "The Raven." Outside of that I had no pleasures. My mother came to visit me once with my brother, then an infant in arms, and I spent a few days at home during an interregnum caused by scarlet fever in Richmond.

But in those four short months I had left behind me the childhood not yet completed when I came away from home. Life in a city for a homesick girl, shut up in narrow conditions, with responsibilities she had not dreamed of, and some dangers she did not know of but avoided by instinct—all these made the blithe *young, very* young creature begin to be old before her time to begin. I came away at the end with many affectionate words and tokens from my pupils—one or two clung to my neck with tears, and wished me *not to go, not to go.* Strangely enough, W. D. H. never saw that side of my teaching. He criticized me as *cold* and lacking *magnetism.* The fact was that whenever he came into my class I was frozen with terror and did not know what to do—could not even go on with my set program rightly. He was one of the most nearly perfect men physically I ever saw—tall, dark, with waving, abundant black hair which always fell about his forehead and had to be put back by a shapely white hand, dark eyes, long lashes, olive

[156]

skin, a magnificent figure, and a dazzling smile which he seldom used. His wife was little and blonde and beautiful; I used to see her at the teachers' meetings which were sometimes at his house. It was he who had made the remark about me and Nazareth at the examination. I do not know whether he was a good superintendent or not. He may have been. Certain it is, he was not a helper of young teachers; he never by chance or by look suggested a word of advice, or a better way. A few words in private from him or anybody else would have set things to better ways for me.

One thing which was entirely new to me in the Richmond community was the pervasiveness of the Quaker modes of thought and action. This was so then as it happened because a number of Quakers taught in the schools; Miss Fulghum in the next room to mine was one. My love of singing and the songs I taught the children offended her. A Mr. Wilson of the high school surprised me at the first teachers' meeting by calling Mr. Henkle "William" and "theeing" everybody. The yearly meeting in the big brick structure at the station-end of the town took place while I was in Richmond, and I saw many of the friends. I did not go to the meeting as I might have done if I had known more.

I find at this date (February, 1909) that I can recall the names and faces of almost all of the thirty-odd children in my first regular school. Not only so much of them individually, but I can characterize them by some physical or mental quality; as thus: William Brady, a thickset, solemn, phlegmatic boy of ten, with a very serious defect in his spelling. If, for instance, I should give him to spell such a word as *particular*, he would say: "p-a-r-t-i-c-ness"— or *less* or *ment*. No matter what the word or ending, he invariably began right and ended thus. It was some weeks before I succeeded in correcting the habit. His little classmate, Frank Kitson, was a boy with yellow-brown hair, thin features, and restless glittering black eyes, who had the curious habit of spelling all his words backwards. When I had taught these two boys to spell correctly, the whole school noticed it with approval.

Peter Plunkett, a tall, pale, melancholy-looking boy with pale hair and dark lashes, silent, unsmiling, usually dressed in what looked like tow linen, not very dirty, but not clean; Annie Poe, a pale

little child with quiet ways, the daughter of a school director;
Annie Casely, an English-born child, loose black curls, a throaty
voice, and unorganized h's; she often wore an orange calico dress,
buttoned either before or behind, as convenience dictated; Nora
Robinson, a dear, dainty little maid with blue eyes and a perfect
figure, responsible and wise, for her age; Emma Fulghum, a pretty,
stormy-tempered child, who used to sit flat on the floor in front
of her seat when she got angry. She was sister to the pretty girl
in the class in which I substituted.

And all the rest: Lorenzo Dow Randall, a pale lad of ten, who
seemed weighed down by responsibilities of some kind. He never
allowed his eight-year-old brother Napoleon Bonaparte out of his
sight one minute. Their father, a prosperous-looking gentleman in
silk hat, fine linen and broadcloth, and a conspicuous watch fob,
called at the school one day. Hugo Wiggins, an aristocratic-
looking boy, with dark eyes and nice manners. Emma Peterson;
Johnny Dempsey; William Barmer; Isabella Barnett; Elbridge Hall,
a fine-natured, blond lad, was especially tractable and obedient and
usually the leader in playground sports, the principal one of which
was plain old-fashioned football: a choosing of sides, a lot drawing
for the toss-up, and everybody kicking at the ball to drive it to
one or the other end of the long grassy yard, without teaching
with the hands. And so I might fill out a record of the whole class,
but these will serve. I may add here that my memory is quite as
retentive of faces, forms, manners, and qualities of children in all of
the schools I taught in Ohio.

I do not remember what I read in those months, or whether I
read at all. When I went home, I found my mother ill of typhoid
fever, the two youngest girls ailing, and my father stone-deaf
from a cold in his ears. My own illness disappeared in the stress of
things, and we all soon came back to health again. By the end of
January I was going to the high school again for two months, when
I studied physics, higher arithmetic, and what else I do not
remember.

In April, 1858 I began teaching a district school in the backwoods of
Lanier Township, among people whom my father had taught a few
years before. Here I found out many things about myself as a

teacher. I taught two terms, which were pleasant and profitable to me. It was in the woods, among large spaces for me in more ways than one.

The Deardorff School in Lanier Township was in some respects better than the usual country school, owing to the fact that it had for one of its directors Benjamin Deardorff, a man who had once taught school, and a man therefore of some views on education that would be of advantage to his neighbors. The schoolhouse stood in the corner of a woodland, near the crossing of two roads, and with a field opposite. It was of brick and fairly well furnished, with two doors and two entries for hats and luncheon baskets, and a raised platform and desk for the teacher between the doors. It was considered as good as the best of those times. The people were mainly comfortable farmers, two or three only having acquired a competency. Among these was Mr. Henry Harter who lived about a mile west of the schoolhouse in a substantial brick dwelling. Near was the old hewn log house of earlier years, then occupied by his son, Mr. Geo. Harter, whose wife was the Hannah Banta mentioned as one of the big girls of my first school days. On the basis of that early friendship, these good young people took me in for a few weeks till I could find a boarding place.

Strangely enough as it now seems, these few weeks made a link connecting my later history with the earliest period of my school days. Two or three distinct memories have their place here: one is of the amiable and cheerful character of the lady who had been the merry, good-natured girl of my childhood, the other was of the weird, melancholy, shouting cries on rainy nights, of four or five peacocks which roosted on a big pear tree just outside my window.

The remainder of the term I boarded with the family of Jacob Fisher, who lived in a story-and-a-half log house with an L. The first old log hut still stood in the yard, and was used as a kitchen and dining room. Here I found every Sunday evening on my arrival from home a chicken supper with cake, pie, at least four kinds of preserved fruits, and often what was more uncommon, *four* kinds of molasses—tree molasses (maple), New Orleans (because my host liked it), apple molasses, and tomato molasses. The house was a model of neatness; the two rooms below had freshly ironed curtains, I should be afraid to say how often. But I have seen Mrs.

[159]

Fisher come in, snatch off the sitting-room curtains, which looked as if they had just come from the iron, and put them into the wash for the day. When I came home from school they would be in their place, ironed with creases to the very thread, it seemed.

The front room, which was never used while I was there, had in it two high-posted bedsteads much built up with feather beds and hung with canopies and valances. The floor was covered with a rag carpet. On a bureau stood various plaster images, one of a preternatural mottled cat which stared at me every night as I passed through to the staircase to go to my room in the attic— a large room with two beds. Mine had a canopy and curtains made of a dark red chintz covered with vines, on which perched at regular intervals life-sized partridges in very life-like attitudes. Opposite the opening of my curtains was a mahogany bureau on which stood a colored plaster image of Napoleon I, about two and a half feet high, with the most disconcerting and, as I thought, malignant stare—always directed to me wherever I was—the first thing in the morning, until I had to turn his face to the wall.

The life on these farms still had many of the aspects of that which I had known in the neighborhood where I was brought up; especially was this so among the many families still living in the old hewn log houses of the earlier time. There was, however, a difference in opinions and shades of thought, which will perhaps be best illustrated by the fact that the Dunker form of religious belief prevailed among a large number of families. This was observable in manners and dress, as well as in conversation and restricted outlook. They did not read much and were somewhat influenced by signs and superstitions. As I looked one night at Donati's Comet, while we stood in the yard admiring this beautiful visitor my host suddenly said, "That means war." When I answered that the movements of the stars and other heavenly bodies did not concern themselves with our affairs, he said, "Well, you'll see."

On Fridays I went to my own home five miles away, walking almost always unless the weather was bad, when my father usually came for me on horseback.

The children of this school were easily controlled, coming mostly from families where obedience had been the bringing-up discipline.

An amusing experience or two of the usual sort common to young schoolmistresses fell to my lot. One was the result of a too-evident admiration of the new "school miss," who of course was as good as and no better than other girls of the neighborhood; therefore to be courted, "set up with," as they were, so please you. Acting on this, one of the young men decided to come "to court" the "school miss" on a certain Sunday night. My hostess explained to me that he had told her he was coming, and that I should have to receive him, as otherwise he and his family would be offended at her. I protested, but finally agreed to let him be introduced and sit to talk with me while she went to milk the cow. He came and was introduced—a red-faced, heavyset man in a white, woolly felt hat with yokel shape, a blood-red necktie with flowing ends, a brilliant waistcoat, and trousers of large green-and-black check, a trifle short. He sat down on the opposite side of the room, leaned against the wall with his foot on his chair-rounds, grinned, and said, "You must 'a got purty wet last week when I seen you."

"Yes," I assented, "it was rainy weather."

Silence—in which I sat straight and quiet in my chair, he fidgeted, redder still in the face, if possible, let one foot down from its perch, then took it back and let down the other.

" 'A—ye—y'—must ha' got pretty wet that day I seen you."

"Yes," I again assented.

Soon after, my hostess appeared, and a few minutes later, her husband. Candles were lighted and we sat stiffly, the men talking crops. At eight precisely, I took my candle, said good night to each separately, and went to my attic.

Much I might write about the experiences of this school, which had very little in them that was disagreeable. The children were docile and teachable. Little by little here, as in other and later schools, I picked up bits of teaching knowledge through passing experiences. I had no occasion to use corporal punishment in this school, although I once made the mistake of coming very near it. But as I was not yet seventeen years old I may be partially excused.

Among the children was a boy of eleven who had lost the use of his feet and legs by a fever when he was very young. He made a great deal of trouble in the schoolroom by moving his ears and wrinkling his scalp to make the younger children laugh. He rarely let anyone pass him without striking a blow with his fist or giving a vicious pinch. None of the children ever resented by retaliating, as it would have been a shame, in the neighborhood opinion, to strike a cripple, no matter what he did. He had been indulged at home for the same reason, as the parents, like most, under similar circumstances, could not see that they were doubling the child's misfortune by crippling his disposition and thus permanently injuring his character. I had tried all my theories on this case without any effect.

I spoke of the matter at my boarding place with the assertion that I was afraid I should have to whip the child. "Oh, you mustn't do that!" was the exclamation. "Everybody would blame you." "But," I said, "he is spoiling the school. I shall do it."

Next day I took the lad alone at the noon recess. I talked with him about the matter, and got no response except a grin. Then I said, "You are perfectly well and strong as any other boy here. You think because you are a cripple you cannot be punished for wrongdoing. But since you are perfectly well, you will have to be treated like other boys. You see the little elm tree across the road? I am going out there now to get a switch which I will use on you, hard, the next time you do these things, or any of them." Then I went across the road. Got the switch, deliberately stripped off the leaves, took it into the house, and laid it on my desk.

The school had seen and understood what I meant to do. Nobody said anything. In the afternoon nothing happened nor did I have any further trouble with the boy. In fact we became very good friends, and he often came in at the noon recess to have a friendly talk. At one of these talks he told me that his cousin Joe was an "Awful high-lernt feller. Why he can write Injun." After some questioning I found that Joe could write shorthand.

One Saturday when I was on some errand on Main Street, Eaton, and during the second, or summer, term of my school in Lanier Township, I met Gen. George D. Hendricks, who stopped and asked me at once, "See here. Don't you want to teach in town next fall? What's the use o' your going 'way down to Lanier? We'll need you here for a primary school."

"Why, I should like it—yes."

"Well, then, it's settled, and you'll begin in September in the Old Public Church, with Mrs. Blythe."

General Hendricks was, and had been for many years, as I have said elsewhere, director of the Eaton schools. He had been a teacher in his younger days. He was an old-fashioned man in some ways, eccentric, clever, and individual. His keen gray eyes looked out from bowed spectacles, straight into you, in a way "just like George Hendricks." He had a droll word for everybody he met. His visits to the schools were always welcome to us children, as he had something interesting to say which was not so much like preaching as many of the speeches speeched at us.

Mr. Hendricks's word then put me into the Eaton schools, in connection with which I knew him until I left for college. The first year I taught in the corner of the Old Public Church diagonally opposite the right "pulpit corner" occupied by Mrs. Blythe and her class. Indeed, when the school assembled, all the entering infants were given to me, and Mrs. Blythe kept the Secondary grade. The room was so large that we did not interfere with each other by the noise of work. Beginnings, singing, recesses, and openings were simultaneous. I had a happy, easy year's work there with little to disturb the routine.

I taught little children to read, spell, count, and write on the slate. I had my first experience in trying to teach a child who did not know a word of English to speak and to read. He was a clever little German boy and spoke and read as well as the other children before midwinter. His speech at the time was without foreign accent. I take no credit to myself for method, for I think the child learned most on the playground.

The two years following went by in teaching mixed, primary and secondary, grades in the old North Building.

School hours began at 8:30 and continued till 4 o'clock, with an hour and a half at noon. Except in very bad winter weather I walked home to dinner, a mile and return, which saved me from headaches, as I soon found out if I had to stay. I was my own janitor the first year, made fires and swept, brought in my own wood, if I forgot to ask some of the small boys to do it for me. Afterwards we had the luxury of a sweeper and fire-builder.

I could say something pathetic enough about a slim, pale young woman under twenty who stood all day to teach anywhere from fifty to seventy-five children; who saw the last one off with its hood and shawl fastened on, its mittens found, and often its dirty face kissed, then turned to the broom to sweep out the big dusty room, stooping to every small desk to see that all the dirt was taken from under. I might tell of the same weary creature covering the fire, placing the kindling for morning, locking the seven big windows which she herself washed, whenever they were washed; whose curtains too she laundered when they grew beyond decency with dirt. I can see her now locking the outside door at sunset and starting home with her weary soul, too tired to eat the supper waiting for her.

The school year ended early in June, and three months of rest at home illumined by the Teachers' Institute term in July made the regular routine of the years from '57 to '61.

I gradually learned to make practical some of the theories I had accumulated in my studies at the Teachers' Institutes. There was very little oversight by the principal and the school board. I was absolute mistress in my own room, and taught, in whatever way seemed best to me, reading, writing and spelling, from McGuffey's *Speller*, *Primer*, *First* and *Second Readers*, and added of my own accord some object lessons in the woods. I used the blackboard a great deal in all the studies. At one time we were expected to teach beginners by the Word-Method, by printing words on the board. In one of these years I was required to teach geography from the first twenty lessons of Colton's *Primary Geography*, which concerned themselves mainly with the definitions of the natural divisions, mathematical geography, and forms of government. I wasted a good deal of energy in trying to teach infants, as required, what parallels and meridians are, and to say word for word the definitions of "absolute" and "limited" monarchies, and other bits of, to them, lovely learning. I am glad to say they forgot all this before they entered the class of the man teacher who had required it.

I should have been glad then to begin by teaching the children the geography of the school grounds and the town. I frequently took my class on Friday afternoons at three, to Aukerman's Woods east of the town, where we "spoke our pieces," played games, and learned something about the trees. Singing by ear was common to all the grades at this time, and I taught the children many little songs.

Many pretty and pleasant incidents of these years come to my recollection, with many childish faces that I still readily recall; one of a little, pink-faced, blue-eyed Irish girl in a red-and-brown-checked flannel dress, who came close to me with her slate pressed against her breast, looking up to the height of my face, saying in a whisper "How do you spell *tungcantell*?" "Tungcantell?" said I, "why, there is no such word." "Yes, yes," she said, shyly showing her slate on which was written: "I love you more than _____." "Oh!" I said, spelling the words for her. Then she went to her seat with the same cherubic smile illuminating her baby face. Strangely enough, and amazingly stupid enough, I did not then understand that that lovely sentence was meant for me.

At this time in my teaching career I knew no better than to stand all day; but this was the general custom. In fact, standing was required in some towns. A few years later, in the middle '60's, I heard a superintendent of the Columbus schools answer, when asked if a teacher should stand or sit,

"Stand, of course!"

"What should you do?" asked the same man, "if teachers refused to stand?"

"I should get teachers who would."

This was in a lecture at the Teachers' Institute in Eaton. I kept silence, but I had some thoughts and "my heart waxed hot within me."

At the beginning of the winter term of '59, I had 125 children of two grades crowded into one room. At the end of three weeks I was relieved of thirty-five of these and, except in stormy weather, averaged seventy-five in attendance to the end of that three-months' term. I cannot say that the children learned much, and I wonder now, what with the bad air and other ill conditions, that any of us lived through it. I may add here that there was but one water pail and one tin dipper from which all of these children drank.

At the end of the eight-months' term in the spring of '61, I went the following Monday to begin a summer term in Dougherty's District west of town, for it had been decided that I was to go to college in September, and some more money must be earned. As I had never had more than thirty dollars a month up to this time, I had been able to save only $250 in the four years. I could not go to the institute that summer, and managed to get in eleven school months from September to September '61.

As may be supposed, I was not very fit to begin a college course. But the change from the big crowded room in the Eaton School to a pleasant schoolroom in an open woodland, a comfortable mile's walk along a country road, a small school of thirty pupils, and change of scene and diet restored much of my strength. The summer was that first eventful one of war times, when not much else was talked of among the country people. Runners carried the daily papers to all the farms, each farmer taking a week in turn to see that his neighborhood was served with the news from Cincinnati as soon as it could be brought from the train. My host's daughter, then fifteen, and very enthusiastic, was one of my most interesting pupils. She and I shared the same room and more than once discussed seriously the plan of offering ourselves as government nurses to go to the hospitals; which, since neither of us knew anything about nursing, was of course impracticable, even if the call for nurses had included women so young as we were.

I can yet remember the names and faces of almost all of the children of that school. The schoolroom was the most pleasant I had yet worked in. I never used the rod there; but on one occasion, as at the Fisher School, three years before, I did use it as a threat in a curious case. One day during the first week of school a pretty, little, quiet girl, named Sarah, brought her younger sister, Eliza, just arrived at school age. In the middle of the forenoon little Eliza began to cry in a sharp, continuous high key, so loud that classwork was impossible. I tried to find out what was the matter without avail. Supposing the child to be ill someway, I sent her sister home with her. At noon one of the older girls told me that this child ruled at home with that cry, and that all of the family would give up everything to her to stop it. At the table, it was said, she would not touch food until she had everything she wanted on her plate. If she was not served at once, as she wished, she would turn her plate full of food upside down on the table and begin that terrible cry. "Ah," I said to myself, "if that is all, I think I can manage Miss Eliza."

The next day the child fell asleep during the warm forenoon and when she waked, again began the cry which I then observed was without tears or change of expression. I went to her, walked quietly, told her she made so much noise that we couldn't hear the lessons. The cry continued without a single moment's cessation. Then I took her to the front door, told her to sit down until she could stop crying, then shut the door and left her. Truth to tell, we could hear little better than before, the cry was so shrill. At the end of half an hour she stopped, I opened the door and asked her if she was ready to come in. She glanced at me, set up the cry, and I again shut the door.

At the noon recess, after the children had eaten their luncheon, I brought Eliza in by the hand, put her on the bench in front of me and told her the facts in the case, and called her attention to a beech rod, left by my predecessor in the corner over the blackboard. She listened without a sign of any emotion. Then I said, "The next time you cry like this, Eliza, I'm going to take down that switch and whip you with it." She looked at me with a steady gaze which seemed to have no expression except a sort of calculation as to whether I meant it or not. All the time she kept fumbling at her perfectly exquisite little right ear with a perfectly exquisite little dimpled right hand which was now and then covered with her lovely light curls, but she did not speak a word. After waiting a minute I said, "Now, Eliza, when you feel like crying you may cry but *you are not to make any noise about it,* either in the house or on the playground." After a few minutes I led her out to the other children, somewhat dubious as to the result.

In the afternoon the child fell asleep, and I made her comfortable on one of the benches. I awaited her awakening with some anxiety, for I still feared I had not mastered the situation, but when she awoke and sat up I saw that the tears were rolling down her pretty cheeks but she was silent. The episode was closed for the term, and the pretty little creature soon liked her school as well as the rest.

My life with these children was so quiet and happy that I was really grieved when I had to leave them. This pleasant neighborhood lay along the West Road, a few miles from Eaton, among prosperous farms. Here and there a new house had lately appeared and here and there still remained the comfortable old hewn log houses of an earlier time.

My walks from home in Eaton at the beginning of the week were pleasant in spite of their length and an occasional storm. But one Sunday afternoon, early in June, on my way back to my weeks' work, I suddenly found myself in the middle of a host of army worms which were moving eastward and covering the whole width of the road, the grass on either side, the fences, and even the weeds in the roadside pools. Fortunately my walking dress was short enough to clear the ground, and I went safely through the seventy-five yards or more of the crawling multitudes. I could not pick my steps and had no choice but to run to the other end of the army.

One day in that week the children were called out from school to help some farmers to keep a similar army from crossing the road into the grassy open woodland opposite the schoolhouse, but their help was little needed. The V-shaped ditch made by the plow trapped the caterpillars which fell into it. They were then killed by dragging a log through the ditch from end to end. The invasion by this pest was widespread through Ohio and Kentucky.

8

A Visit
to Antioch College
and a Backward Glance

In the latter part of June, 1861, I took a week's leave of absence
from my West Road School, made convenient for the people by
wheat harvests, and went with my father and mother, Mr. Isaac S.
Morris, a Miss Chrisman, and John I. Bailey, who drove us in his
big family carriage, across country forty-five miles, to commencement at Antioch College. Our way followed the National Road to
Dayton, beyond which on the Mad River we stopped an hour to rest
ourselves and horses and to feed both. We saw along the road
beyond a piece of prairie on which thickly grew field lilies, or
flame-colored tiger lilies, with tall stalks full of flowers with their
curled-back petals of such an air as no other flower ever has. The
road all the way from this place was through a succession of
grassy fields and fine old woods. Diagonally across one fine level
field of grass rose a great wall-like row of close-set willows, with
the white underside of their leaves showing in the slight breeze
that turned them from the road.

We arrived at Yellow Springs early in the evening and were soon
"quartered," after the hospitable fashion of that time for commencement visitors, at the house of a Mr. Armstrong, whose sons
and daughters were in college. Of that first glimpse of college life, I
have comparatively few detailed recollections, but the whole
impression made by the visit was one of a confused panoramic sort
that left little behind, except that this was a thing I wanted to be in
for myself.

After the commencement exercises the next day, we started
in the evening on our homeward drive, as it was pleasanter traveling
in the cool of the night, and the heat had greatly increased since our
arrival. There was no moon, but the road lay straight before us.

Some miles west of Dayton we stopped by the roadside to eat supper, which was funny enough in the dark. Roast chicken, pie, cake, bread and butter, and pickles were handed about by feeling with laughter and jokes, while the unharnessed horses munched their oats near us. The sky was full of stars, and Mr. Morris, my father, and I traced some of the constellations, while the others finished supper and put away the remnants.

Somewhere about halfway to Eaton Mr. Morris said, "I remember well when I was over this road last. I was on the Underground Railroad then, driving a Negro man slave from our home near Wilmington. Our place was a station on the Underground Railroad to West Elkton, the next station. I had been engineer before so that I knew the track well. Before I came to the tollgate we have just passed, I got out of the covered wagon, walked on to the tollgate, which was closed after midnight, told Sam, my refugee, to sit well back in the shadow and drive on. I waked the toll man, who came out without a light; I called out, 'Drive on, Sam, I'll catch you in a few minutes.' Well, I got my man through to Stubbs's at West Elkton, and my father heard from him from Canada a few months after."

September came and I went to college. A big grassy common full of thistles with their balloons flying about in the low winds is what remains of the pictures of the first few days while I waited for the opening day—a little homesick and lonely after my father and mother had gone.

Such a history would be incomplete without some more definite details of the interior life of my home. Although I went regularly to school except during a long illness in my thirteenth year and except some months during a long illness of my mother's, I helped much about the household work and had always some responsible part of it to do. During my mother's illness my sister Laura and I took turns about the larger business of baking and cooking, washing and ironing, milking and making butter, and housecleaning. My younger sisters did their share of the work which was within their strength, all of us working directly under my mother's oversight.

My father was absent from home five days in the week much of the time, which of course added to our necessary work.

Before I was sixteen I had learned how to make my own dresses and other clothes, which, like all the family sewing, was done by hand. The simple styles of those times made this easy, which was fortunate, as it was, and had to be, the custom in most families.

Our evenings were spent around the fireplace reading, knitting, or sewing and sometimes listening to what my father might read from the papers. We never had any lessons to learn at home, as all studying was done at school.

The four open fireplaces in our house contributed not a little to our comfort through a large part of the year. I may say too that they counteracted much that was unsanitary in the lower rooms of the house which, although built on the hill, had poor underdrainage. The open fireplace found in nearly all houses of this region and of this time was in truth a great factor in the preservation of health, as it was the principal ventilator in the winter and made it easy to have fires night and morning in other seasons of the year. The fireplace furnished the only indoor cooking convenience and, of course, the only source of heat. The one square room of the settlers' cabin, with its two beds and trundle beds and possibly its loft with straw mattresses on the floor, very often sheltered a large family whose whole indoor life in the wintertime was spent in this one room. The wide fireplace and great chimney gave the main part of the ventilation.

But over and above these material values the open fireplace ministered to the intellectual and spiritual life in ways which cannot be put into words. On my own life it had so marked an effect that every year since when the open fireplace has not belonged to my surroundings I have been conscious of deprivation, not merely of the creature comfort but of something of what must have been the feeling of the fire worshipper around his altar.

But the intimate life with my father and mother and their direct and indirect training of their children had, of course, more to do with forming character in these years than all else besides. While there was no change in the underlying principles of their training, there was a gradual recognition of the fact that what had already been done gave more responsibility to the children, and required the exercise of less authority; in other words, more liberty was given, and more was required of us in the way of managing ourselves.

My mother had the usual experience of mothers in applying her basic theories to the training of several children. These worked very well as a whole and in details with the first two, but their application to the third child showed that a different kind of wisdom had to be made use of. For she was born with an abnormally strong sense of justice and with a personally fearless determination to resist what she felt to be unjust. Her manner of doing this both at home and at school took the form of a refusal to speak in her own defense. If she had been wrongfully accused she would take the severest punishment rather than to say a word for herself. This was accounted obstinacy and sometimes made trouble for my mother and once or twice for the school teacher. But it was entirely from want of understanding the child, who was, in reality, tractable enough by nature when rightly treated. It was a clear case, as I now think, of inheritance from an English strain of blood reinforced by several generations of Virginian and Kentuckian ancestry. Different also the discipline had to be for the fourth child, who was of an artistic temperament, which showed itself early in a great love for music. But, as I now know, the elder children of the family were of great help in the management of the younger.

Our opinions about people and conduct were formed by our parents unconsciously to us, not by direct precept but by the natural order of expression in daily life. We were not told that this or that man or woman or boy or girl was bad, but that this or that kind of conduct was bad. We knew, and had known for a long time, what our parents thought about the ordinary facts of life, and when we looked at these facts in the years of more experience our opinions were determined by that knowledge but only to such a degree as left room for the individual equation.

Two or three incidents of my father's life as a teacher in these years recur to me. One of these relates to a boy of phenomenal mind who attended a winter school taught by my father in a district a few miles northwest of Eaton. He was the seventeen-year-old son of a Dunker farmer and did not know a letter when he started to school. The first day he learned his letters and to spell and read a few small words. Before the week's end he was reading almost as well as anyone in the school and had begun arithmetic. By the end of the month he was coming to school but three days in the week, for he was quite able to do the week's work in that time. He left school in the spring with as much reading, writing, spelling, and arithmetic as the other boys of his age had acquired by their past years of schooling.

My father was so astonished and so interested in the case that he went to see the father to ask him to give the boy opportunities for an education, but although the man was in good circumstances his Dunker point of view on the subject of education made him think that his son already had enough. He had sent him to school to learn to read, write, spell, and cipher. The boy had done it and neither of them had interest in anything more, though my father tried to persuade them to a different course. Since that day the point of view of the Dunker sect, on the subject of education, has greatly changed, at least in some parts of the country.

Another recollection is of my father's showing us some verses in heroic couplets, which he said he had written in a contest with a young man student of his at West Florence. I remember nothing about the poem excepting that it was humorous and very fluently written. On a vist from this youth, whose surname was Kelly, they had another riming bout and with it a good deal of amusement. The Carrier's Addresses, several of which my father wrote about this time, were usually in the heroic couplet.

The Carrier's Address, it may be explained, was an annual New Year's poem, addressed to the patrons of *The Eaton Register* and written by someone chosen by William B. Tizzard, its editor, for the benefit of the boy who carried the paper. The carrier delivered the printed Address at the houses of the subscribers to the paper, receiving therefore twenty-five cents from each. The Address was usually looked for with some interest as it was a sort of political review of the local as well as of the national history of the year. I wrote such an address myself for January, 1866.

Our amusements during these years had their center largely in the home. They were, for the most part, connected with outdoor life. Now and then we went to a panorama; now and then to a concert or church festival. Sometimes a travelling menagerie,

Barnum's or Van Amburgh's came to town, and we saw their processions, the best parts of which were the elephants.

Of the panoramas, one, painted by a Cincinnati artist named Inscho Williams and called a panorama of the Bible, made a great impression on me. It gave me, for the first time, some knowledge of what landscape painting might be. Much of it was indeed beautiful, and it was considered, by those who knew about such things, to be a great pity that such a piece of work should be dragged about the country thus and worn out. It was said at the time that the artist, who was capable of great things, was compelled to do such work for a livelihood but that he put into it much more than could be paid for. "That was where he saved himself," said one to whom I have told this lately.

"Parties," say you? I went to one small party at the house of Mr. Morris. To another, an afternoon party, at the Garrison Spring, at both of which we played games and had simple refreshments. There was no dancing and, of course, there were no cards, as both of these were held in disrepute. At such dancing parties as were now and then given in a small way in private houses among the Presbyterians, the cotillion or square dances prevailed, indeed I think these were the only forms of dancing then in use. The grace and beauty of these dances gave them some excuses for being, which cannot be said of the stupid and ungraceful two-step of the present time (1910) whose lack of beauty and fitness makes it unmoral. In my young womanhood, however, no interest in dancing was felt among the young people of the village, as the greater part of its families were connected with the Methodist or the New Light Christian churches in both of which dancing was believed to be wrong. The church, the Sunday school, the singing school, the day school, teachers, meetings, lectures, the yearly county fair, the neighborly life of the village streets, the afternoon visits, or the "spend-the-day" visits between whole families helped to make a simple, natural social life which had many advantages both positive and negative.

The manners of this time were distinguished by the absence of conventionality and by the presence of kindliness and consideration. Men did not take off their hats to women or to each other, nor were boys taught to observe this courtesy to their elders.

Both women and men shook hands when they met. The custom of kissing among women and girls on meeting was not in use.

As few people in the town, even among the wealthy, kept help in their homes or gardens, all the work was done by the various households for themselves. This brought it about that all the girls grew up with a knowledge of housekeeping. The help employed in those families which needed it was for the most part drawn from the surrounding farms. Without exception the farmers' daughters who took places to work either on other farms or in town were treated as members of the family, and were so considered socially. This was true also of men who were hired to work on the farms. There was no servant class. Though there were many families that might have been called poor, there were none that were dependent and very few that lived discreditably. There were but two saloon-groceries in town, which existed in spite of general disapprobation.

People who went shopping or marketing carried home their purchases themselves. There was no such thing as a delivery wagon. Even as late as in the early sixties my father used to bring home a barrel of flour in a wheelbarrow.

Through all the last half of this decade, in which I had taken my place among grown-up workers, there was, of course, along with the widening intellectual growth, the less recordable acquisition of those perceptions which look toward spiritual things. But of these I was reticent even to myself. My mind was in a state of unrest on questions of religious doctrine, but I did not suffer the anguish common to many, because I had been spared the task of finding my way through the intricacies of a man-made creed. All those terrible words ending in *ation* I escaped with no knowledge of the terms which they invoke to haunt the beds of the willing and unwilling sinners upon whose necks they have been laid as yokes. My problems were to be settled by myself by direct application to the Bible and such interpretation of what I found there as I was equal to. Whatever I heard at church or Sunday school was supposed to be a help to such enlightenment.

[175]

COLLEGE, AND AFTER

1

Antioch College

A brief but vivid recollection still clinging to the log walls of my early home revives a short conversation between one of our neighbors and my father, as he stood leaning on his ax in the yard. They were talking about Antioch College, the walls of which were, as I understood it then, part way up. My father said with a smile, "*I* have a brick or two in those walls." Then followed some other talk which I cannot remember.

Thus in my tenth year I heard the name of Antioch College. This institution was projected in 1850, and incorporated and named in 1852 by the Christian (New Light) denomination. Much of the endowment and building funds had been given in small sums by farmers and other people of limited means, who were looking forward with a large hope to educational opportunities for their children. There went with these small gifts the mute expression of a great ideal.

Among the men whose zeal and labor contributed to the movement in the Christian denomination which resulted in the founding of Antioch College, the Rev. John Phillips was preeminent. He never lost courage, and never failed to make the most of any opportunity to further the interests of the college. He travelled about visiting obscure country churches and neighborhoods, to which he glowingly preached education. He thus stimulated the minds of young and old by showing them the way to ambitions already alive in their minds. I frequently saw and heard Mr. Phillips at the college in the early sixties and remember that his enthusiasm was still alive and active. His speech and manner were characterized by a certain quaint kind of humor which, underneath, had the seriousness of profound purpose. Whenever Mr. Phillips appeared in

[179]

a neighborhood church, people expected to hear something about Antioch College. He was spoken of, more or less affectionately, as "Old Antioch."

The site of the college had been determined in 1852 by the gift of a plot of twenty acres of ground at Yellow Springs, Ohio, then a favorite summer resort of people from Cincinnati and other cities. This plot of ground, together with a generous sum of money, was given by Judge Wm. Mills, a resident of the town. The place was then a small, picturesque village, situated among groups of beautiful forest trees which the inhabitants had had taste enough to save from the ax. Immediately eastward of the village are the springs which give name to the place and flow down into a beautiful wooded gorge known as "The Glen." To the south of the village on higher ground which slopes gently eastward toward the woods of The Glen stands the college. Although The Glen was not a part of the college grounds, it belonged to the pleasures and privileges of the college community, as it was then free to everybody. In it, as the years of my college life went on, I found continuance and enlargement of that close acquaintance with nature which had begun in the Big Woods and the Little Woods, and had gone on in the woods and other natural surroundings of my girlhood's home near Eaton.

The village as I first knew it was essentially a college town, the large part of which was made up of families settled there for educational reasons. The life was quiet and simple and surrounded by an atmosphere of intellectual seriousness which had its expression in uninterrupted and thorough study. The main interest flowed on in a steady stream with no crosscurrents. The numberless social and other distractions of twentieth-century college life had not then relegated to a second place the main purpose of an educational institution.

The college and its two dormitories were built on three sides of a quadrangle on the west end of the campus. The main building, facing east, is in the form of a Roman cross with two large square towers at the head and two small octagonal towers at each of the other ends. It contains the chapel, which occupies the space of the second and third stories of the central part. A wide hall, with entrances at north and south, extends the length of the building, crossing the main hall at right angles. A large lecture room occupies the west end of the first floor under the chapel. The president's and treasurer's offices are on opposite sides of the main entrance. All the rest of the building is occupied by classrooms and laboratories and the library, except the fourth or attic floor, which contains rooms used by the literary societies and finished and furnished by them. I speak of these things as they still were in 1870.

The men's dormitory on the south, the women's dormitory on the north side of the quadrangle, are four-story buildings 170 feet long, exactly alike inside and out, except that the kitchen, dining room, and main college parlors form a part of the North Dormitory.

Although the college grounds had been entirely denuded of their native growth of trees before they came into possession of the founders, they were already, when I first saw them, beautiful with groups of maple, elm, native evergreens (particularly clumps of red cedars), and other trees and shrubs. The red brick towers and walls of the college and dormitories were soon softened by the vines of the native Virginia creeper.

The only other building belonging to the college is the president's mansion, a square, two-story brick house surrounded by a wide verandah and topped by a square observatory or cupola. It stands north of the college buildings just outside the campus.

My years at college were through the stirring, tragic times of the Civil War, until its end and the death of President Lincoln. So much of what connected itself with the war was intermingled with my years of study there that it seems difficult to speak of one without the other.

Early in September, 1861, before the opening of the fall term at Antioch College, I was settled in the rooms which I was to occupy for the year. Two other girls, strangers to me, were to share the rooms and house privileges which my father and mother had arranged for in the house of Mrs. William Cleveland. My chamber looked out upon a piece of unfenced common covered with grass, then thickly studded with tall stalks of thistle, from which were flying innumerable puffs of down. The red walls and towers of the college buildings directly east of the common rose in what looked to me a great and noble group. A slight wind from the west carried the white fleets of thistledown sailing toward the red towers. A few cottages to the south interposed their blocks of white or gray between my view of the common and a distant wood. Thus looks the permanent picture of my first days in Yellow Springs.

When my father and mother and our friend John Bailey, who had driven us over, left the next day, a cloud of homesickness settled down over me. There were still three days before the opening of college. My roommates had not come and perhaps would have increased my loneliness if they had, as they were entire strangers to me. I had nothing to do and shrank from going out alone to look about me. I was too awkward and shy to begin for myself an acquaintance with Mrs. Cleveland and her little girl, and I find the memory of these three days recording nothing but the picture from my window.

When my roommates came we planned our housekeeping in accordance with Mrs. Cleveland's prearrangements for her own and our convenience; that is, we were to have two sleeping rooms, the use of a little tower room for study in warm weather, of her living room, which was also a dining room, with its fire in company with her and her little girl, and her kitchen in which to do our cooking. We had also accommodations for laundry work. Many groups of girls boarded themselves in a similar way in other families. As I afterward learned, many students had thus been provided for from the beginning of the college. Others still boarded themselves in rented rooms for which they had brought furnishings from home. Those who were able paid their board in accredited families in the village or at the Commons table in the North Dormitory, where most of the girl students from a distance roomed. Most of the men students roomed in the South Dormitory and had their meals at the Commons table.

The problems of our self-boarding were early settled by arranging that each of us should do the kitchen work week about in turn, at the same time furnishing all the food for that week. Boxes from home containing cooked food and other provisions replenished our larder at frequent intervals, so that, in the main, there was no cause for apprehension, on the part of the president or professors, that we were not feeding ourselves properly. Though we were not, of course, so well fed as from the country tables we had left at our homes, we were generally very well nourished, quite as well at least as those who boarded at the college table.

My wardrobe for college had been brought and mostly made by myself; much of it was old, and what was new was mostly for the summer. I remember a pink barege, a blue-black-and-white net-worky wool, some lawns lavender in color, a pink calico, a white calico with little wreaths of violets in lavender, a red calico with dark brown spots, a brown debêge worn with a white low waist and a white linen jacket, two or three delaines for winter, a green shawl with a plaid border for fall, which (save us!) I wore with the pink calico a few times till I learned better; a black waist and two or three sacques, then worn in the winter with delaine dresses. This may seem an unnecessarily large number of dresses, but it was the custom in our town in the early sixties to have as many, especially of summer dresses, as one could afford. Indeed it was a matter of reproach to be greatly limited in this respect, since materials were cheap and one could make and launder her own dresses. One did not like to be called "Miss One-dress." I was very soon enlightened on this subject by what I saw at the college receptions, where the president's wife and the wives of the professors and other ladies wore a "best dress" on all occasions throughout the season. Fashion in those years decreed that women's gowns should be made of figured materials summer and winter. Especially was it true that one seldom or never saw a young person dressed in solid colors.

I try to include in this narrative minor matters which may hereafter have some historical interest; otherwise my sense of humor would get the better of my judgment as I review such trifling details and would counsel me to be more careful in my selection. But I shall let them stand though I laugh at them myself.

Antioch College prepared its own students in its own preparatory school under the immediate direction of the college faculty. The curriculum of the school had been carefully arranged by Horace Mann, according to his theories of what such a course should be. It was based on the opinion that the student could follow profitably but three studies at one time, and that these three subjects must occupy the whole of his fifteen hours of weekly recitation. It was expected to educate as far as it went, not merely to prepare for college, and it presupposed a thorough grounding in the common branches. Entrance examinations to this course excluded those who could not read, write, or spell accurately.

Entrance to the freshman class was had only by passing examinations in all the subjects laid down in the three-years' preparatory course as there given. As my advanced studies had not been consciously in preparation for college, they had had no definite direction toward a given curriculum. I had had no Latin and no ancient history except my own desultory reading, and was therefore obliged to begin these studies in the preparatory school and to take such others as were required beyond what I had already studied. However, I was admitted to partial standing in the freshman class on my examination in mathematics, elementary physiology, and physics, and one or two other branches, and on such general scholarship as I had shown in my examinations.

After teaching eleven school months in sixty and sixty-one, I was naturally not in good condition for college work; but before the end of the first term I was permitted to take up the study of Greek, which enabled me to finish the preparatory course in two years. At the same time I carried such freshman studies as were available.

2

The Old President and the New

Not long after my arrival at Yellow Springs, and by the time I was beginning to be acquainted with a few townspeople, I began to hear anecdotes and other bits of interesting information about Horace Mann. There was evident in each of these, no matter from what source they came, a note of profound reverence and admiration. I soon gathered from all that I heard a feeling which expressed itself to my consciousness in an image of this remarkable being as he appeared to the village people. He still seemd to me to be walking up and down the streets of the little country town as he had done for the last time but two years before.

Among the stories told me was one of Mr. Mann's wonderful faculty of getting at the substance of a book at a glance. It was said that he used to drop in at the college bookstore on Xenia Avenue, pick up any new book from the counter, and turn through it slowly, taking in every page as he went and knowing all there was in the book when he laid it down. It was related as a curious bit of information that nobody ever saw Mr. Mann carry any kind of a parcel. This, in a country village, was of course exceptional, but it was not spoken of by way of criticism. I heard his dress commented upon for its immaculateness, much in the same way as I have elsewhere spoken of it myself as affecting me when I saw and heard him lecture in Eaton at Teachers' Institute.

A few comments I heard also on Horace Mann's relations to the student body; of his constant care in the form of advice given in the morning assembly in regard to exercise, sleep, personal hygiene, and other matters relating to health. As his govenment of the college was of the closely personal and parental type, it illustrated all the characteristics of that responsibility. The use of

[185]

tobacco in any form was forbidden to students not only on the campus, but on the streets of the village. I never saw a student smoking on the street, and a tobacco-using professor was unheard of.

In letters written in the earlier years of his life at the college, Horace Mann speaks with pride of the fact that there was no rowdyism, no drinking, no card playing among the students; and that the men's dormitory, filled with students, was so orderly and quiet that there was no need of tutors or proctors. As further illustration of Horace Mann's relations with the students I include the following letter written to a prospective student:

Mar. 14, '59.

Mr. D. Cronyn.
Dear Sir:
The 'Price Current' of board here is $2 a week. I understand there is a Club here which boards for about $1.50.

We have a rule against boarding in the Dormitory because it would fill the building with unsavory smells, and would sometimes necessitate fire even in the summer. A more serious objection, however, is its effect upon the health, where one lives alone and takes all his meals in that dissocial and unnatural way, especially if the diet is purely vegetable.

I cannot fully explain this matter in a letter, but the cases are exceedingly rare where those who abjure all flesh do not permanently injure health. We have had many cases of that here. Your better way would be to live well and work in some way to make up the difference. All our work about the College is done by our students. No one loses caste or standing here on account of labor. Labor is considered honorable. You may be able to obtain a private room and board yourself, but I should advise you against it strongly. You had a hundred times better borrow money of some friend to be repaid after you graduate, and when you can earn at least twice as much, if not three times, in a year as you can now.

Should you come here and conduct yourself as a man, we shall do all we can to make your residence with us pleasant as well as profitable.

Yours very truly,
Horace Mann.

Public reproof, the severest punishment given to a student who had transgressed but was permitted to remain, was of so severe a type that it was seldom necessary. The offender was called to his feet in the assembly and reproved by the president in terms which could be used only by a man of such power and eloquence and such a lofty standard of conduct. The reproof left its object white-faced and subdued, and perhaps mainly thankful that it at least saved him from being sent home in disgrace, which was always the last punishment resorted to.

In 1852 Horace Mann had been nominated to the governorship of Massachusetts. In the same year he was called to the presidency of this newly founded college in Ohio. He laid aside the more than probable honors of a brilliant career of statesmanship to undertake the direction of a new venture in education. The provisions of the articles of incorporation of this institution in respect to coeducation and other important matters were of a liberality hitherto unknown. The opportunity given to Mr. Mann by these liberal conditions for carrying out his theories of education were far more attractive to such a mind as his than any political honors. He became the president of Antioch College in 1852, and began his work there in 1853. The courses of study for the sub-preparatory and preparatory schools as well as for the college expressed his idea of what an education should be.

I am told by Major Wm. L. Shaw, who was a student and was with President Mann the last night and day of his life—he died in August, 1859—that he asked early in the morning to be taken downstairs where he might see all the students then in the village for a word of farewell. As each student was brought to him in turn, he took him by the hand and spoke to him such words of counsel as were suited to his individual need. For though but few of these had been under his personal instruction, he knew and remembered all that they were. Though Mr. Mann was distinguished for his eloquence, it was said by those who heard him then that they had never listened to such words from the lips of any human being. Nearing his end, as he knew himself to be, he seemed to prolong his life by sheer force of will that he might speak to each his last word.*

*For Horace Mann's thought and growth as an educational statesman, Louis Filler, ed., *Horace Mann on the Crisis in Education* (1965), and for his college establishment, Louis Filler, ed., *Horace Mann and Others* (1963), by Robert L. Straker. [Ed. note]

Dr. Thomas Hill was president of Antioch College in 1861. He was at that time, I think, about fifty years of age. His big blue eyes, not yet covered with glasses, his rather long blond hair, and his abstracted air, gave him a childlike look which a nearer acquaintance deepened, as he was characterized by an exceedingly simple and straightforward glance and manner. He was an unworldly man absorbed in his own thoughts, and yet not so absorbed but that he easily became interested in any who addressed him or asked his advice. He seemed to know everybody whom he had once met. He was very fond of trees and wild plants, and of planting and tending them. He was so simple and democratic in his daily life that he thought it not beneath the dignity of a college president to mow grass in his shirt-sleeves on the campus, when he wished to, between lectures.

On one occasion he started from his mowing to his classroom on the second floor with his coat on his arm, as he thought; but when he arrived at the room, already filled with students, he found the scythe on his arm; explaining to his class he added that it was too late to go back, and with their permission he would proceed as he was with his lecture on philosophy. Various other amusing tales were told of the president's absentminded behavior; one especially so in respect to Horace Greeley, who had come to lecture and stay over Sunday. Dr. Hill left his visitor in the library while he prepared for the Sunday service in the chapel. When he came down he was to take Mr. Greeley with him to church, but went serenely over to the college, and preached his sermon without thinking of his distinguished guest, until one of the professors said, "Why, where is Mr. Greeley? We thought he would be at church."

I was greatly interested in observing the president's oversight of the education of his own little children, for whom he had written a baby geometry. I have often seen him walking out at sunset by the house where I lived to show his little daughter Kitty something about the perspective of the college towers. I once chanced by when he was talking to her and pointing out the various lines from a spot some distance away. Many of the students were deeply attached to him personally; he was always approachable, behaving toward us as if we did him a great favor to come to speak to him. After his election to the presidency of Harvard in 1862, I had several letters from him, which I still keep.

[188]

I have heard it said that Dr. Hill was a remarkable teacher in any mathematical subject. He sometimes made short addresses to the students in the general lecture-room, when he usually chose mathematical subjects and discoursed enthusiastically on such topics as the catenary curve and the cow's-foot curves in a bowl of milk. I once heard him use, in one of these lectures, the phrase "My Nineteen Systems of Coordinates," which thereafter became to me a superlative way of expressing my ignorance of any subject, for I never knew what this phrase meant, and only that Dr. Hill had discovered these amazing things. "Oh, I know nothing more about that than I do about the Nineteen Systems of Coordinates."

Of Dr. Thomas Hill a friend (W. L. Shaw) quotes to me this anecdote. Someone asked him this question: "What are you going to do when you enter the next life?" His reply was, "There are enough problems, mathematical problems, connected with the arc of a circle to keep me busy and happy for at least a thousand years."

After morning prayers Dr. Hill sometimes gave advice or direction about certain practical matters connected with the use of the recreation hours. One of these I remember, as it was related to our use of The Glen. The rule that odd days of the month should be used by the men for excursions there and the even days of the month by the women had been established at the beginning of the college. Botanizing and collecting, walking and wandering about at all times of the year, were student privileges, with this one restriction. But Dr. Hill requested us to be careful about our plant collecting. "Do not take all the flowers from any one plant," he said; "leave most for seed. When you see a plant which needs help, give it. Do not pick plants or flowers for the mere pleasure of picking them."

Dr. Hill dug up with his own hands and planted on the edge of the sidewalk by the president's house certain young elms, which he frequently inquired about after he went to Harvard. He was very fond of the native vines, especially the white clematis, the bitter-sweet, the large, wild white morning glory, and the Virginia creeper.

3

School and Studies

I was now for the first time to come under the influence and instruction of college-bred women. Hitherto my schooling had been under men teachers, except in the log cabin dame schools of my infancy and a few terms under "Female Seminary" women employed as an experiment in the Eaton schools. Mrs. Weston and Mrs. Caldwell were women of very different types, alike in that they were cultivated, refined, and greatly interested in their students.

Mrs. Weston was the wife of Prof. John B. Weston, and was that Achsah Elizabeth Waite who had left Oberlin College at the beginning of her senior year, because she found that she was not to be permitted to graduate on equal terms with the men. For although Oberlin College, as early as 1833, had under pressure admitted women to the same courses as those taken by men, it had provided a special course for women and did not graduate them on equal terms with men. Miss Waite joined the first senior class at Antioch College and graduated with it in 1857. And this, be it said, was the first time in the history of the world in which women had graduated from the same college platform on equal terms with the men of their class. Behind this fact stands the college charter. The gentle and amiable qualities of Mrs. Weston's character were not out of harmony with the decision shown by this incident. Her teaching in elementary Greek was lucid and accurate and pervaded by a steady enthusiasm that prevented the slightest suspicion that one was doing any drudgery while learning Greek verbs or struggling with Greek accents. I for one at least got more than Greek grammar, as she gave it to me, out of my sentences in Ollendorf.

Mrs. Rebecca Wilmarth Caldwell, the teacher of Grecian and Roman history, was a woman whose character was marked by dignity and repose. The effect of this on me was a sense of grace and power, which added itself not only to what she taught in subject matter, but to whatever she implied in connection with it, especially with reference to the conduct of life. It is difficult to say just how her mere presence had its effect on my manners and dress, over and above what her words and actions may have had. Mrs. Caldwell's teaching of history compelled us to be entirely dependent on ourselves in recitation. There were never any leading questions. "You may begin the lesson, Mr. Sheldon." "That will do, Mr. Sheldon. You may go on, Miss Weeks." Her questions, when they came, were never of a sort to serve as crutches for the lame. We were required to draw maps and to write exhaustive abstracts. Mrs. Caldwell frequently read important chapters from the original sources of our textbooks.

Another woman instructor of my preparatory years was Julia Maria Church, a student in the college and a pupil-teacher. I read Latin to her part of a year. Although she was a bright and interesting teacher, the memory of her remains with me rather as the friend than as the teacher. But even here her attainments and personal qualities were a matter of wonder to me, especially when I compared her learning and her ability to use it with my own. It was then I saw the contrast between what five or six years (she had entered the preparatory school at fifteen) in a college community had done for her and what the same length of time occupied in teaching in a country town had done for me.

John Burns Weston, professor of Greek in the college, was at this time principal of the preparatory school. But as he taught in the college only, I did not come under his instruction until I had completed two years of Greek.

My Latin teacher in the preparatory school was Professor Claudius Bradford, then a somewhat feeble old man. He actually drove us before him in a few weeks through the declensions and conjugations of Stoddard's *Grammar* into the sentences, fables, and easy Roman history of Stoddard's *Reader*. He had many kindly familiar ways of speaking to us, calling us by our first names: "Now, Irene, which means peace, begin." He interspersed our sometimes dry grammar lesson with Latin jokes, which he used as illustrations to the point: for instance, of the boy who wrote *tu doces* on a tea chest outside a shop door; of another who gave *quid rides* to a newly rich tobacconist who wanted a motto for the coat-of-arms on his new carriage; and of the *"g"* removed from before the last word and placed before the first noun of an inscription, *pro rege, lege, grege,* written over a door in London. Mr. Bradford was never severe, but not even the most thoughtless quite dared to take liberties. His failing health deprived us before very long of his excellent instruction, which was to me the opening of the door to a new language, in all that that means. I read Caesar and Cicero's orations to him and remember that they were both frequently lighted up by a quaint kind of humor which he interjected between questions of syntax and translation. He sometimes read to us his own clever metrical translations of selections from our Latin reader.

Among the students in these classes were John Adams Bellows and Harry Hill, the nephew and son of Dr. Thomas Hill, the president. Bellows and Hill, two boys of fifteen or so, I may say in passing, were interesting and friendly youths, Bellows especially, whom we older students liked very much. For some years afterward, when they had left Antioch after Dr. Hill's election to the presidency of Harvard, I had pleasant letters from John Bellows while he was a student at Dartmouth and later when he was literary editor of a New York paper.

In all of the classes where it did not interfere with the recitation we were permitted to work for the soldiers. In Greek and history lesson times then, we used to knit stockings or scrape lint or do other things to fill up the boxes to be sent out by the local branch of the Sanitary Commission. This commission was fathered, as most people know, by Dr. Henry W. Bellows—"Old Sanitary"—the uncle of these two boys and Dr. Hill's brother-in-law. Dr. Hill was much interested in this work and when the women met, after battles or before great movements of troops which called for comforts for the soldiers, to sew, plan, pack, and collect, he was almost always present. I remember that he invented some simple machine to wind bandages and came to do it while we sewed or packed in the hall where the townspeople met; also that he was greatly interested to see that plenty of anti-scorbutics were sent—sauerkraut, onions, pickles, and horseradish—and gave the women advice about such stuff.

We were encouraged to knit, as I have said, in the recitation hour, and it was not an uncommon thing to see almost a whole class scraping lint from old linen rags, or heeling or toeing-off stockings, while reciting the principal parts of "drive out" [*exelaunô*], "send" [*hiêmi*], or "run" [*trechô*] or such suggestive verbs in Greek. Harry Hill and John Bellows joined the girls in this work, and sometimes Harry Patton, who soon afterward enlisted. This lad came back once on a furlough with a long army overcoat dangling at his heels, and the same sunny, saucy, boyish manner.

Indeed those war days were hard days on us all. In that first year the classes began with an ominous uncertainty in numbers; day after day at roll call more names were unanswered. "Does anyone know where Mr._____ is?" "Enlisted, sir." Once his students went into a classroom where the professor's chair was empty, and found on going out by the bulletin board, "Professor Bardwell will not meet his classes today," only to learn that he would not meet them at all. Or "Dr. Warriner's class in geology will meet Mr. So-and-so tomorrow at eleven."

The courses in English at Antioch College in the early sixties were much the same as they had been in Horace Mann's time. They consisted of a lecture and textbook course in literary history and criticism, and a course in rhetoric with lectures and textbook, combined with some practice in writing. The literature course, as I knew it, confined itself strictly to the recitation of from ten to twenty pages, five times a week, in Shaw's *History of English Literature*. So far as I remember there was not even a suggestion of books to be read in connection with it. There were, however, occasional scholarly lectures to his classes by Professor J. K. Hosmer, who added much to our knowledge of the lives, works, and times of the authors studied.

But I was fortunate enough to have a three-month's course in rhetoric under Professor Suliot, the least part of which required a knowledge of a book on the subject. His lectures and detailed criticism of our composition were illuminating in all directions. His use of classical English in profuse quotation for illustration of his points was more than rhetorically significant, as it led us to read what he recited from so enthusiastically. Many a time we were incited to read other books by some kind of a gleaming hint from him that he should like to suppose that we had read it.

My course in English literature, however, was outside of,

though in a sense subsidiary to, my college work. It was pursued in a sort of comradeship of chosen friends whose tastes drew them together. We read the *Atlantic Monthly*, then full of that rich contemporary literature which characterized the early years of that journal. The young people of 1910 can hardly have such sensations as the opening of those current pages of the "Autocrat" and the "Professor" in the making gave to us, and they can never have the joy of waiting for the next number of Lowell's "Bigelow Papers," fresh from the hand of the author. Thoreau's "Wild Apples" and "Excursions" and "Walden"; Mrs. Stowe's and Harriet Prescott's stories, Thomas Wentworth Higginson's essays, and essays and verse of many others who have now places on the shelves of American literature in libraries, came to us month by month. We read Emerson, Hawthorne, Whittier, Bryant, Longfellow, and talked them all over in our elementary way. We steeped ourselves in Tennyson and knew many of his poems by heart. We loved Jean Ingelow and her lush and grassy poems, full of the brooks of Lincolnshire. We read Mrs. Browning's *Aurora Leigh* and carried the book about with us until we could quote amply for any occasion, especially in our literary-society essays, wherein we heartily concurred with Mrs. Browning in the saying that "Souls are dangerous things to carry/Through all the spilt saltpetre of the world"; and in our superior moods exclaimed with her, "With what cracked pitchers do we go to the world's deep wells." We read Robert Browning's *Men and Women* a little, and I by myself bought and waded through *Sordello*, lured on by the not infrequent jeweled phrases, words, and rimes, though I understood little of the content of the poem, as I was wholly ignorant of Italian history. But I got my time's worth out of that, and a great deal more out of more than one reading of "Christmas Eve" and "Easter Day."

We read too in those three or four years Wordsworth, Coleridge, Lamb, and De Quincey, and talked about them all to each other doubtless with much crude and limited criticism. But the main thing was that we read widely and lovingly and talked our readings over. The "each other" were Maria Church, Zella Reid, Ellen Van Mater, and I. The first of these was our Mentor, the second also in another way, the third was our enthusiast, and I was the pupil of all three, as it were.

My year and a half as librarian of the college library, added to what I have just catalogued, gave me other opportunities for reading. The library hours were limited to afternoons from two to five every day in the week except Wednesday and Sunday. I was thus able to be practically alone there in any of my own free hours. I read then much from the older English poets, a little from the dramatists, and a good deal of philosophy, some translations of Goethe and Schiller, Richter, and some French translations. Shakespeare I did not read very much then, nor Chaucer and Spenser. Scott and Dickens I had read before in the main. My novel reading, however, included some of Dickens, all of Charlotte Brontë's and Elizabeth S. Sheppard's novels. Jane Austen and Mrs. Gaskell I did not meet at this time, and on the whole gave very little attention to novel reading. I may, however, include several novels then current in the *Atlantic Monthly* and several others, among which were Henry Ward Beecher's *Norwood*, Rebecca Harding Davis's *Margaret Howth*, Mrs. Stowe's *The Minister's Wooing*, and Bayard Taylor's *The Story of Joseph.*

After the Battle of Ball's Bluff, which ended the life of Theodore Winthrop, we read three novels found in manuscript in his desk and published soon after his death. One of these, *John Brent*, had as extraordinary an influence on my life that it needs must be mentioned here. This was not because of its ethical significance, but simply through the effect of its narration and description of the episodes and scenery of an overland journey on horseback, perhaps combined with the romanticism of the story. Whatever one may say about the style of this tale or the defects of its plot, certain it is that the elements I have mentioned so affected my imagination that I said to myself and even to others, "I shall make that journey some day." I have often wondered since just how circumstances in my life came to be so ordered that without any conscious thought or effort to bring this about, it came to pass not many years afterward.

There was no teacher in my time in Antioch College whose instruction did more in helping us to a better use of the English language than Professor Suliot's. He taught us English composition and French. He was the only instructor I ever had in composition, though I had at one time, perhaps twice in a term, some criticism of papers by Professor Hosmer, whose help I did not then know enough to benefit by.

Mr. Suliot understood how to take the student where she was, intellectually, and to teach her how to go on rightly from that point. Besides all that, he was a genuine inspirer to work, and a creator of the "expression-impulse," as the new educator puts it. He knew how to wake us up to the recognition of our already acquired knowledge. He was a gray-haired, bald man of sixty, French-born, brought up in Ireland, a Quaker in religion, when I first met him, with big blue eyes, a ruddy complexion, very active habits, and excessive shyness with strangers, unless those were his own newly come students. He was the neatest man I ever saw, in old-fashioned clothes—leather slippers, homemade blue stockings, trousers a trifle short. He never wore a hat except when he went downtown.

He usually finished up his hour's lesson with some important statement, flung the door wide, and smilingly showed us out saying, "Now go." He always stood at the door of his classroom impatiently awaiting our arrival, shut the door promptly, hurried to the desk, and began at once. His remarks at odd times to each person were individual. His plan of teaching composition was also wholly individual. He enclosed in each paper returned a sheet containing numbered comments on points similarly numbered on the student's paper. Pithy remarks, pointed questions, light on the use of a word or phrase, positive commands about this or that usage, mild ridicule of some careless phrase, commendation and even praise of a part or the whole made up these priceless lessons. Every such lesson was a season of close companionship with the mind of this imcomparable master. The whole of his moral and spiritual force seemed to be brought to bear in his intellectual touch. I have heard it said that Professor Suliot would not accept the call to the professorship of mathematics until he was assured that he might teach English composition to the college classes.

Among distinguished visitors was Edward Everett Hale, whose frequent visits as trustee of the college were always occasions of delightful intercourse with that most approachable of men. His commonest words, like most of his writings, were full of the suggestiveness inseparable from the charm of his personality.

Others who added their unconscious gifts of intellect and spirit to that which their formal lectures presented were Robert Collyer, Edward L. Youmans and his brother William J. Youmans, Henry W. Bellows, Mrs. Sarah J. Lippincott (Grace Greenwood), Caroline H. Dall, Olympia Brown, and Amory D. Mayo. Of each of these I have some distinct recollection of value to myself, as a recorded influence.

When the Rev. A. D. Mayo* gave his lectures on education he doubtless must have set forth much that was worthwhile. But as I had heard lectures on that subject every summer for six or seven years, he increased my knowledge in that direction but slightly. Nevertheless he did me a great service by the excellence of his speech, for he spoke with elegant precision without the least pedantry. I was thereby put to shame by the condition of my long *u*'s, which were of the flat Western variety. I felt my cheeks burn when I thought of my pronunciation of such words as *duty*, *institution*, *institute*, and the like. I knew, as I listened to him and noticed what distinction the right pronunciation of this letter gave to his language, that I, like all of this Middle-West province, said *dooty*, *institootion*, *noos*, *institoot*, and so following. I resolved then and there to begin to reform that much-abused sound and after much difficulty and great strife succeeded.

Later, at irregular intervals, I became aware of various other defects in my spoken language, and found that I had been ill-treating the word *like* by forcing it into the place of a conjunctive adverb. Other provincialisms I swept out of my speech one by one. But I still cherished a bit of unconscious pedantry and some righteously grammatical superiority in my careful use of such an expression as *might better go* or *would better go* for *had better go*. This was taught by most of the grammar books of the time, and especially by Pinneo's *Grammar*, by repeated precept, and by pages of "Examples in False Syntax." The logic of it was that you couldn't parse *had go*, therefore it was wrong. Of one sin against

---

*Amory Dwight Mayo (1832–1907) was a Unitarian minister and public school teacher who served on the Cincinnati and Springfield, Ohio, school boards (1863–1880). He supported the Christian Amendment Movement, which attempted to incorporate into the U.S. Constitution a provision to guarantee Bible instruction in the public schools. [Ed. note]

common sense in the use of language we of the Middle-West were not guilty: we did not say *different than*, as many people do now, both east and west. But I am afraid that most of us did say *awn* for *on*, *gawn* for *gone*, *dawl* for *doll*, and the like.

My later Greek studies were, by good fortune, with John Burns Weston, professor of Greek in the college and principal of the preparatory school. He was all teacher, by which I mean that he so gave himself to the work of the hour that it seemed the one interest of his life. Greek he was for the time being, and Greek we had to be as well as we could make our halting steps follow. Greek verbs and Greek participles, accents and quantities, had life and color. But the master's enthusiasm was of a quiet kind, burning with a steady flame which nothing ever seemed to dim. I have known him to go into the classroom very weary as if ready to drop down with fatigue, and forget it in a few moments and make us forget it.

When I read Xenophon my only classmate was Louis Adrian Rosecrans, afterward a Paulist priest, son of General William Starkie Rosecrans, whose family was stationed there. He was a lad of sixteen or so, blue-eyed, with curling fair hair and delicate features. Whenever I think of him I recall one of Xenophon's phrases, "From here he drives [*enteuthen exelaunei*]," which we found such a good starting point for a brisk run of a few parasangs along the text.

I began the *Iliad* with three others, all of whom dropped out for one or another reason; so that I read on alone a whole hour a day five days in the week with Professor Weston, at the end taking as many pages as I could read through in the lesson hour, often five or six. I remember no greater intellectual joy than came to me in that work. Even then, by the training of the Westons, I had got into Greek literature, into which, as I have observed in these later years, not all Greek "majors" come by a full university course. But they do know the grammar.

My Latin studies continued, and included a great deal of Cicero, Tacitus, Plautus, a little of Horace, and not much else except more of Cicero.

My formal studies of natural history, as I have said elsewhere, began with lectures of Daniel Vaughan in geology, zoology, astronomy, chemistry, and physics, excepting for the little done in celestial geography under Isaac Morris, and somewhat in geology with my father. In my freshman year I studied systematic botany, working also by myself in the summer vacations in this branch. Later I took a course of lectures in zoology under Dr. Edward Orton, whose knowledge and enthusiasm led his students to a good deal of outdoor work, and on my part to some special field study in entomology in the intervening vacations.

Dr. Orton required us to know a system of classification as laid down in our class textbook and as apportioned by himself from day to day. He gave us also, in tabulated form at the blackboard, a classification of his own, particularly of the vertebrates, based on the structure of the skeleton, with a running commentary on the differences and likenesses of structure, which opened the way for us to such investigations as we might wish to follow. His knowledge was so wide that it compelled our admiration; his enthusiasm was so contagious that we should have felt ourselves struggling against it, if we had not been drawn into its current completely and permanently. His lectures and illustrations by specimens and otherwise put us into possession of a good working knowledge of systematic zoology. This course I found of the greatest use in organizing my already acquired knowledge of animal life, and afterward in later studies of this branch under another instructor and from a biological point of view.

4

Societies and Social Life

The literary societies in Antioch College in 1861 were four: the Adelphian Union and the Star Society for men, and the Crescent and Philalethian Societies for women. The Adelphians received college men only into their membership. The other three societies selected from the preparatory school older and more promising students whom they added to their numbers, believing as they did that it would be to the advantage of all that the sub-freshman students should have such preliminary training. Character and scholarship were the basis of choice, which therefore prevented haste in making the elections.

The exercises of these societies, which met on Friday afternoons and evenings throughout the year, consisted entirely of literary work of some kind: original essays, poems, reviews, orations, debates, selected readings, and recitations. In each a debate alternated with the society paper, which was edited fortnightly for six weeks by one of the members. The programmes were prepared a month ahead by a literary committee, and no one came on duty with any exercises of importance more than once a month, unless he chose to do so. Music had no place on the programmes in these years.

One of the most important officers of the society was the critic, who served six weeks at the critic's desk. He or she was usually a senior and always a student of recognized ability. Manner, manners and conduct, as well as literary merits and faults, were subjects of criticism in the report which closed the exercises of the literary session.

Formal invitations addressed by one society to each of the other three gave occasional opportunities for visiting at open meetings, at which the regular programme was presented. Such meetings were mutually advantageous, as they stimulated individuals as well as the separate bodies of students to better work. All the meetings, business and literary, were open to the president and faculty. Public meetings were given in commencement week in the college chapel by all the societies; but at this time the Star and Crescent held a meeting in union, the other two taking their turn the next evening. Later when the numbers had been greatly depleted by enlistment for the war, all the societies were permitted by the faculty to unite and held their meetings in the Star and Crescent chamber on Friday afternoons.

I was at first elected to membership in the Philalethian Society, which was composed for the most part of women who had been students formerly and were still living in the village, though not then otherwise connected with the college. It was here I first met Mrs. Lusina Gates Lewis and other women who made up the circle of my non-college friends and acquaintances. Among these were also the Misses Sarah, Celia, and Cornelia King, who lived in a large English-looking brick house on a farm northwest of the village. Later, however, this society was discontinued and those of us still remaining in college became members of the Crescent Society.

I speak for others when I say for myself that the training I received in these literary societies throughout my college life was of more importance in my education than any one part of the curriculum itself. This would be easily understood if the personnel of these societies could be more fully described than is possible here. Among those who may be mentioned as members at different times, of advantage to me in these years because of their characters, tastes, and acquirements, were Maria Church, Ellen Van Mater, Louisa Philbrick, Zella Reid, Susanna Way Dodds, Catherine Oakes, Fidelia Foote, and Harriet Botsford. After the consolidation of the societies we had the further advantage of association with such men as David Cronyn, George E. Church, William H. Deming, Channing Butler, Benjamin R. Gass, Thomas Hirst, George W. Hufford, and others.

Recollections of several entertaining and otherwise interesting incidents connected with the open meetings of the societies still brighten for me the memories of those times. One of these recalls a debate in the Star Society in which a student named Judson Applegate forgot an important part of his argument. He stood for a few seconds, then said, "Mr. President, ladies and gentlemen, I have something more to say on this subject and if you will wait a minute I shall be able to recall it." Then standing perfectly still in his place on the platform for two or three minutes, he went on without embarrassment either to himself or to his audience and finished his speech. At another public meeting of the joint societies in commencement week a student who had prepared and memorized his oration with the greatest care forgot his peroration and finished his speech extemporaneously and so admirably that the audience was unaware of any hesitation or change in style. A brilliant debate on *Hamlet*, a highly ornate essay on De Quincey, a clever burlesque on the same in the next public meeting of the rival society, and various clever poems more or less humorous by Thomas Hirst stand out in pleasant relief.

The debates of the literary societies, it may be said, sometimes discussed questions of public interest, perhaps more often than questions on literary topics. A debate on some question connected with the purchase of Alaska by the women of the Crescent Society recurs to me as a good example. Debates on woman's suffrage occasionally called forth the expression of opinions more or less emphatic on this subject, although the suffrage question did not so often come to the front either in the societies or in the daily life of the college women as that subject does in these days. The women of the college, however, were in various degrees, ranging from enthusiasm to indifference, in favor of the enfranchisement of women. I was myself as yet unpersuaded as to its expediency. I felt that I did not know, I wanted to know, and I wanted for women what was to their advantage as human beings. Susan B. Anthony Elizabeth Cady Stanton, Mary Livermore, Anna Dickinson,* and others were fighting the battle for women without fear or favor of men or women. We others were mostly looking on and consenting, but not actively taking up shield and spear. To be sure,

*Dickinson was a phenomenon of the time: a young girl, born in 1842, whose emotional speeches, first favoring the Union, then broadening to include women's work, the suffrage, and education, drew audiences and, in book form, readers. Her *A Ragged Register (of People, Places, and Opinions)*, published in 1879, reflected her career. [Ed. note]

in the greater part of the time of which I write, that is, in the years between 1861 and 1871, the Civil War and the Reconstruction Period following filled the public mind for the most part. But the suffrage leaders still moved forward, gaining inevitably though often imperceptibly.

As Horace Mann and other members of the faculty considered the main business of the college to be study, social entertainment, recreation, and literary or other college activities took second place. A monthly Friday evening reception at the president's house or at the parlors of the girls' dormitory, to which students, faculty, and village people were invited, Saturday walking excursions, a public lecture in the chapel on Friday or Saturday evening, an open meeting of some one of the literary societies on a Friday evening constituted the principal diversions. The receptions began at seven and closed at ten. No refreshments were served. On Friday evening after Thanksgiving it was customary to have a fancy dress party in the college dining room, at which students and faculty were present. The costumes were invented and made by the students for these occasions. There was no dancing at these parties until late in the sixties, when the square dances were permitted. Occasionally one of the professors or some other resident of the village who had a large house would receive the students and faculty. The same customs were observed at all these receptions.

Rarely students gave theatrical performances in the college chapel. Among these I saw for the first time a Shakesperian play, *The Merchant of Venice.* John Murphy, a young Irishman from Cincinnati, took the part of Shylock so successfully that he received much praise even from those who were well acquainted with the theatre. The garden scene was made particularly beautiful by the employment of trees, bushes, and vines brought that day from The Glen and set up on the stage for that act. Another good piece of work of this kind done by the students was the dramatization and acting of John Townsend Trowbridge's *Coupon Bonds.*

By the terms of the college charter, Greek-letter fraternities and other secret societies were forbidden. Partly for this reason and partly on account of the general democratic spirit of the sources from which the student body was drawn, there were no social distinctions. Students grouped themselves according to personal preferences much as children do. Character seemed to be the determining factor in the choice of friends. Men who earned their way, as a considerable number did every year, gained rather than lost in the opinion of all. More than one man sawed his way through college on hard hickory wood in the cellar. More than one rang his way through by pulling the rope of the bell in the great tower nearly every hour in the day from six in the morning till nine at night. Another pumped the college organ. A few men did chore work on farms near the college. A few women washed glass and silver in the college dining room. One I know of made all the bread used on the Commons table. Two or three places as pupil-teacher in the preparatory school were open each term to young women. I taught one hour a day several terms in that capacity myself. In later years a young woman earned her expenses by playing the college organ.

All the students of my time were either of the Middle-West American type, mostly rural, or distinctly New England, and all of generations of American blood. An occasional sprinkling of Southerners and of Far-Westerners (that is, Minnesotans or Iowans) made up the remainder. I do not remember a single foreign-born student, or even one of recent American stock.

There were now and then at Antioch College very good examples of what might be called the Eastern inability to understand the West, which really might be said to illustrate a general law. The piece of ancient advice often repeated by Horace Mann to his students might have been reversed and followed with advantage by certain professors and teachers who came from New England in the middle sixties. Horace Mann often said "Orient thyself," and it was certain that under his instruction and that of the eastern-bred men who filled the college professorships the students as a body laid aside much of their provincialism and took on the graces and intelligences of cultivated people. But it sometimes happened that in the changes of administration a larger number of the faculty would be men and women entirely unused to the West and unable to understand its people. They sometimes took it for granted that we were ignorant of things with which we had been familiar from our childhood; for example, one of the newly arrived professors stood up between the parlors of the president's house at a reception and explained to us how to play charades, which diversion he was intending to introduce among us. We listened gravely and followed his lead, although we had not only played ordinary charades at the college receptions for years, but had presented some of them in the form of dramas in the college assembly room.

Trifling examples of this kind were common. Eastern students now and then wondered at our flat *a*'s and healthy, round *r*'s, and laughed at our "umh-huh" and "huh-umh." Occasionally one took pains to learn these things to carry home to Boston, where they still did all their shopping even to their shoestrings. The old lady from New Hampshire who, as a certain well-known story goes, took a jar of apple butter out to Ohio with her, because she was sure they had no such thing out west, and who asked the conductor to tell her when they came to the Mississippi Valley because she wanted to look out and see it, is perhaps a goodly type of the person who lives in the geographically personal center of things. The same state of mind, however, is sectionally perennial. A few years ago a middle-westerner said to me, "Why, do they have churches in San Francisco?" Another said, "I had a cousin go out to California about twenty years ago. You didn't happen to meet him, did you?"

Among the professors in the college whom I observed in 1861 was Adeline Shepard Badger, the professor of modern languages. She was the wife of Professor Henry Clay Badger, in whose class I was after the enlistment of Professor Warriner. Mrs. Badger interested me by her looks and manner even before I came to know her as slightly as I did afterward. I saw her for the first time one winter day on the gravel walk as I went toward the college door. She was tall, slender and very fair, with a shower of golden curls whose airy quality seemed to suit the spiritual expression of her very delicate face. I met her blue eyes as she passed and wonder now that I remember the effect of her soft round cap of gray and blue wool with its gray-and-blue cord and balls that fell among the curls.

A peculiar interest attaches to this lady because she was that Adeline Shepard who went abroad with Nathaniel Hawthorne and his family as governess to his children. Hawthorne so admired her character that he made her the original of his "Hilda" in *The Marble Faun.*

[205]

5

College Friends

College friendships are proverbially potent, one way or another. That they are usually made more by temperamental choice than by accident adds much to their power and permanence. It was not my nature to allow mere chance to determine what friends I should come to have; but a good deal more than half, so far as I was concerned, had to depend on the others interested, for I was shy and reserved as well as discriminatingly cautious about making friends, partly owing to my home training and partly to such experience as I had already had. Further than this I can take no credit to myself for the good fortune that gave me such friends as soon came to be mine through acquaintance with Ellen Van Mater, Maria Church, Zella Reid, Louesa Philbrick, and Jane Weeks. The first of these and one of the youngest, Ellen Van Mater, entered the preparatory school with me, and we at once became acquainted in the Latin room. This began a friendship which extended over all of my college life. When we met in the Latin class I was twenty and she was a growing girl of fourteen. Her short curling hair was light brown, almost golden, her eyes were large and blue-gray, and her complexion a healthy white and rose pink. It seems strange now, as I recall her at this time, that so many older girls were so attracted to this girl-child that permanent friendships between her and us began at once.

At first with them and with me the acquaintance was that of the classroom and college halls and the campus. But through her own seeking and my own liking for her we began to read and study together. I found her mind as mature as my own in matters pertaining to poetry and other literature. She had friends of her own age among Dr. Hill's children and others, but more and more we spent time together, walking, studying, or reading, until the year when I lived in the same house with her, either at the college dormitory or in her own home in the village.

Her father, John Van Mater, a business man, was then treasurer of the college and found it more convenient to take his family to the college dormitory for a time. But my association with Nelly was most intimate after their return to their own home in the village, where I lived as one of the family, by the generous invitation of Mr. and Mrs. Van Mater. Words of mine would fail to tell what the excellences of John and Nancy Van Mater were. The kind of life they lived with each other and their neighbors may be partially described by saying it was that of people to whom discipline of life and profound religious experience had given a spiritual poise which showed itself in every action and every word.

Nelly had, as it were, inherited herself; that is, it seemed as if she had attained the poise and discipline given by experiences which she herself had never had. In no other way I can account for the moral and spiritual insight of so young a child as she was when I first knew her.

She had, it was thought by her latest teacher in music, a real genius for musical expression. She played the piano with distinction, even at the age of sixteen or younger. Her manner of practice of heavy exercise-work was so interesting that I often sat in the drawing room to hear her practice. If she were doing scales or arpeggios or mere finger exercises, after a certain length of time she would suddenly break into a joyous song without words, with a few interspersed chords, then go back with modulated notes to her exercise. Her voice was a pure contralto of most lovely quality, and seemed to have come to her almost suddenly, as did a fine soprano come to her friend and mine, Jenny Weeks. As my own voice was a fairly good mezzo-soprano, with a good range, we three sang together a great deal in three-part songs.

Whatever musical knowledge I have, I owe for the most part to this time and to Nelly. I then first heard and learned to love the sonatas of Beethoven, the songs of Mendelssohn, the chorals of Luther, and other music of other forms. My own study of instrumental music was so slight and was begun so late that although I learned to play a few pieces well enough to please people who knew as little about music as I did, I never acquired skill enough to

[207]

express myself in musical terms. My short study, however, helped me to understand and appreciate music well enough to be further educated by listening to my friend's playing.

I never knew anyone who enjoyed the beauty of pure sound so profoundly as Nelly. Sometimes after striking a single note on the piano, she listened to its latest vibration with an expression of ecstatic enjoyment. "Listen!" she would say. "Did you ever hear anything so beautiful? O I know my piano has a soul. It cannot be just wood and wire and ivory." So strong was this feeling on her part that in moments of grief when she was alone she felt as if the spirit within the piano understood and sympathized with her. On my own part I was aware of this half-defined feeling in myself when I sat before her beloved instrument after it had become mine through her last will.

Nelly's love of the beautiful showed itself quite as strongly in her enjoyment of color and form. The aspect of the sky, the spring and autumn, woods and even the beauty of a single little flower or a feathery patch of golden-green moss, stirred in her the profoundest emotions. I never knew a happier child.

With Nelly I read, almost from the first, the *Atlantic Monthly*. We read *Aurora Leigh* and other poems of Mrs. Browning, and talked about everything that we read, and had some sort of opinion of these and other books. As it will be impossible for me to give any just estimate of this friend of nearly fifty years ago, I may perhaps but conclude by saying that to my years with her, to her idealization of me, and my continuous effort to become what she thought me, I seem to myself now to owe more than to any other influence of my college years.

Zella Reid was one of the small circle of girls who made the center of my college life socially, and I might say in every other way. She was from southern Indiana and of a Scotch Presbyterian family, directly descended from the Clydes of whom Thomas Campbell, the poet, was one. She, like him and others of the Clyde family, was mathematical to a degree unusual in a woman, and a poet as well. But above and better than that, she was a rare creature in many other ways: clever, with a shy, beautiful humor, and a keen sense of the life all around her; gay, sometimes with an airy evanescent kind of joyousness in our company, which made her peculiarly fascinating to those of our circle who knew her well; profoundly religious, but mostly reticent about what she thought, and so well grown out of her creed as not to think other systems of belief disqualifying, yet never discussing any.

Our time together was all too short, for although she herself wished to complete her course at Antioch College, a certain uneasiness in the mind of her father because she was at a college considered unorthodox decided her to go to Oberlin.

In '74 Zella Reid came to California from Antioch College, where she had been teaching, to be married to David Cronyn, an old college friend of us both, and a Unitarian clergyman then preaching in San Jose. They were married in Oakland at the house of a mutual friend where I was living. The next day I left Oakland for Ohio, having already resigned my position to take the place of Zella Reid in my own college. I did not see her again until the fall of 1876 after my return to Oakland, when she came with her baby to visit friends there. Nor did I ever see her after that, as her husband accepted a call to San Diego. There they lived until their return to Massachusetts where the family home still is. She died in 1905, in far-off Virginia, with her husband and children about her. Some of her verses had been published in the *Atlantic Monthly*. These and others of her verses, together with a brief sketch of her life, were published soon after her death. A letter from her not six months before contained an allusion to our friend Nelly Van Mater in which she said, "I have sought all my life to find another Nelly but never found anyone in the least like her."

Julia Maria Church was a brilliant, beautiful woman, then in the junior class, and a pupil-teacher in the preparatory school. All the rest of the group had a profound admiration for her and a great affection. To her we all owed a literary stimulus that came from her personality, and from her breadth of acquaintance with books. She read to us, recited pages of poetry, English and German, helped us in our Latin and Greek, and was a most delightful and bewitching companion. The days were made every one like a storybook chapter, by an unconscious expectation of something she might say or do. And it was never the same twice, never anything one expected—but always some delightful thing. I remember once that in a vacant hour in which I had planned to finish learning a Greek lesson, she met me in the college hall, took my hand, and said in a whisper, "Come on, come one! Let's walk." "Ah, no," I said with regret, "I must get this lesson." "What is it?" she said, taking my book; "Come on! I'll teach it to you in fifteen minutes and we'll have the rest of the hour to walk."

We sat on the steps at the little-used front entrance of the college and in a few minutes we had finished the lesson, closed the book, and started off across the campus, toward an open common. That walk I cannot forget. The sky was full of bright sailing clouds, with brilliant blue between; the wind was blowing briskly, and as we walked May Church recited German poetry, English ballads, and I know not what else delightful. She was but a few years older than I, but she had come to Antioch at fifteen, I think, and had years of training there, while I was teaching infants in a country town. I read Latin to her in class one term. Her influence on the little group I have named, besides its incitement to the love of literature, was daily evident to each, in her own life at least.

Mary Louesa Philbrick was another girl from Northern Ohio— a farmer's daughter of New England birth and speech. She was afterward a roommate with me for a year at Mrs. Cleveland's. She had taught a year or two, and was a few months older than I. We became good friends and until she left college and married she was one of a little circle who became very intimate, and were indeed each to each a good part of "a college education." Although our acquaintance began through Latin and Greek grammars, it grew more rapidly into friendship through our love of singing than it could have done in the devious ways of declensions and conjugations. Her voice was a contralto of extreme sweetness, and its quality so perfectly harmonized with mine that we rejoiced in using them together. She had a faultless sense of time and pitch and read music with the greatest ease, while I had to depend more or less on my ear, as I was then a poor reader.

When I started college in 1861 there were still several students of the upper classes who had been in the college in Horace Mann's time. Among these was Mrs. Susanna Way Dodds, a physician. I made her acquaintance first in the Crescent Literary Society, of which she was then one of the prominent members. She would have been a conspicuous figure anywhere, as she was a strongly individual type. Her tall, well-formed figure, her dark complexion and eyes and fine, large features, together with her short black hair, beginning to turn gray, all gave her an Indianesque or Indian-princess look, which had a peculiar fascination for me.

I admired her then greatly and later came to know and love her. She was incisive and logical of speech and had more insight than most people. Her debates and other exercises in the literary society were looked forward to by the younger members with an eager expectancy which was seldom disappointed. Later, when the literary societies were all united into one, it was more than a treat to be present at the debates in which Mrs. Dodds crossed swords with some of her classmates among the men. Her ability and dignity compelled respect; and the fact that she then and always wore the reform dress, otherwise known as the Bloomer costume, detracted in nowise from that feeling either in the college or in the village. Indeed those who knew Mrs. Dodds very well at this time never thought or cared about her peculiarities of dress. She was the only woman in the college who wore the reform dress then, and, as it happened, the only woman member in the graduating class.

Among the recently elected trustees in 1864 were two or three New England Unitarians, men of culture and breadth, no doubt, but essentially unwestern in their ideas. When they met the members of the graduating class, they observed with some curiosity the dress of the only woman, and at once decided that it would not be expedient to permit her to wear such a costume on Commencement Day, as visiting strangers might think that a part of the curriculum, as it were. So in spite of President Craig's protest, the lady was notified that she must wear more conventional garments on that day. This she refused to do. The men of her class threatened to withdraw, and all the students and village people were excited and indignant. When the diplomas were awarded by the president and her name read as being one of the graduates, she arose at her place in the audience, and said, "I decline to accept the diploma." I am sure she felt, and certainly all of her friends felt, the sympathy of the whole audience behind her, as well as that of President Craig.

The Bloomer costume of that day was the original dress worn by Mrs. Bloomer herself. It consisted of a one-piece dress, usually cut princess style and falling below the knees, sometimes but little below, sometimes to within six inches of the shoe tops. It was worn over trousers, straight and narrow, made of the same material as the dress, and reaching to the shoes; the general effect of this was much the same as that of the little girl's dress in Queen Victoria's childhood. In winter there was a coat-like jacket, and at all times a hat; never a bonnet. The hair was always short.

Mrs. Dodds's graduating dress was made of dove-colored silk, beautifully finished with real lace. The wearing of this costume was, with her and with other women who had worn it at the college, a matter of principle. I have been told that at the very beginning of the college in the early fifties, many young women wore the dress for a little while, as a mere fad. But to those who still continued to wear it in the sixties and seventies it was something more. On most of those who did wear it, it was usually very ugly, either on account of the ill shape of the wearer, or poorly chosen material, or both. It is said that Horace Mann disliked the dress very much, but made no regulations against it.

Another friend of these college years, not only to me, but to many another student in the successive classes, year after year, was Mrs. Lusina Gates Lewis. I first knew her in the Philalethian Society, of which she was an honorary member although not a student. She lived in a little cottage on a small farm a mile south of the college. Her plain little house was the home of many a homesick student and her motherly hospitality made a bright spot in the lives of young men and young women whose claim on her kindness was merely that they needed it. An invitation to dinner, or to tea (which meant supper at six o'clock), was always gladly accepted, especially by the self-boarding student who had a vision of a big baked sweet apple in a bowl of cream or some other unusual goody as an addition to the homemade bread and butter and tea of the simple meal. But the friendly bits of news about old students, the kindly talk, never commonplace, and often more profitable than she knew, made the finest part of her hospitality.

Among the students who entered college in one of my later years there was an interesting young woman of unusual type, whom, for convenience, we will call Octavine. She was the only child of a widowed father who had placed her in a Canadian convent to be educated. Finding that she was preparing to take the veil he promptly removed her, and brought her to Antioch College. This, being a coeducational institution, gave her an entirely new field for the operation of the peculiar faculties which controlled her conduct.

Octavine was what certain novelists would describe as *petite*. She had a graceful, elegant figure, a beautifully modelled head with very long dark hair, always perfectly dressed. Her features were small and fine and all pretty excepting her nose, which was inclined to be aquiline. Regular dark eyebrows and long lashes emphasized the variable gray of her eyes. Her complexion was pale but healthy, and her cheeks were finely dimpled. Her clothes were conspicuously better than those of any other girl in the dormitory and were always neat and well fitted. This minute description of her appearance seems somehow necessary to the understanding of her personal qualities.

To be the center of any group of people among whom she was even casually thrown was essential to Octavine's happiness. She had a way of taking hold of the interest of a number of people at the same time, as if by some invisible threads of personal power. She was a born intriguer, and seemed to have had a great deal of practice in that character. If, for example, at a reception she wanted the company of any otherwise engaged person there, she was capable of getting what she wanted by the most subtle maneuvering, and usually by making someone else, who was wholly unsuspecting of the part she was made to play, an actor in the little comedy. Some of her intrigues were founded in her inordinate jealousy. She did not like to be surpassed in any direction. She took the sting out of the inferiority of some of her literary society performances by laughing at their shallowness before anybody else had a chance to criticize them. I once heard her make fun of her own speeches in a debate for which she had not prepared in the least, while her opponent, Miss Catherine Oakes, ably presented the other side of the question. In spite of their recognition of Octavine's faults her acquaintances in the classroom and literary society were generally on friendly terms with her, though now and then relations between her and them were more than strained.

My first experience of dormitory life was with my sister Laura in two third-floor rooms of the North Dormitory. We were permitted to board ourselves there and did our cooking on a little parlor stove.

Our larder was frequently replenished by boxes from home containing, besides the substantials, various goodies which our mother's thoughtfulness added thereto. It sometimes happened, however, that our cupboard was bare either because we had no money or were every day expecting a box. Once, I remember, we were reduced to baker's bread and sorghum molasses for two or three meals.

Among the twenty-five or thirty girls we each found interesting companions with whom we became more or less intimate and with whom our recreation hours, when we were shut in by stormy weather, threw us into more or less close companionship. Our Friday evenings were often spent in the parlors singing, listening to music, in talks, often of a speculative kind, or in girlish nonsense and fun led by some of the gayer spirits. Now and then a "comb concert" in impromptu costumes by three or four of the giddier group broke the ten o'clock silence of the third floor.

A good deal of current slang was used by a large proportion of the girls of this time until, I know not how, a spirit of reformation swept over the whole dormitory. Those who were greatly afflicted with the language distemper had to be encouraged by those who were free from it; they soon grew tired of trying to cure themselves. Fines and self-reporting in council every evening were a part of the discipline agreed upon.

6

Religious Exercises

Attendance at morning prayers at Antioch College was still, in 1861, obligatory seven days in the week. Later the Saturday prayers were omitted and the Sunday morning preaching service at eleven o'clock was all that was required on that day. The only other regular religious service was the Sunday evening prayer meeting, attended by professors and students voluntarily. Sunday preaching was usually by the president, sometimes by professors who were ordained clergymen; occasionally by clergymen invited from other places. To these last we seldom liked to listen, because, unused to preaching to college audiences, they thought they must show their learning and usually got upon some intellectual stilts which they were incapable of managing.

The college prayer meetings were usually led by Professor Weston. Other professors were often present and took part by speaking of some thought awakened by what had been said by the leader or suggested by a hymn. Another might speak of something of which his mind was full from some other source. The words of Prof. Suliot were, in the rare times when he was moved to speak, full of spiritual insight. Few other details of these meetings remain with me, except that my friends were generally present; but I do remember that the effect of these meetings on the entire student body, through the comparatively large numbers who attended, was evident in the daily life and conduct. For my own part, I found many perplexing questions settled there, without my knowing how or when.

The Sunday chapel services in Dr. Hill's time were of the simplest order, as they were throughout my college life. They consisted of hymn, prayer, hymn, sermon, hymn, benediction, though afterwards I think responsive readings were added. Dr. Hill's sermons were profound but simple and practical. They were always expressed with deep feeling and not without a touch of poetical imagination. They left me (at least) with a sense of certainty with regard to things concerning the future life and the serious import of things pertaining to this, which had no little influence on my after life and my attitude toward it. Indeed I may say that many theological problems which at times had disturbed my mind were either solved satisfactorily here, or put aside for the time without difficulty. I learned to reserve judgment on what I knew I did not understand. I remember no one particular sermon of Dr. Hill's, nor indeed any specific thing said by him then, except the beginning of one sermon in which he turned aside for a moment to speak of the authenticity of the narrative in the chapter he had just read, and showed us how the article "One," used as it was there, was evidence of the truth of the story.

Dr. Craig's sermons were very often more than an hour long, which nobody ever resented, for Austin Craig was a man who held all minds captive while he spoke. His oratory was nothing more than a mild conversational voice, uttering the sweet gentle oracles of the Christian religion. His face always beamed with the joy of life. I met him once when I was on the street with my friend Zella Reid. He stopped and spoke to us under some blossoming locust trees, and leaning his tall, gaunt, linen-clad form against a fence, with one arm around the top of the paling, he talked to us like an archangel, and yet I do not remember what he said. It was full of such heavenly philosophy as I never heard from any other. He was a great admirer of the character of Moses, and sometimes said that he should have been a much better man if he had been named Moses; but we did not think it possible or desirable.

Dr. Hosmer was perhaps a more finished speaker than other presidents of my time. He was an old Harvard man, and had the culture and grace of many years of preaching to large city congregations. He always wore the Geneva gown when he preached, as did Dr. Hill. I confess that this always pleased some sense of fitness in me. His sermons were, as were those of others, practical and full of things one might live by. Two of his subjects I recall. One was on Pictures of Imagery. Dimly enough I remember, but I do remember how he took us into the chambers of our own thoughts, and showed us there pictures of imagery painted by ourselves, and made us realize that since we could not get out of these picture galleries we had better hang there such pictures as we should like to live with. The other sermon was drawn from a recollection of his own when he was a boy. He had thought it very strange, but very beautiful, that his own home was directly under the top of the sky, and had wondered to himself how other boys liked living where the house was not under the top of the sky. One day when he went for the first time with his father to the neighboring town, he bethought himself to look up to the sky while he waited in the wagon, and, behold, he was still under the top of the sky. Then in the preacher's very wonderful application of this story, we saw how each of us, if he only knew it, lives under the very top of the sky.

But perhaps none of these men surpassed Professor John Burns Weston in tireless service to the college and the townspeople. The sermons he gave us, good and suggestive as they were, were the least of what he did for us; his informal talks in prayer meetings, his illumination of the text of our Greek studies with him, his friendly interest in what we were doing, and his readiness to help at all times, giving himself as a matter of course, really made a large part of our instruction—how large a part we did not know until we had left it; and this latter fact was perhaps a proof of its greatness.

The occasional sermons of President Dr. Edward Orton were of an entirely different type from any of the foregoing. They were searching, epigrammatic, with a certain kind of nervous insistence, which made him seem at times almost impatient that it should be necessary to say such and such things. But what he said was wise and kindly withal.

In the later years of my college life, the hour of the chapel service was changed to three o'clock. This permitted those who wished to do so to go to churches in the village. At this time the Christian Church was the largest and seemingly most interesting to the students. Many of us had church membership there and sang in the choir. In fact the choir at one time was made up almost entirely of my own group of friends, with Ellen Van Mater as organist. We were in the college choir as well.

Colored Students in College

Sometime within my first three years in college there appeared at
the opening of a term a Miss Randolph,* a tall, severe-looking woman of forty or thereabouts, with a very straight, proud carriage,
and determined look. She called herself an Indian descended from
John Randolph of Virginia, and had come from Oberlin College,
where, as afterwards appeared, she had been offended by the treatment she had received. At that time I was reciting in advanced
algebra to Professor Doolittle, whose class was full of men, with perhaps seven or eight women. Miss Randolph entered this class one
day, and the next day but one man appeared: all the others had left,
"because Miss Randolph had negro blood in her," though I believe
this was not true. We women said to the one man who stayed, "Why
don't you go too, Mr. Butler?" "Oh, I stand by such principles as I
have—and the college charter."

This secession was odd enough, indeed, as there had always been
people of negro blood in various classes, and besides the phrase
"without distinction of race" or its equivalent was conspicuously in
the college charter. But this incident showed the effect of the
influence wielded by a single Southern man, a fellow from Cincinnati, who was obnoxiously Southern in his conduct and conversation, as was another man who "hurrahed" for Clement L. Vallandig-
ham once in the college hall, between classes, about the time I
think that that notorious personage had been sent south over the

---

*In the typed manuscript the names of Miss Randolph and other black students
were spelled out as given here. Later editing in Miss Hardy's hand, however,
reduced the last names to initials—Miss R, Miss Fanny H, etc. The use of an
initial for a full name elsewhere in the manuscript is apparently a matter of for-
getting the name or of delicacy. The lower case spelling of Negro throughout the
memoir is Miss Hardy's and has been retained.

[Mason-Dixon] line by President Lincoln. But students of Southern opinions and politics were, it is perhaps unnecessary to say, never interfered with or sent away for any other reason than failure in studies, or violation of college rules.

Miss Randolph afterward came to me for private coaching in arithmetic and Virgil's *Aeneid.* It was a matter of special wonder to me, and is yet, how she ever contrived to learn as much Latin as she had. I think I never saw a denser but a more persistent mind. When she asked for explanations of a passage or a construction, she was quick in her praise of the lucidity of my exposition. Two minutes or less afterward she would ask a question or make a remark which showed me that she had not comprehended a single point.

In the same literary society with me was a Miss Fanny Hunster, a young woman of colored blood, refined, elegant in manners, fault-less in dress, with shining, smooth black hair, a beautiful olive complexion, always somewhat pale. She was much liked by the women. At one time she sang in the college choir. Once when there was to be the usual annual exhibition of the societies, a double quartette was needed. Doubts on the part of some as to whether it would do to have Miss Hunster were met with, "You'll be lucky if you can get her; she's the best singer and the most lady-like person in the whole society!" As a matter of fact, she would not consent to sing until she knew that it was agreeable to all those who were singing. I remember that the young men said when someone asked them about it, "Not have her sing, because _____? Very well, then we'll not sing." Of course, she knew nothing of the discussion, which had been started by some dunce of a girl.

The night of the exhibition there were present some eastern people of importance. One of the women was heard to ask who that distinguished young woman who sang contralto was, and was much surprised when some stupid person explained that she was colored, instead of saying simply "Miss Hunster." The woman who asked the question said she was beautiful and her voice was heavenly. Her dress was a shimmering silvery gray poplin with an opalescent sheen of violet and rose intermingled, and she wore a single large pink rose in her belt. Altogether she was the most noticeable figure in every way who had appeared on the platform that evening, although the cream of the societies was there. One of the sisters of this young woman was in college later. To end the color-question as connected with my college life, I may add that I had one student in English (I was a pupil-teacher then), a black man of failing health, of good mind and a beautiful spirit in whom I became much interested.

8

Vacation Exercises

A long walk in the woods with my sister Laura and a cousin of my mother's in the winter of '63 has yet a distinct place in my memory on account of the pleasure of seeing once more the woods in winter in rain—a soft-falling, quiet rain which made the gray boles of the beeches fresher, and heightened the tender green of the lichens and mosses everywhere on ground, tree, and log. The brown, faded leaves, the odors of the wet ground, the stems of shrubs and vines, the buds folded away tightly to fend from the winter's cold, the few gray and all-so-silent birds spoke a most eloquent mystery into the rainy air. I walked as in a pleasant dream of soothing music.

We were on our way from our Eaton home to the Banta Farm two miles or so distant to spend the night and New Year's Day by invitation of my uncle and aunt who lived there. A sudden change in the weather in the evening to severe cold and freezing, followed next morning by what was called the "cold New Year" shut us all in the house and kept us close to the big open fireplace all that day and the next. Our walk home was by a different path broken through deep snow that creaked under our footsteps.

I was at home in the summer vacation of '63 when Cincinnati was threatened by General Jubal A. Early. The Squirrel-Hunters, as they were afterwards called, were to be got ready for the defense of Cincinnati at once.* Men who had thought themselves Southerners in sentiment, men who still said bitter things about the Government and Abe Lincoln, gathered up each his comforter bed, his tin cup, plate, knife and fork, his little "house-wife" bag of buttons and thread, and any rusty gun he might have, and started, on the run

---

*For the "Squirrel-Hunters," *History of Preble County*, pp. 54–55. [Ed. note]

as it were, to the defense of house and home; for it was coming very near to that in southwestern Ohio, when Cincinnati was threatened. Women sewed and cried and laughed, men talked excitedly and grew jolly, with anxious brows, however, over a chance to see a little of the reality of war. All looked unutterable things over the alacrity of the "Butternut Democrats" who snatched up their guns; it was now their ox that was in danger of being gored, and talk would not avail. Every man carried three or four days' rations of coffee, ham, and bread. Every pack was more or less salted with some woman's tears. Lawyers, doctors, editors, merchants, everybody, walked to the railroad station laden each with his own new outfit.

But the sights in the early morning of that first day after the news came! Look what way we would from our hill-top house, we saw wagons filled with men with guns and bundles, in clouds of dust—the North Road, the Camden Pike, the West Road, Brookville, New Paris—flying processions in clouds of dust, of dusty excited men. We could hear the rattle-roar of their wheels and see the flash of their guns. The whole town was in a turmoil of excitement as these country roads emptied their numberless loads into its streets.

Our part was then helping to sew, to make lint, to cut flannel night caps, for none knew how long the men might have to stay, nor where they would sleep. They would be digging trenches, throwing up earthworks, fortifying as they could in that time. Meanwhile I presidented the Teachers' Institute then in session in the Old North Schoolhouse, but little studying was done that summer, I think. Going to the front ceased by order in a few days as Cincinnati was full of soldiers everywhere, sleeping in churches, in public halls, working in the earthworks, and standing guard—soldiers who had done no more soldiering in their time than we women had done. A few days more, and back the most of them came, covered with such glory as there was; and Cincinnati and all Ohio were safe. But Ohio had its lesson—for many of the stay-at-homes, a good one. But, indeed, the number of men who might have been in the field then in our part of Ohio was very small.*

*As a sequel to this bit of history I add a news item cut from a late paper.

Preble County had sent to the army a large number of men, young, very young, and middle-aged. Necessarily it had its share of losses and these were later followed by the funeral trains of those who fell in battle; for, generally, when they could be found, the bodies were brought home by relatives. Among these I recall the funeral of Captain Mulharen, a handsome Irish lad who had been a near neighbor of ours, and a schoolmate of mine. He was killed in battle and brought home to his mother and father. They tell that a little dog of his, long a pet at his home, sat under the coffin and could not be dragged away until the flag-wrapped body was taken to the cemetery, when he tried to follow. Captain O'Caine, another man idolized by his soldiers, was buried among his kindred also, and followed by the sorrowing affection of many comrades. Captain Ed Cottingham, another schoolmate of mine, I saw after his return from months of imprisonment in a Southern prison. He was almost starved to death, and when I saw him driven out by his sister in a buggy some weeks after his return he still looked a living skeleton, and had to be held up by his sister's arm as she slowly drove him out for air. He recovered later and went back to the field.

At the close of the war, William Smith, my cousin by marriage, was taken from Andersonville on the transport ships that brought that ghastly brigade home to New York to be distributed thence to their homes. Smith did not know his name, where his home was, his regiment, or indeed anything. It was known that he belonged to an Indiana regiment, and he was sent to Indianapolis, slowly coming to himself with such care as he got on the transport train. At night in the hotel in Indianapolis, where he had been placed by the attending officer, he was able to recall the name of his native town (Portland) and lay awake till morning fearing he might forget it again. When he reached Portland he knew nothing to tell those who asked him where he wanted to go. His name or place he did not

---

UNION VOLUNTEERS FINALLY RECEIVE PAY.

Get Checks 47 Years After Service in Army.

Cincinnati, O., Nov. 8, 1909. Forty-seven years after they served as volunteer soldiers to protect Cincinnati from a threatened raid by Confederate troops, "the squirrel hunters" of Cincinnati have received their pay. In the mail received by a number of Cincinnatians yesterday were checks for $13, a month's pay for a private soldier in the United States Army.

know. Nobody knew him; after some hours, he was seen by a neighbor who recognized him and took him home to his wife and child. He recovered to a degree but did not live long.

Uncles, cousins, and friends of mine fought through those battle years. The stress of the time bore down upon us all from day to day, and we never lived an hour of that time without the undertone of war in our hearts—impending battle, or battle just over, with the very sound of all its tragedy beating like a bell in the air. We all were touched on this side, on that, by private griefs. None escaped without scars somewhere on the very heart of life.

An isolated traveling experience of my young womanhood sometimes recurs to me when I am traveling now. I was once alone on a C. H. & D. train going to Richmond, Indiana. I had on a thin summer hat of some black-braided straw which did not fit my head and needed repeated replacing, as it slid off at the back. My gloves were off and my hand perhaps looked very white on the black hat crown. When the train stopped and I rose to go out, I was aware that a large, well-dressed man was coming toward me with a smile on his face; he pushed by others to come alongside of me, carrying a handsome valise and overcoat on his arm. "Which way are you going, Madam?" said he insinuatingly.

"The other way, sir," answered I, glancing at him with a startled look. He turned away into the crowd and I saw him no more.

Although I was periodically on the trains on my way to and from college, I seldom met anything but courteous and respectful treatment. I think this was the only exception.

9

Teaching Interlude

In September, 1864, I left college for a time to teach in West Florence, a little village six miles west of Eaton. The district lay in a flourishing farming region of which West Florence was the little post village—a few houses, a general merchandise store, a blacksmith shop, and no saloon. The schoolroom was the large basement of the brick church on the hill, away from the cluster of houses. Its windows looked over the region round about, and up and down the West Road on which the church was situated. The bell in the tall steeple called daily to the school as well as to the service on Sundays.

Many of the children of this school were from families long settled there. Some of the young men who came in the winter months were older than the teacher. Some of the youngest had come to school for the first time. The larger part of the school of forty-nine pupils was made up of boys and girls between the ages of twelve and fifteen. Although a teacher or two had been in recent years compelled to leave, by some of the unmanageable boys, I had no difficulty with the discipline; though if I had not been fore-warned by my host, one of the directors, about the peculiarities of a certain sharp-eyed young fifteen-year-old tyrant among his fellows, I might have inadvertently antagonized him before I had time or knowledge enough to make him my friend. As it was, I secretly enjoyed the evident attempts to come to sword's points. I treated him as if I thought him a gentleman, and conquered him by the most studied and careful politeness, at the same time not relaxing the least of my own notions of discipline.

In about three days he knew who was master of the situation and was my most excellent champion the rest of the year, and in this was followed by his two brothers, and several other boys of about the same age, all of whom were his abject followers. Among the older young people were three brothers and their two sisters who were very fond of singing and led the young people of the neighborhood in the hymns at church and the songs at school. I think I never heard better congregational singing than in this church. Perhaps because there was an uncommonly large number of good voices, most of which were in one family and its connections. It was something worth remembering to hear one of those young men begin the singing on Sunday, as soon as the minister had given out the hymn. One of these, named John MacW., had a voice of remarkable sweetness and power. He used to spend much of his noon recesses hovering about me with a singing book in his hand, asking: "Please how does this tune go? Won't you sing this?"—as he could not then read music. If, by chance, I sang any song unknown to him, I had to sing it again two or three times until he had learned it.

Whatever advantages the school term gave to the children and young people of this neighborhood, it was quite as profitable in many ways to me as to them. Nothing particularly noteworthy interrupted the quiet movement of the school through the winter months to the end. The children went on learning and so did I. They were at peace with each other and with me. Sometime during January there was a religious revival of a very quiet nature, in the church. Some of the young people and one or two of the elders of the neighborhood joined the church.

The teaching of this school went a long way toward making a teacher out of me. Hitherto I had hardly realized the responsibilities and privileges of the work as a life business. I have always thought that the district school is the best training place for teachers. I have always advised college graduates who have asked me for advice to go away and teach a district school. For there one learns the limitations of her knowledge and of her disposition and character; and not only that, but what is of equal importance, she learns the rule of averages, that is, if she has real teaching timber in her makeup. It is perhaps a narrow estimate to say that in any ten children she may teach, she will find the average of development physical, intellectual, and moral. At least she will meet the greater part of the kinds of material she will have to deal with afterwards.

[226]

The West Florence School was of course not my first place of instruction in these matters, but I was now more mature in mind, and slowly coming to the realization of what I had undertaken. Certain it is, that all the pupils I have since taught profited by some of the things I learned at West Florence.

Some time before the Christmas holidays, one of the school directors came to see if I would take in the scholars from the adjoining district, saying that the older boys had turned the teacher out and shut the door on him, and wanted to come to my school. I said that I thought I had as many as I could do justice to, and perhaps more, already, as there were forty-nine enrolled and in pretty constant attendance, and of so many grades that they did not classify well. "However," I said, "I will take the school if you think best, provided that I am to profit by the fees they bring in." This seemed to settle the matter and they did not come. The ring leader of the trouble went to the teacher's examination the next week, took a certificate, and taught the term out himself.

As for myself at this time, I did some considerable amount of growing in experience and thought. My two years at college had widened my horizon and the regions bounded by it, so that I was better able to judge of people and their actions. My correspondence kept me in communication with my friends still in college, and those gone to other fields. The kindly and intelligent people among whom I lived gave me many new ideas about life and living. In the large family, part of which I was at this time, most generous and hospitable living prevailed. All the household work was done by the family in the most regular and systematic ways, and although so many comers and goers were entertained, there never seemed to be any hurry and confusion.

It was at this time that I learned to appreciate fully what my mother and father had meant when they said, as I often heard them say: "Lucinda Conger is such a fine woman." Strength, gentleness, tact, intellect—all entered into what she said and did, from the making of bread to the entertainment of visitors. Perhaps the character and convictions of the people of this neighborhood can be illustrated by Mr. Eli Conger, who raised a great deal of corn on his farm, but would not sell a bushel of it for fear it might get into the hands of the distiller. He therefore turned it into pork and beef, by feeding it on his own farm. Men did not talk so much about their convictions on this or that subject, but they lived them as simply and directly as they managed their farm work.

Another illustration of the character of these people is connected with that dark time in the war when the Last Draft was made. The country was well-nigh stripped of its men already. Every township had had its quota declared for this draft, and some had raised money enough to buy substitutes to clear themselves of the drawing entirely. Dixon decided to do this, and a mounted troop of farmers rode about to all the township dwellers to take up the share each man should pay. Where they met refusal they drove off cows or horses to make up the sum, or started to drive, which always brought the owners to terms. I stood in the door of my church basement schoolroom on the hill overlooking the country east and west and saw this troop, that muddy, foggy March day at sunset come splashing up the hill and down again to the finish of their day's work. Their horses with bunched-up tails were covered with mud and sweat; they themselves were spattered from head to foot, tired and stern-looking, and well ready to attack the hardest man to deal with in the district.

He was a rich man with five sons, three or four of whom were "liable to draft," but he was determined to let the chance come. I saw the troop go into his yard, saw the parleying though I heard nothing but the voices, not words. Presently one of the men jumped from his horse, went to the stable-yard, and took two horses to lead away; whereupon with an angry gesture, as I could see from my door, the owner gave in, and took out his purse. Then the troop rode away, breaking up on the hill in front of my schoolroom, with jokes and laughter, though with half-dead, weary looks. At the supper table I heard a recital of the day's adventures by my host, who was one of the "Persuaders."

One of those unexplainable experiences which come to many people at some time of their lives came to me while I was teaching in this school. As I had no room in which I could be alone at my boarding place, I generally stayed in the schoolroom to write, read, and study until nightfall. Here I wrote all my letters and my journal.

One evening, while I could still see the red and yellow of the winter sunset through my windows, I sat by a desk in the middle of the room near one of the supporting pillars writing to Ellen Van Mater. Suddenly, as I wrote, I saw her standing just in front of me, to the right, as vividly as if she had been there in the flesh. The color of her eyes, the gown she had on, the scarf about her neck could not have been more real had she been there. I stirred and looked up intently and the vision was gone. I immediately wrote of it in the unfinished letter mentioning the exact time. In her answer three days afterwards, she said that she had been in a greatly disturbed state of mind exactly at that hour and had said "O I wish Rene were here."

10

College, Eaton, and Sorrows

When the end of my six-months' term at West Florence came, early in March, I left these people and the school with many regrets. At the beginning of April I returned to college for the spring term. As I was to be in the library I again took a room in the dormitory. Changes in the faculty had brought several new professors to the college during my absence. Among these was Professor W. H. Russell, with whom I studied German. I remember his teaching as particularly emphatic and forcible, as if underneath he felt like using compulsion to drive his instruction home. It was a slight manifestation of intellectual impatience with dullness.

Sometime during this term Professor and Mrs. Russell gave a reception to Dr. and Mrs. Edward L. Youmans,* to which he invited all the students of his own classes. It was at this time that I first saw a large private library. The Russells had lately bought and remodeled the old Hermann house on a small farm near the college. One of the large rooms facing The Glen had been made into a library. Here from floor to ceiling were shelves of old books, rare books, beautiful books such as I had never seen before.

On one side of the wide fireplace was a painting of a quality entirely new to me. It was a lifesize picture of a French prince twelve or fourteen years old, of the time of Louis Quatorze, in the gorgeous costume of that time. The beautiful dark-eyed, dark-haired lad stood holding up his right hand, which held the leash of a great

*Edward Livingston Youmans (1821–1887) is best remembered as an outstanding popularizer of science. A disciple of Herbert Spencer, he was sought after as a lecturer, organized a famous International Scientific series of monographs which was both popular and authoritative, and initiated the influential *Popular Science Monthly*. [Ed. note]

greyhound by his side, and looking at you with a bright smile on his lovely lips. The group stood on a marble terrace with distant sky and landscape in the background. Professor Russell took great pains to explain this picture to us that we might understand its merits. Seeing it made an important era in my education in that I began to know something about the art of painting otherwise than from books.

April 15, 1865, the Saturday after Good Friday, I came downstairs to the porch from my room in Mr. Van Mater's house where I had been spending the night; it was a bright, fresh day full of spring promise; the orchard and garden showed signs of awakening, though no leaves had yet come out. As I went to the orchard end of the porch, Uncle Jimmy, an old mulatto ex-slave, came up from the garden behind the house, and said with tears rolling down his yellow, seamed face, "O Miss, I must go home! Our President has been killed and we all must be slaves again. I cyain't work no more." "Why, no Uncle Jimmy; it is a mistake. I have not heard it. Nobody has told us anything. Somebody told you this to scare you."

"No, no, Miss," he said, weeping bitterly, "I know we must be slaves again," and he went off down the street with the stiff steps we knew him by. It was from his lips that I knew what had happened to the world. In an hour or two we went to the church to drape it for the funeral service that was to be a part of the expression of sorrow, as of personal loss felt in every family. The college women and the village people put on outward signs of mourning. All life seemed to stop and words meant nothing; indeed, few had words to say. People went about the mournful task of putting signs of death on their houses mutely, and with a bewildered sorrow expressed by the very attitudes of the body.

In September, 1865, as my sisters Laura and Adelaide had decided to go to college for the fall and winter, it seemed best that I should take my place in the schoolroom again. The secondary grade which I had left when I went to college was open to me with little difference in the conditions which had existed four years before. One or two patches of light appear on the picture as I recall the crowded schoolroom. My only brother, a shy, little round-faced lad of eight, was there at school for the first time. His brown eyes and his quiet ways as a child belong there at a school desk in my memory rather than in our home where I lived at the time.

My former absences from Eaton had given me the advantage of a slight perspective in looking at various matters which concerned the life of the people there. I was better able to comprehend and classify specific facts and generalize for myself about what was going on around me.

I had been made aware at rather an early age that there was a difference, and a damaging difference, of some kind between the people who went to the "New Light" Christian Church and those who went to the Methodist and Presbyterian Churches. But though I went to the Methodist Church and Sunday school often myself, I could see no difference except at Thanksgiving time, when the two village papers announced that "union Thanksgiving services will be held at the Methodist Episcopal Church, to which all *evangelical* churches are invited." My mother's comment made me know that that did not include the Christian Church, nor the Disciple Church. This state of things continued through the sixties. I remember going to such a service in the Methodist Church in about 1867 and seeing our minister, the Reverend J. D. Lauer, sitting in one of the pews behind the middle third, while the other ministers of the town sat in the pulpit with the officiating clergyman. As Mr. Lauer was a tall, distinguished-looking man somewhat of the Lincoln type, this could not have been because he was unnoticed. This I-am-better-or-righter-than-thou feeling did not show itself aggressively or even in an unkindly way so far I knew, but continued to exist until after I left Eaton in 1871.

Sometimes even before that time, whenever we had a visiting preacher of more than usual ability, like H. K. McConnell for instance, men from other churches used to come to listen. It was not until after the beginning of the pastorate of Reverend Levi Purviance that the other churches came to understand that the Christians were not heathen or other kinds of infidels. This enlightenment, as I have been told, came primarily through the discoveries made by a Reverend Father Charles Swain, a retired Methodist preacher who had settled in Eaton after his last pastorate. He was for many years a conspicuous personage in the town; a director of schools and frequent visitor; and a privileged person in the church who not infrequently, I have heard, used to get up and rebuke, openly, any frivolous young persons who, as he thought, had behaved in an unseemly way during the sermon.

I had not expected to return to college in September, 1866, for want of means, when Franklin Hill wrote me that the position of librarian was open to me, at enough salary to pay my expenses, and a trifle over. I had already served one or two terms in that capacity. I returned then in the fall of '66, and took up my college work with this privilege which was to me enough of itself, in that it meant the freedom of the library at all hours of the day. The room was open from two to five only, every day except Wednesdays and Sundays. And my duties were simple: arranging magazine tables, recording loans and returns, finding subjects for students, and returning books to places. (Students and others might take books from the shelves, but must leave them on the tables.) It was not long before I could put my hand at any time on any book on any subject in the seven thousand volumes.

The freedom of the library where I might spend hours and hours alone, since the door was open at limited times, gave me such opportunity as I could not have had in any other way. I read and browsed, and explored many an author whom I could not get my own consent to read, many another simply to know what kind of things he wrote, and others still to make acquaintance which has lasted till now. Many a lame and injured volume have I restored with paste and care to a respectable shape among its fellows. I remained in charge of the library until I left college in 1867.

The episode of the purple barège connects itself with the memory of my days in the libary. In the last year of my regular life there I boarded at the house of a good lady who had a genius of a certain kind for bargains. The bureau drawers were filled with a strange assortment of things bought at sales in Cincinnati, a greater or less number of years ago, but sometimes there was a successful purchase of good stuffs.

At this time my library salary gave me enough to pay my board and other expenses and left me six dollars with which to buy a much-needed gown for the commencement season. My hostess was going to Cincinnati on a yearly shopping tour and offered to buy my dress for me. With some anxiety I consented, giving her these cautions and directions:

"As I have neuralgia of the face so often this spring, I must not wear a thin dress, I cannot afford the fashionable stuff now used for summer gowns, besides; so do not get barège. My best winter dress is purple, I have a purple muslin and a white calico with purple violet wreaths; I have also a purple calico. So do not buy purple; and use your judgment as to color and material, with these restrictions, if you please, Mrs. Blank."

Well, she bought me a *purple barège*, "because it was such a bargain." What happened then? I told my story to a student friend who lived near, and showed her the bargain. "Oh," she said, "that is just what I want. I'll take it off your hands." This enabled me to make another venture which resulted more fortunately and I became the possessor of a shimmering blue silky-looking cloth of more substantial quality than the purple barège.

In President Craig's time, there was about the college a black-and-white cat which had earned the title of "Old Antioch" by her fearless way of taking possession of everything and every place about the college buildings, including the chapel, lecture room, and halls. Everybody petted her and enjoyed her extraordinary impertinences. She always seemed to know when there was to be service in the chapel, or lectures in the same place in the evenings. She had an eye—or a scent—for audiences, and usually walked deliberately up the north aisle, mounted the steps to the rostrum, took her seat, and placidly surveyed the audience as if giving her sanction to what was said.

At one time a distinguished Dr. Somebody from Michigan University had come to look at the college with reference to accepting the presidency offered to him by the trustees, as Acting-President Craig found the duties of the office irksome and wished to retire to the work of his professorship. The visitor, a rather large, imperious, and not altogether agreeable-looking personage, was to lecture in the chapel one evening. The audience was assembled and the lecturer was well under way, when in marched "Old Antioch" as usual, mounted the steps, and was about to take her customary friendly look at the audience, when she noticed the elegant silk hat which the speaker had set upon the carpeted floor not far from him, about where Pussy commonly sat. She went at once and looked into the hat as if with some thought of making a bed of it, but changed her mind and walked behind the speaker to the other side and sat down. All this was very greatly to the annoyance of the speaker, as was seen by his nervous bearing and evidently annoyed glances. He made the episode the subject of severe remark before he left the college, including it in other criticisms which formed the base of his refusal of the presidency. The secret amusement of the audience, especially of the student part of it, was more than equalled by their feeling of relief at his decision.

"Old Antioch" also took a lively interest in the meetings of the Literary Societies in their rooms on the fourth floor of the college building, and sometimes went to the president's recitations in philosophy. She counted the members of the small senior class as personal friends. Indeed Dr. Craig had one morning called the class back to the great wood-box by the door in the hall and said, as he showed them Pussy and her three kittens, "I wish to introduce you to the new members of the senior class."

In the spring of 1866, my father, after selling our home in Eaton, removed the family to a small place near Paint Creek Church, not far from the farm on which he was born and brought up. The little place, which he had bought two or three years before, was about four miles southwest of Eaton. The old hewn log house, built by the original owner, was still standing, though it had been unoccupied for a number of years. My father had built what was to be the ell of a new house which was to stand on the site of the old log structure. In the meantime we made use of the large living room with its big fireplace for a kitchen and thus enjoyed a partial return to log cabin life for a season.

Both houses stood near the edge of a high bank along which were planted apple trees and below which was a stretch of bottom land bordered by a branch of Paint Creek. The situation naturally suggested the name of Brookbank which I gave it without much encouragement from my family. Nor indeed was the name much used, as it was not the custom in the neighborhood to name farms except from the owners.

Among the happy summers of my young womanhood were two or three spent here among the fields and woods and the lovely prospects of hill and farm and winding roads. The daily companionship of my three sisters and my father, mother, and young brother was infinitely satisfying and almost compensated for the exile from home required by a teacher's life. As I recall those summer days, vivid pictures with their settings of orchard, field, garden, or household, wherein each of us moved amid the pleasant occupations of a simple daily life, I feel that there could be hardly anything better for body and soul.

In one of these summers, that of 1867, my friend Nelly Van Mater made what proved to her last visit at my home. I had closed my college life at the commencement in June, though without knowing that I had done so. In September I again took up the work of teaching in the Eaton schools. In the next March the cloud of uneasiness concerning the health of Nelly, which had been hanging over me for some months past, took definite form in news of what proved to be a very serious illness. As soon as my school closed early in May, I went to her and was almost constantly by her bedside all summer. During these months of pain and much suffering, the natural brightness of her spirit controlled every hour of the day. As I sat by her all the mornings, we talked or I read and sometimes sang to her the songs we had often sung together. We talked of what we would do when she should be well again.

Then suddenly I was called home in August by the illness of my mother. A brief convalescence, after my return, gave us hopes of her recovery which, however, were destroyed by the relapse followed by her death in September.

News of Nelly's death came to us during my mother's last days. Added to these sorrows, though making little impression at the time on account of them, was the final separation from other near friends, so that the autumn of that year was, for me, a time of inward grief that had no outlet save in work. Teaching and its heavy demands in the grade schools of Eaton, together with boarding myself a part of the time, gave me but little space to think of my own troubles. Additional care on account of my young brother and anxiety for my sisters who were struggling to get an education filled my days with other than selfish griefs.

Memory still lingers with varied emotions over days and episodes of these years at Brookbank between '66 and '71. At one time when my sister Adelaide was teaching her first school, nine miles distant, my father was teaching at West Florence and my sister one mile south. They walked home on Fridays, my father waiting for Adelaide and sometimes going to meet her and both joining my sister Laura on their way home. When they had arrived at the edge of a wood a mile away, they saw the light set in the dining room window for them.

I had usually arrived a little before. The hot supper, the recital of the week's events, the warmth and light and family cheer turned every hardship and mishap into subjects of merriment. The droll experiences of my sister Adelaide and her account of them gave the comedy touch to our little family drama. The wealthy farmer and his wife at whose house my sister boarded could neither read nor write. They had built a large, expensive house, but their manners and ways of living were in many respects of the one-room log cabin style. My sister's introduction to some members of the family at the supper table two hours after her arrival was, "Addie, these are my two boys, Bill and Sam. You may have whichever one you want."

11

Farewells

I began to write verses before I was twenty, but printed nothing that I remember until after I went to college—at least not more than two or three things in the county paper, *The Eaton Register.* Mr. Morris was then its editor and asked me to write some things for him, which I occasionally did. I do not remember what they were about, except that one was a metrical attempt to answer Jacob Chambers's criticism to the effect that I ought to be ashamed to hide my talent and not use it. At college I wrote some things for the society paper, for occasional exercises, and for a magazine at Ann Arbor University, whose editor had been at one time a member of the same literary society at my college with me, and had asked me for contributions.

Through all my college years I kept a journal which was simply a record of what I thought and not a diary of happenings. In that journal I wrote many fragments of limping verse, very little of which was ever used again for revision or finishing. Occasionally I did keep a few lines of some more promising stuff to finish. But for the most part the journal in every respect was a practice book as it turned out.

In the ten years between '61 and '71 the history of the college was eventful and clouded with many misfortunes. Its numbers were depleted at once by the breaking out of the Civil War. Thomas Hill resigned in 1862 to accept the presidency of Harvard College. A greater part of the faculty resigned also because the college expense fund was too nearly exhausted to pay the salaries. Some of the college classes therefore were closed. Professor John Burns Weston, however, stepped into the breach, as was his wont in times of a forlorn hope, took upon himself the acting-presidency, and carried the burden successfully until 1865. Austin Craig, D. D., professor of philosophy, then assumed the acting presidency until 1866, when the Rev. G. W. Hosmer, D. D., was elected president and held the office till January, 1873.

As the four years and a few months of my college life were distributed between 1861 and 1867 they gave me a somewhat wider range of intellectual experience because of the frequent changes in the faculty. Perhaps this was still more advantageous in matters relating to the social life, as it brought the students into contact with a greater number of cultivated people. Perhaps also the necessity of going out to teach, although it broke into my various courses of study, was in no great sense a misfortune to me. For I was thus compelled to make practical use of newly acquired knowledge even though I still worked in grade and district schools. I was much more *I* than I had been.

I was dimly conscious also of better manners in myself and of greater poise. I had partly acquired control of a troublesome shyness and awkwardness which had been the painful obsession of my first years at college. I was no longer so afraid of people.

Some readers may be curious to know why I write nothing more personal of my life as a young woman, since I have been so frank about my life as a child. My answer to this should be obvious. I was, when I was young, a timid soul. I did not talk of my feelings; neither of my admirations, except of the intellectual sort. Life was early a stern discipline to the emotions, and I had myself well in hand by the time I was twenty. Moreover, my ideals were dominant, then as since, and I was saved from that sort of blunder which I saw some of my mates making for their own lives, not by my own wisdom but by that in me which was more like the judicial action of a man.

I have lived a happy life. Whatever personal tragedy it has had has gone to the enlargement of life, and as I look back over the inter- vening years, I have been thankful for whatever saved me from going the way of many women into a commonplace, "good-enough," or even tragic marriage. More than this I do not care to say. Let none set me down as cold and without sentiment. There are hundreds of young men and young women, students of mine at one and another time, who would tell another story. Many of these I came near to in the capacity of teacher and mother; to not a few, I was all the mother the world had for them. To a few, one here and there in the passing years, I became the mother I might have been to my very own, if I had married and had my own. The maternal faculty was large in me, and satisfied itself deeply by this feeling for the motherless and by giving itself out in help to them; to those also who had no relation of confidence with their own parents in the flesh; to those who had never remembered a mother; to those whose unthinking mothers could not know what their children needed. That was my happiness, especially when as a mature woman at thirty I began to understand life better. It was after this time that I lived most profoundly in that side of my nature, and did most for humanity and perhaps grew most myself. These were the years of my teaching in the Oakland High School, the history of which is still to be recorded.

Reliving my college years, vivid though brief and fleeting recollections come to me of incidents, faces, personalities and hear-say traditions. I see, for instance, General Rosecrans walking one windy winter day from the college gate past the window where I sat and of noticing his strongly marked features, the color in his cheeks, the care with which he picked his steps over the wet ground, and the blowing back of his long overcoat in the wind. Associated with this recollection is one of seeing Mrs. Rosecrans, then a very beautiful woman, at the door of her house.

Connecting itself directly with these two pictures is one of an evening spent with a few other girls from the dormitory at the nearby house of General Kirby Smith,* whose family was stationed there some time during the Civil War. We were entertained by the general's sister, a very tall, elegant society woman, whose brilliant conversation, or monologue rather, was picturesque and amusing in the extreme. Among other people and things that she talked about was the poet-painter, Thomas Buchanan Read, who, as she said, was an old beau of hers. At this time he had painted the portrait of

*General Edmund Kirby Smith, 1824–1893, was an important Confederate officer in the Kentucky campaign and commanded the Trans-Mississippi Department from 1863 until the end of the war; see Jon L. Wakelyn, *Biographical Dictionary of the Confederacy* (Greenwood Press, 1977), pp. 388–89. [Ed. note]

her niece, then a beautiful child of six, which portrait hung on the wall in the drawing room where we sat. It was a most ethereally beautiful picture, painted with a poetic understanding of the evanescent graces of childhood. Of course I could not have thought or expressed this then, but the memory of the picture and its coloring is still so vivid that I am as sure of these qualities as if I had seen it yesterday. When, long afterwards, I read Read's poem, "The Closing Scene," I seemed to recognize in its rich coloring the same poetic tones I had seen expressed in the portrait of the child.

Among interesting people whom I heard of as having been students at the college in former years was Edgar Hamilton, a grandson of Alexander Hamilton from Tarrytown, N.Y. The fact that he always dressed in white seemed to be all that anybody made a tradition of. I have been curious to know if certain letters of this young man which are said still to exist, would show any signs of qualities inherited from the illustrious grandfather of their author.

Another tradition of a student of distinguished lineage has a vague place in my recollection, since it was but a name, with no title of itself to remembrance. It is that of a youth by the name of Speed, who was the grandson of George Keats of Kentucky, the brother of John Keats the poet. When he was there, what he was, and what he did I have not been able to learn.

One afternoon Professor Clarke came into the library to open a case just received. No boy anxious to get at the contents of a Christmas box of goodies from home could have been more excited than this mathematical genius, who handled the hatchet but clumsily. His excitement communicated itself to me, as with eager hands he grasped a volume of Laplace's *Mecanique Celeste* translated by Nathaniel Bowditch, whose widow had sent a copy to the library. So I have still this memory-portrait of Professor Clarke's face radiant with the joy of the mathematician, his dark eyes glowing and delighted smiles flickering over his face. I was myself thus impelled to read a little of this ponderous work, to see what it was all about with not much enlightenment possible to me at the time.

If I were a painter of the human figure I could after the lapse of so many years make a portrait of another man of distinguished appearance whom I saw a few times in my first years in college. It would be the picture of the Rev. Matthew Gardner, a minister of

the Christian Church, from northern Ohio. I remember particularly
seeing him at one of the called conferences for the discussion of
ways and means of increasing the college endowment fund. He was
a man of great stature and magnificent proportions. He wore over
his shoulders a long and voluminous broadcloth cloak then still
worn by clergymen and other professional men. It was a cold winter
day and he had just come in when called upon to speak. He stood
in the middle of the floor, a grave and admirable figure, bearing his
sixty or seventy years like a soldier of twenty. His large features
were gloomed over by dark eyes that added to their stern expression. His rather thin gray hair was parted in the middle and fell to
his shoulders. The movements of his hands had the unconscious
grace of power. His mental attitude toward whatever was said and
done at that meeting was uncompromising. I remember nothing of
his speech excepting that it had here and there a slightly Scottish
accent and that he thus pronounced what he called the *endooment*.

In the summer of 1869 I was appointed to the principalship of a
grammar school in Eaton. I had been teaching for a year in the
grade schools under Major W. L. Shaw, then superintendent and
principal of the high school. My appointment carried with it
responsibilities for four classes and the North building and grounds,
but no advance in salary. My protest against this to the president
of the school board was answered by a smiling remark to the
effect that I ought to consider the honor worth something. My
answer was sufficiently plain, but I ended by accepting the
position.

Most of the pupils of my own class in that school had been with
me in the grade below for a year, and in many respects this class of
fifty-two gave me opportunities for minute study of character and
development. Two or three there were also, who had been in the
infant class of my pre-college days, and rather a large number from
families whose antecedents were well known to me. In some
respects this was to myself the most satisfactory teaching thus far;
though in one respect, at least, it resembled all that I had done
before, and differed from all that I did after in the public schools,
namely: that the "credit system" was not then and there in use. The
only legitimate motive for study, the love of learning, was all that

I had to concern myself with in teaching these children. I began to see some results not merely intellectual.

Theories aplenty I had had about the teacher's responsibility for the moral culture of the children under her care, and in some dim fashion, through a few successes and many blunders, I had come to feel that if I failed in this I failed entirely. So I think that in these two years I came to my own, in that my mission of "preacher" became evident. About the state of my own classes I may say that intellectually they worked with eagerness. In a few cases I feared overwork. Nothing was required to be done at home. As there were two grades in the room, one studied while the other recited. Daily reading aloud was one of the most important lessons. I took time and pains to teach the children how to study a reading lesson for the thought and how to express that thought with the voice. Each class recited from benches immediately in front of my desk, so that conversational tones took the place of the high-pitched unnatural key of the "public-school voice" so often heard in children today. Large numbers of the children of these classes took real joy in their reading, and many of them began the reading of real books for themselves, a matter in which I guided them with advice outside of school hours.

Whatever were the general or specific results of this era of my teaching, of one thing I feel sure: I put into the hands of every child the principal tool by means of which an education is to be had. I taught him to read. It may be well in passing to give some slight hint of how I did this. Perhaps the merest incident of the schoolroom will suggest this better than a long explanation: A twelve-year-old girl comes to the desk with her reader in her hand, before she leaves the room at recess: "Please, Miss Hardy, I can't read this sentence at the end of the paragraph, because I don't understand it. I know all the words, but I don't know what they say." I ask her a few pointed questions, then take the book from her hand, and read the sentence without explanation. Her face lights up. "Oh thank you! I understand now." I speak of this the more emphatically because in these days the public schools "sweep with extreme flounce the circle of the sciences," and fail to teach plain reading, composition, spelling, and elementary arithmetic. The high schools "prepare for the university," they do not educate.

[243]

I may add here that I was wholly independent in my management of the school, for Superintendent Shaw gave the largest liberty to his teachers, while he expected from them the limit of efficiency. He was a man of energy, system, and perception. Exacting with himself in matters requiring promptness and accuracy, he expected no less from his students and assistant teachers. Severely just and vigorously cheerful, he commanded not only the respect and obedience of all his pupils, but also their affectionate regard.

There were some experiences in these two years as principal of the North Grammar School which had not hitherto made a part of my training as a teacher. I was compelled to know, through my care for the buildings and playgrounds, that there were some morally ill-conditioned boys whose lives at home and on the streets were already turning toward depraved instincts rather than toward healthy and clean habits and ideas. This knowledge, however unpleasant as it was, became of some use to me in dealing with other cases with the greater wisdom that a few more years added to my judgment.

I recall, and often with delight, the schoolroom experiences of this time, the singing, the enthusiastic map drawing, the beautiful reading, and the general willingness to observe rules which characterized the whole school. The boyish faces of Rolla, Clarence, Martin, Louis, John, George, and Joe came before me as they sat on the recitation benches. The half-a-dozen Marys, the three Kates, fair-haired Ella, dark-eyed Louie who had to be scolded for studying too hard, blue-eyed Lina, and scores of other bright young girlish faces dear to my memory, rise before me as I write.

In imagination I have taught these children again and again, using the knowledge of better ways learned since, by later experiences. I have set them to doing original investigation in local history. I have worked with them among the townspeople to create a library to help us all in our reading and study. But the omissions of that time and the other mistakes made then merely serve now as a sort of pastime of regrets. But perhaps the day for these things had not yet come in Eaton. At least the prophet of them had not arrived. How effective and serviceable a local history society would have been to the town I did not then realize. I could not then see, through lack of perspective, what rich material for the work of such a society lay all around going to waste and slipping away from the memory of men as the older people, the natural historians of the place, themselves slipped away one by one.

When I left Ohio in July, 1871, I did not then know that by thus turning over the leaf of the third decade of my life story, I was practically closing the Ohio volume of my history. For although I did later return to Ohio with the intention of remaining, circumstances brought it about that I was henceforth to be a Californian.

The thirty years of my life thus far had been an apprenticeship for work that I was afterward to do in the schoolroom—a kind of apprenticeship in its earlier years which seems now, as I become acquainted with other persons of my profession, to have been unique. It included the log schoolhouse, before the days of the public school system; it included also the education of the pioneer home, of the field and woodland, and later of the village school, and a touch of western town life. It was continued by the training of the summer institutes for teachers, the teaching of village and district schools, and some years of college life followed by more years of teaching. Hitherto my professional work had had the faults of a beginner; for the greatest apprenticeship must be that which comes from experience. In my opinion it takes at least thirty years of life to make a teacher whose wisdom is anywhere near sufficient for this task. If I were choosing teachers for a school of my own, other things being equal, I should choose none below the age of thirty. And I should be unwilling to choose any who had not had an early and close acquaintance with nature, and to whom nature had not spoken her various language.

CALIFORNIA

1

Beginning Again

My last year in Ohio was a hard and busy stretch of time. I was principal of a grammar school in Eaton where I taught a class of fifty-two preparing for the high school; I kept house with two other teachers in a house which we had partly furnished for living. My youngest sister and my brother were with me some of the time, she, studying music; he, going to school to me. In January my health was evidently breaking under the strain of work and responsibility which continued to be too heavy from that time until the end of the school year in June. In April I had a letter of invitation from my old college friend Louesa Philbrick C. to spend a year with her which opened the way for me to go to California for a year's rest. I had decided to make the trip with a large excursion party which was to leave Indianapolis in July.

In 1871 the journey to California was a formidable undertaking to inlanders like us who had never been from home. I longed to get off, and felt better before I had been two days on the way, and by the time our train had begun to climb over the rolling hills of Wyoming I was looking with interest at every weed or wisp of grass, to see the lands over which Richard Wade and John Brent had taken their ride "to save and to slay."

By the time we had arrived at Salt Lake, where we stayed all night in our own car, I was already much better, able to eat and to walk several blocks. A few vivid pictures of that strange city remain with me—its fresh brooks in the streets instead of gutters; the wonderful beauty of the view from the top of the boat-shaped tabernacle; the service there on Sunday morning, the choir of young Mormons, and the great organ; the reception in the Lion House by the acting Mormon president (who took the place of Brigham

Young), the speech of welcome, and the introductions. At night after we had returned to our car, a Methodist minister of our party began to sing hymns and all the excursionists who could came in to what grew to be a fine singing evening of familiar hymns. Crowds of Mormon women and children gathered outside in the shadow to listen. The next morning we went back to Ogden through long verdant stretches of farms and orchards, the very blue Salt Lake always in view, and still to be seen long after we had left Ogden.

The Nevada desert west of Ogden took hold of my imagination with a strength that no other scenery had ever till then or since approached. I seemed to feel the terror of those primal experiences of childhood with regard to Space and Volume that I have otherwhere tried to describe. The remote desert mountains brought near by the clear air, the long and wide fields of gray-green, yellow-green, or black sage brush, appealing both to the sight and to the sense of smell in some mysterious large way, as of struggling to suggest some forgotten familiar thing, fascinated me almost to the point of hypnotism.

We stopped in Sacramento on a hot July day and an hour or two later went on to Oakland, arriving after dark at the Mole where my friend Louesa Philbrick Cutting met me.

The following Sunday after my arrival in California, I went with my friend to the little Congregational Church on Ninth Street. There I heard the Rev. D. B. Gray, who with his family, was among the earliest of my friends in my new home. In the congregation that day was Judge Hinkson of Wilmington, Ohio, whose acquaintance I had made coming overland and whose old-fashioned courtesy during the journey had added much to my comfort and pleasure. He was at that time seventy-five years old and coming to California to surprise his daughter by a visit. Strangely enough, as it turned out we found ourselves next door to each other. A call from his daughter, Mrs. Niswander, next day began a friendship which continued to the end of her life.

In October, immediately after the news of the Chicago fire, I went with Mrs. Niswander to a meeting of ladies of the various churches, held in Brayton Hall, to work for the sufferers from that calamity. The hall was full of women with sewing machines busy cutting, basting, sewing, and planning. Men kept coming throughout the day with clothing and material to be made up; other men packed into boxes clothing, shoes, and general supplies. My friend and I sat and basted undergarments for a lady who sewed them on the machine as fast as we could baste. A little later I found out that this lady was Mrs. K. B. Fisher who was some years after my colleague in the Oakland High School. It was rather interesting to me to notice with what sidelong approaches of the conscience some of the ladies considered the raffling of a hand some music box and some other articles which had been sent in for that purpose. One lady I noticed, who wanted the music box very much, rather shamefacedly bought a ticket for the raffle although her conscience was conventionally against it. She was afraid that she should get it but was disappointed when she did not.

When the necessity for any further aid to Chicago was over the women who had thus met on common ground for benevolent work formed themselves into an association known as The Ladies' Relief Society, which later founded, built, and equipped an Old Ladies' Home and an Orphanage. Both of these institutions they still manage and support.

Not long after this I went to an Old Folks' Concert given in the same hall for an additional fund to be sent to Chicago. A curious recollection of the entertainment seems worth recording, as it was characteristic of the time. The Niswanders had invited me to go with them to the concert, partly that they might enjoy seeing the effect on me of the California custom of ending every kind of public hall entertainment with a dance. As Mrs. N. was herself but recently from an Ohio town which, like my own part of the state, had what would be called puritanic standards, she knew that I should be affected by what I saw as she had been. After the concert was over in this case almost everybody stayed to dance. We lingered to look on for a few minutes and saw men and women of all ages taking part in the square dances then in vogue.

Mr. Niswander was a man of parts almost amounting to genius in several directions. He was descended from a family of Swiss-German goldsmiths, in a line unbroken for three hundred years. He was born in Virginia but had come to California from Ohio. He could make a watch from the ores, and there seemed to be no limit to

[251]

his power of invention. But in the years in which I knew him he worked at these arts only as a pastime in the intervals of mining business.

Although a very quiet man, Mr. Niswander sometimes told stories of his mining life, when he happened on a reminiscence. Among these, one of a prospecting trip is still vivid in my recollection. It was of an experience in "Scorpion Gulch."

"I was once," he said, "returning from a prospecting trip among the mountains of Calavaras with my partner, Doc. Doane, when, by some mischance, we lost our way among the barren canyons of those mountains. As we had been out for two or three weeks our provisions were exhausted excepting a little corn meal. For several days Doane had been sick but had kept going without saying much about it. I saw that he was scarcely able to go on and now and then he showed signs of delirium. I began to feel ill also but saw that I must not give way on Doane's account. Either because we were too ill to pay attention to our surroundings or because we had become bewildered, we seemed to get further into the maze of canyons and gulches. At last it was evident that Doane could go no further. We had come to a sort of cul-de-sac, the end of a narrow, steepsided gulch in which were a few scrubby oaks clinging to the sides. Near one of these, which slanted along the slanting ground, was a small spring. Here we camped; Doane was now delirious with a raging fever. There was so little level ground that I had to lash him to the tree to keep him from rolling down to the bed of the dry stream.

"By this time Doane's fever must have been at its height for he raved continuously with a few short intervals of restless sleep. I slept not at all, but besides giving the sick man water occasionally there was little I could do. I had no food to give him except corn meal stirred in water which he generally refused. I had no other food myself. Among Doane's delirious dreams there was one which persisted. He thought he had invented a machine which would turn all the sick, infirm, and old into blooming young men and women, when they were put in at one end and ground out at the other. He saw it at work up among the branches of the tree over his head. 'Look,' he said, 'there goes Tommy D., he's older than we are. Nice, but, there, see him now, he doesn't look twenty. There goes M.

and J. Now, they're young too. Look, look! There goes Mary Lize, and there she comes out; but nothing could make her prettier than she is. O, nice, put me in, put me in, put me in.' Then his voice trailed off into a whisper and he slept a few minutes, only to wake again to call me to put him into the machine.

"At last I thought of a device to keep him still, for I was nearly dead for the want of sleep. 'Yes, my boy, I'll put you in, but you will have to do like the others and not speak a word till sunrise and then it will be all right to put you in.' So we both slept.

"One night a heavy rain fell and we were drenched, though we seemed none the worse for it the next day. I lost count of the time and do not know how long it was before help came, probably about ten days.

"One afternoon there suddenly rode into the gulch a little, fat, red-faced Dutch man covered with dust. He came up to where we were, looked at us a few moments, then drawing a bag of gold dust from either side of his fat body held them with outstretched hands toward us and with tears streaming down his dusty face, cried, 'Mein Gott, Mein Gott! take all I haf!' but, seeing that there was no present help in his bags of gold, he turned, and rode rapidly away after telling us that he would bring aid from a camp eight miles distant. In a few hours he returned with a number of men who brought two litters on which they carried us to the camp. Doane was still delirious and I was, by this time, in a semi-conscious state and knew little for some days after our arrival at the camp. Doane's recovery was slow and his mind still affected by the hard experiences long after I had regained health and strength enough to be anxious to return to our own camp."

To this early part of my California history belongs the recollection of hearing two then distinguished leaders of the Woman's Rights cause. I went with my friend to hear Elizabeth Cady Stanton and Susan B. Anthony who were to speak in Brayton Hall to women alone. Hitherto I had not sought to hear advocates of the cause, for the reason that I was coldly conservative with respect to the whole movement, and had not been attracted by the aggressive kind of presentation of the subject by the women I had heard. But I was interested in these two leaders whose names and public addresses had long been familiar through the newspapers, more often than otherwise in terms of ridicule.

Elizabeth Cady Stanton, who was to deliver the address, sat near the front of the platform directly facing the middle of the audience, and talked in an easy conversational tone, perfectly audible to all in the crowded room. She sat throughout the entire address, and used her very beautiful hands but little in gesture. Mrs. Stanton wore a simple but handsome black gown of silk grenadine, trimmed with black lace. Her hair was snow white and done in silky puffs over her head which heightened the brilliancy of her fine eyes and her youthful complexion.

The address, as I remember, was personal and individual as to family relations, training of children, and household management, rather than about civic rights. At the end of the lecture Miss Susan B. Anthony rose from her seat on the platform, came forward, and suggested to Mrs. Stanton that she should speak further on a certain topic. There could hardly have been a greater contrast between two women. Miss Anthony's dark eyes, brunette complexion, and plainly dressed dark hair, her somewhat spare figure in an old-fashioned striped silk, all emphasized the difference between her own and Mrs. Stanton's personal appearance. But Miss Anthony's persistent and courageous adherence to her chosen work had given to her intelligent countenance great dignity of expression. I saw her again, about 1895, standing by Mrs. Jane Stanford at a reception given to the Stanford faculty in her San Francisco house. Miss Anthony seemed to have changed very little. She had before that time begun to enjoy the consciousness of the approaching fulfillment of her greatest hopes.

I could not look at these women and hear their voices without feeling deeply the earnestness of their plea for the betterment of the condition of women. They made plain their belief that equal suffrage was the solution of all the social problems relating to women. It seems now that there is no other way open for the control of those conditions which result in the destruction of thousands of ignorant and helpless girl-children, who are sacrificed yearly to the beasts of the social jungle. But whatever woman's vote may do toward this end, there will never be safety for the unprotected women until good men in private and in public life look upon crimes against women in the light of the highest Christian standards.

[254]

A few weeks before this, in September, I had gone with friends whom I was visiting to spend a week on a ranch near Niles, where I saw much that was different from farming and farm life in Ohio. I had not yet grown used to seeing the earth so brown and dusty and bone-dry, so greatly in contrast to the green of Ohio fields, roadsides, and farm grounds that it gave an impression of desolateness. The large indifference of many ranch people to the minor details of farming added to this feeling. Although the orchards and vineyards were full of most delicious fruits and anyone could help himself at pleasure, these never appeared on the table. A lack of variety in the food was most noticeable to one who had come from the abundant tables of the middle west.

On this visit I saw Refugia, a Mission San Jose Indian woman, the daughter of Old Pascascio, the well-known Indian guide who had run up and down the trails between the missions many years before, in the time of the mission fathers. Refugia still wore her shining black hair cut straight across the forehead in mourning for her father who had died on the ranch the year before at the age of one hundred years. He had retained his faculties and a good deal of physical strength to the end. As he had never worn shoes the soles of his feet were so hard and horny that they were as great a protection in walking as sandals would have been. He was a devout Catholic and up to the time of his death walked every Sunday to the service of the church, at Mission San Jose, some miles distant.

Pascascio often told tales of the old mission days. One of these, now of some historic interest, he told repeatedly with a good deal of emotion and dramatic gesture, sometimes with tears streaming down his face. It was of that cruel time when Ignacio Vallejo, among other Spanish warriors came to take possession of the lands of the mission fathers. It was on Christmas night about 1783. The rain was falling heavily. The priests had gathered all the Indians into the church for a special Christmas service, in which they taught the people by a sort of Miracle Play the difference between being good and being bad. On one side of the altar stood angels, and men, women, and children representing good people. On the other side were hideous devils and bad people. The priest was standing before the congregation speaking to them and pleading with them, when suddenly there came a loud knock at the door and a command to open. In marched Vallejo, resplendent in uniform, followed by his staff and other soldiers. Pascascio, who was an altar boy, then thirteen years old, looked on and listened, terrified, while the Spaniard told the priests and the frightened people that they had come to take away their lands, their vineyards and orchards, and their cattle. He said that the priests might have the people and the church. Pascascio often described himself in Spanish by the phrase "As lonesome as an eagle."

My main business of that time had to concern itself with the recovery of health, which reduced my activities both mental and physical to a commonplace level so that whatever the memory retains is mainly of things external to life. I became a part of the household of the friend who invited me to visit her and helped a little about the housekeeping and care of her only child as I was able. As I grew stronger I took strolls about the place wherever the streets had been made passable by wooden walks, for as yet Oakland Point was a waste of sands in the streets, and sidewalks were infrequent.

Some recollection I have of a feeling of loneliness on these excursions because of the strangeness of the plant life. It was not until I had begun to notice with more attention the native plants and flowers along the streets that I began to recognize their affinities and so to feel more at home among them. Many of the flowering plants and shrubs of the gardens were unfamiliar and baffling if I attempted to place them botanically, as they often belonged to exotic genera.

At my friend's home we often spent the evenings reading aloud by turns or singing, sometimes our old songs of college days or new songs with guitar accompaniment. This practice and returning health had so improved the strength and compass of my voice that I was able to attempt songs which I had not hitherto supposed I could sing. My friend and I sang sometimes at neighborhood evenings, and now and then at church.

I gradually extended my daily excursions, usually following the boardwalks into whatever direction they might lead. I thus, one day, came upon the public schoolhouse of the district, which, after a few days, I ventured to visit. This was the Prescott Grammar School which gave me my first impression of California public schools. Here I met Mrs. Delia R. Wheelock, who was then first-assistant. She was an Oberlin College woman who had taught in California a number of years, in private and in public schools. To conversations with her and a somewhat intimate acquaintance in the few months following, I perhaps owe the directing of circumstances which finally ended in my remaining in California to teach. For by her advice I decided to prepare for the state examinations, which were to come six weeks later in June. To do this it was necessary to cram a good many useless technicalities of state school law, state geography, and large quantities of other matter which could in no way show fitness for the teacher's vocation.

After four days examination in twenty subjects with satisfactory results, I was offered a choice of three positions by W. F. B. Lynch, the county superintendent; but I decided to apply in Oakland where I hoped to be elected to a primary school. But my election was to a head assistantship under Mr. Brodt, then principal of the Prescott Grammar School, who had asked for my appointment. This came about through my having substituted some days for the principal during his examination of the other classes of his school. As Mrs. Wheelock was to be transferred to one of the uptown schools, her position became vacant and thus fell to me. At this time the school term began on the first Monday after the Fourth of July.

On July 17th, a few days after beginning to teach, I went with Mrs. Niswander to the commencement exercises of the University of California in Brayton Hall, on 12th Street, Oakland. I think this was the last commencement held in the building of old Brayton College, which was the nucleus of the University of California.*

The few whom I remember among the many on the platform that day were President Durant, a slender, dark-eyed, dignified man

---

*The University of California was organized by John Le Conte, then acting-president. The university opened September 20, 1869. "Eleven students were inherited from the College of California, which had disincorporated and turned its property over to the University. Twenty-five entered the Freshman class, and one or two enrolled as special students, a total of about thirty-eight." *Autobiography of Joseph Le Conte* (1903), p. 243. Both Joseph Le Conte and his brother John were famous scientists and teachers. [Ed. note]

in a gown, Professor Ezra Carr, and three young men, one of whom I afterwards knew as superintendent of schools in Oakland; another, a professor, was a military-looking personage, a youthful blond, whom I saw at intervals in the years following. The graduating class was small and had a red-haired valedictorian who recited a Latin oration, one word only of which I remember, and that was *Berkeleyensis*, which he used in speaking of the oaks of the new campus. Another minor recollection of the time is that of surprise at the style of decorations, which consisted merely of a wire stretched around the two sides and over the platform end of the room, strung at rather wide intervals, with artificial roses—a yellow rose, a red rose, a bunch of leaves, a yellow rose, a red rose, and so on. I had expected elaborate flower decorations, or simple wreaths and festoons of green.

But the vivid memory of the day centers about a slender young man who might have been one of those described by Shakespeare as "Young-eyed cherubim." His delicate features, soft, dark hair, and a sort of inspired look, together with his vibrating voice, gave an indescribable power to his words. He read that day a poem called the "Venus of Milo." He rose in his place, stood erect seemingly unconscious of himself. His fine head was perfectly poised without the backward tilt so often seen in young speakers who, either because they think highly of themselves, or from some of that awkwardness which grows out of being shy, lift the chin at the same time they lift the voice. His fine gray-blue eyes took in the audience as naturally as a child's. I had gone to the college commencement without expecting anything unusual, and I had happened upon an event, for I saw and heard a real poet in the flesh—a poet whose looks, words, and life, as I afterwards knew them, took nothing away from the high ideal I had cherished in my imagination of what a poet should be. All this, Edward Rowland Sill fulfilled in his whole life. He was at this time teaching in the Oakland High School, which he left in 1874 to take the chair of English literature at the State University.

After I went into the Oakland High School in 1877, I had occasional correspondence with Professor Sill in relation to students who were intending to go to the university. Once, in 1879, I think, I went with a young woman to consult him about some special work for her. We found him in his Mansard recitation room, in the college of letters. He was still at his desk after the last recitation of the day. His advice to the young girl was most wise and kind, and he soon satisfied her by planning the courses she wanted. He then rose and said some felicitous things about the views from his rooms off to the hills on one side, and out the Golden Gate on the other. Then he turned to a picture on the wall, which he saw me noticing, and talked about that in a way to fix it in the memory, even in detail. It was a small photograph of Riviere's "Circe and the Friends of Ulysses," a copy of which I afterwards bought for myself. While he was talking to us an extraordinary-looking young man came into the room, a short, thickset youth with a remarkable head covered with thick red hair. He had the air of one on intimate terms with the owner of the room. As we were just going out I did not hear him speak. He was later and is now known as Professor Josiah Royce.

Somewhere about this time I heard Professor Sill lecture on the English language, when he read most delightfully some Anglo-Saxon verse. I last saw him in a bookstore in Oakland, when he looked very ill. Before he left California he printed for private distribution a small collection of his poems, a copy of which he sent me. This was the collection containing the "Venus of Milo," the "Fool's Prayer," "The Invisible," and other poems. After I went east in '83 for a year's rest, I had some correspondence with Professor Sill about a little composition book he had urged me to prepare for high schools. His advice about the matter was wise and business-like, as well as enlightening as to what would be of most use. After some months of silence, when my book did not appear, he wrote a little letter of inquiry as to what had become of it. He advised me to publish with Henry Holt, "as," said he, "he is a good man to deal with."

I have often been asked by teachers and others what was the secret of Professor Sill's influence on his students, for even to this day (1912), it is a common experience to hear the echoes of his influence among the lives of those who never knew him personally but who have come in contact somehow with his spirit as expressed in the lives of those who did know him. As I have studied these men and women I have observed in them a certain quality of moral enthusiasm which seemed to me to have been handed on to them and through them to others, from him. So far as I can express it from my own knowledge of Professor Sill's personality, he led others by his own moral enthusiasms which burned with a steady light illuminating all that he said and did. Thereby he touched the lives of his students at their highest point and thus led them to "follow the Gleam."

I taught for two years in the Prescott Grammar School. The contrasts between the children of this school and those I had been teaching some years in Ohio showed greater docility and more gentle manners and a decided difference in speech, particularly in the quality of the consonant *r*. I was greatly interested in noticing that this consonant was invariably slightly clipped by the whole class, which was composed of children of various nationalities but mostly Oakland born. The largest number were of Irish parentage; and of those who were American, the greater number were of southern extraction. My relations with these children were of the pleasantest character.

It was thus early in my connection with the Oakland schools that I took the liberty of pointing out to the superintendent that there was great waste somehow in the teaching of the two subjects, arithmetic and grammar, that more time was given to these two subjects than to any others and yet that the tabulated results were lowest. I attributed this to the fact that an attempt was made to teach these subjects without reference to the stages of mental development, while at the same time the methods employed failed to give facility and accuracy in the simple operations of arithmetic and any power of expression in language. As proof of this I showed by an example performed in Mr. Campbell's presence that more than ninety percent of the class, averaging fourteen years of age, were both inaccurate and slow in the simple operations with whole numbers. Yet the course of study required them to be working at examples of various kinds beyond their ability to understand. I further pointed out that this was the case in all the grades of all the schools. He verified this for himself by experiments. However, nothing came of it, as the course of study was not changed owing to objections made in session by school principals and teachers. During the whole time that I was connected with the Oakland schools this state of things existed both there and in the schools of San Francisco, and so far as I know, still exists.

Among the fifty or sixty children of this first school whose names and faces I recall, there were, of course, some types entirely new to me. But my apprenticeship to the business of teaching, served as it had been among a rural and village population, seemed to have fitted me to meet new conditions. As the courses of study included nothing but the common branches, among which reading was still of so much importance that it occupied a lesson period every day, I had time at least once a week to read to the class such poems, and other pieces of literature as I thought might interest them. Among these were Tennyson's "Morte d'Arthur" and Arnold's "Sohrab and Rustrum" which I remember made a profound impression on the whole class. One of the boys, who asked to see the copy of Tennyson, reread the poem, then asked if he might copy the picture of King Arthur receiving Excaliber. He worked at noons and recesses and made an admirable enlarged copy of the print. By the wish of the class this picture remained on the board till the end of the term. Several of the children asked to have reread parts of the poem and of the "Sohrab and Rustrum."

One morning in August of the first year of my work in the Prescott School during a class recitation, there came a knock at the door followed immediately by the entrance of a distinguished-looking gentleman with an extended hand, a smile and the inquiry, "Is this Miss Hardy? My name is Tompkins. There is a gentleman at the door who wishes to see you." It was no other than Dr. Thomas Hill who had landed in San Francisco the day before with Professor Louis Agassiz from the Hassler Scientific Expedition along the coast of South America, around Cape Horn.*

Dr. Hill had heard that I was in Oakland and had taken the trouble to look me up. Judge Tompkins, president of the school board, whose guest he was, had helped him to find me. Dr. Hill looked very much as when I had last seen him ten years before

*The purpose of the Hassler Expedition was deep-sea dredging which partly failed for lack of adequate means of preserving specimens. But Professor Agassiz's observation on the Magellan glaciers made the expedition worthwhile.

at Antioch College. His long ocean voyage had rested and restored him, so that although the sorrows of life had pressed hard upon him in these ten years, he looked very little older. Though I was naturally somewhat excited by the unexpected visit, within I was much moved by the sight of his face and the sound of his voice. In the few minutes that he stayed he expressed himself with deep feeling in appreciation of what my sister Adelaide had been to his daughter Katharine. Miss Hill had spent a year at the home of his nephew, Dr. Franklin Hill, at Yellow Springs, while my sister was at college. She was then suffering from a nervous collapse after months of care of a nervous invalid in her father's family, and was so ill as to have lost the initiative toward recovery, which my sister supplied by her determined effort.

In September, 1873, I took two months' leave of absence for a visit to my home in Ohio. On the journey eastward I met among other interesting people General Bryant, the Commandant of the Pribylov Islands, then on his way to Washington to make his annual report. He was a very tall, powerfully built man with bushy brown hair and weather-beaten features, always smiling like a boy while he talked. His large voice had an agreeable boom through the car as he talked almost incessantly of "my people," meaning the Esquimaux. He was accompanied by his wife, a little, dark, silent lady. They often invited me to walk with them whenever the train gave us time for exercise.

Another fellow traveller was Captain Reed of Salem, Mass., a retired sea captain who had for many years been the chief officer on a steamer line between Liverpool and New York. He also was very tall, straight, and although probably over seventy years of age was muscular and strong. His white hair and ruddy face seemed to belong to the type of which he was a fine example. His conversation was quiet and full of matter without a superfluous word. As we came in sight of the blue waters of Salt Lake he told me the story of a lady whom he had brought over from England with a company of Mormon converts, led by a Mormon missionary. She was a beautiful, highborn, young woman of refinement and culture, and the only lady of the company. The other women were evidently of a very different order. A chance interview with the lady put Captain

Reed in possession of the facts about her conversion and her decision to follow the apostle of her new faith. She had escaped from home, but now she was in a state of doubt. The captain urged her to return to her home, promising to aid her in every way to that end, but on her arrival at New York, she told him that she must go on, that she would write to him from Chicago, or return from there if she should so decide. Her brief letter said, "I must go on." Captain Reed never heard from her again. He ended his story by saying, "I shall stop at Ogden and go down to Salt Lake to see if I can find any record that will tell me if she ever reached Salt Lake City, but I do not believe she would outlive the discoveries she must soon have made." He promised to let me know if he should find anything, but I never heard from him.

My father's home was still at Brookbank, where I spent most of my vacation, again living the simple country life among the fields and woods of that pleasant neighborhood. The memory of that brief time with my father, sisters, and brother adds itself to the memories of the earlier summers there with the family still unbroken. The natural human joys of the daily life with your very own blood and no others about, the simple daily meals, the round of little house and garden tasks, the walks, and talks, and laughter, the looks, the mere words all had something of the effect that lies too deep for either smiles or tears.

A week at Yellow Springs with the Van Maters, a visit to Cincinnati schools where I saw the Phonic Method of teaching reading successfully applied, a day spent in the Indianapolis schools on my return trip to California, a short visit to Bell Center, Ohio, left their impression upon me. It was not without a wrench that I again put distance between me and my own, for now I had no definite plans for a return, and I knew that my father and the family felt the separation deeply.

My class at the Prescott Grammar School celebrated my return with an exhibition. Before leaving I had had an uneasy feeling that the contrast between my discipline and that of the teacher who substituted during my absence would be to my disadvantage in the judgment of the class; for she was reputed to be a strict disciplinarian, and I had never had the reputation. I was relieved, however, from that fear by seeing the class and hearing later the criticism of a fourteen-year-old girl, "Miss Blank has so much 'discipline' and yet we were not very good. You don't seem to have any, but we behave just because you want us to." The same child made a criticism of Swinton's *School History of the United States* which had lately replaced one long in use. "There isn't enough mixed with it to make us remember it, is there? I don't like it." The book in question barely escaped being a handy catalogue of names and dates.

The remainder of this school year went forward without episode or interruption, and my life outside of school hours was quiet and uneventful, with the exception that I had continued my slight acquaintance with the theatre by seeing John McCullough and his stock company in *Coriolanus*. Heretofore I had seen nothing but two melodramas in which the California actress, Lotta, was the star. As in my ignorance of dramatic representations I was then intellectually unable to judge of the acting, I could at most but record the impression made by the spectacle. I have a distinct recollection, however, of a curious feeling in some hidden recesses of my consciousness that I was perhaps doing something wrong in going to a theatre. It was probably the vestige of some early precept heard at church.

Near the end of the school year I had a call to teach in Mill's Seminary but decided to remain in public school work. At the request of Mr. McChesney, principal of the high school and Irving Grammar School, I was transferred to the Irving School at the beginning of the next year.

The one thing of interest that I recall as belonging to this time, was meeting Mr. John Muir, with whom Mr. McChesney and I went to see a collection of butterflies belonging to Dr. John Behr of San Francisco. Dr. Behr's house, an old one-story cottage, stood at the further end of a yard covered entirely with weeds as high as a man's head, a narrow walk of single planks, end to end, led through this forest which brushed against us on either side. The door was opened by a man past middle age, somewhat bald and in his shirt sleeves. He took us to a room which had originally been intended for a parlor, judging from its carpet and an old-fashioned, haircloth, mahogany sofa. "Come in," he said, "but don't you touch anything," he added, as he left the room for his coat. We stood stock still looking around, not daring to move for fear we should touch something. The sofa was piled high with a confusion of large, thick manuscript books which barely left room at one end for a seat. The table and the two chairs were full of specimens or boxes and papers. One end and one side of the narrow room were stacked nearly to the ceiling with wooden specimen cases. From these the good Doctor took down and opened box after box showing us the marvels of Lepidopteran beauty. I suppose our exclamations of wonder and delight and some of our questions may have been amusing to the naturalist but he showed no signs of it. I was interested to hear Mr. Muir's comments, none of which, unfortunately, I remember except one, when a box containing some very large white butterflies from South America was opened. "Oh! Sunday lawn!" said he, with an appropriateness of description characteristic of all Mr. Muir's speech. The wonderful widespread wings of diaphanous white bore out the phrase, which, however, nobody else would have thought to use. All imaginable colors, tones, tints, added to by flashes of irridescent bars of brilliant color, passed rapidly before us as one case after another was opened.

Although I was well satisfied with my new place in the Irving Grammar School, I resigned in August, to take a position in the preparatory school of Antioch College, which included matronizing the young women of the college dormitory. My friend Zella Reid, who had held the position for two years, was coming to California to be married to the Rev. David Cronyn of San Jose. My father and sisters had long been urging me to come home, and for many reasons it seemed best for us all that I should again make a change. My father's increasing deafness made it improbable that he could teach much longer. Two of my sisters who had been teaching some years, and my young brother, wanted to go to college. My acceptance of the Antioch call would make this possible.

Late in August, a few days after her arrival, my friend Zella was married at the home of our college friend with whom I had been living. Four out of the five persons present were old Antiochians. The simple marriage service, by the Rev. Dr. Horatio Stebbins, ended this period of my life, for the next morning saw me on my eastward way with my friend Louesa and her two children.

A few evenings after Miss Reid's arrival we had the great

2

Two Years at Antioch College

Such ideas as I had about the duties of a matron of college women were naturally based on my recollections of what I had known of that office when I was a student in the same place. Unfortunately I did not know that while the same rules were nominally in operation, many of them were in reality a dead letter; as a consequence I frequently put myself in the wrong by requiring conformity to rules that were no longer enforced. The curious part of it was that in two or three cases I found myself held responsible for judgments made in imitation of decisions on similar cases by other officers of the college.

There were but few among the young women of the dormitory who were not self-governing, and therefore most were without need of supervision in matters of conduct. The exceptions made all the difference between an atmosphere of confidence and liberty and one of uneasiness and restraint. Under these conditions my relation to the office was, in my own opinion, a failure, during the first year, although my personal contact with most of the young women was pleasant. The second year, however, was without disagreeable experiences.

The two hours of teaching every day in the week seemed a light task compared with that of other years and the subjects were more to my taste: Caesar's *Commentaries*, English literature, physical geography, rhetoric, reading, two subjects each term. I had taught none of these before except the last. It was in the second or third term of the second year that I discovered English literature and rhetoric as my subjects. With Hale's *Longer English Poems* and the Clarendon Press edition of *The Merchant of Venice* I made my first acquaintance with my own capabilities, and their chances of expression by teaching; for I perceived then, though but imperfectly, that I had found my work. I felt the touch of mind on mind as my class of eleven young men and women began to show enthusiasm for the content of the pieces of literature they were studying, and when they began as well to carry that enthusiasm over into their own attempts at written expression.

One morning as I had called the class of eleven men and women to the blackboard to write a ten-minute composition exercise, before the usual lesson, the door opened, and in walked some visitors. One of them took a piece of chalk and wrote with the class. The exercise was a simple piece of invention in which certain words were to be used. Its purpose was to give the student freedom of expression in the use of his already organized knowledge and to make him independent and natural in such expression. The visitor wrote this exercise with the zeal of a boy who knew how, much to the delight of the class, which was at that time studying *The Merchant of Venice.* Although the little composition had nothing to do with the play, it was copied into the flyleaves of the textbooks by every classmate of the newly arrived distinguished student, Dr. Edward Everett Hale.

Mr. Hale was at this time president of the board of trustees of the college. I saw him often in those two years but more especially in commencement week when he presided at various meetings and at the annual dinner. It was a great privilege to see and hear him as toastmaster, and to hear the brilliant speeches made on such occasions by him and by Henry W. Bellows, Dr. Thos. Hill, some of the alumni of the college, and other distinguished visitors. On one visit Dr. Hale with some other members of the board of trustees called at my rooms in the dormitory. As I stood talking to him, one of them, who had been moving around the room said, "See there, Hale!" pointing to the end of the room where hung a framed motto done in Old English text, which read,

"Look up and not down.
Look out and not in.
Look forward and not back.
Lend a hand."

He smiled and nodded.

Dr. Hale once read at the college his story "In His Name," at another time "The Man without a Country." Some correspondence with Dr. Hale before and after this time was of much value to me as suggestive criticism. I owe much to him and his books in the way of help towards more simple expression than I could easily have achieved otherwise.

As so little of my time was occupied in teaching, I spent some of my spare hours in study under Dr. Edward Claypole, then professor of natural history in the college. He was an English university man, of very broad and liberal education, as strong in the humanities as in the sciences. A primary object in his teaching of the sciences was the training of his students to accurate use of the senses, particularly of sight. In the most painstaking way he lead everybody to the knowledge of how to see. Every object studied was reduced to terms of the pencil. Everything learned was drawn. The country for miles around was ransacked in all seasons for materials for study. No student, however dull, ever left Professor Claypole's classes without definite knowledge of some one kind of things.

Standing at the blackboard, Dr. Claypole began his lecture and illustrated each step in the description of structure by drawing. The student followed with copious notes and a copy of the outline drawing as it grew under the master's hand. At the end of the lesson each student had a completed drawing of the general anatomical structure of the subject, followed in detail with enthusiastic interest. The next step for the student was a discussion of the creature (oyster, snail, earthworm, or caterpillar), directly under the eyes of the teacher, with drawings made from the result. For myself the main thing was a revelation as to the manner of presenting any subject whatsoever. In a certain sense, the instruction under Dr. Claypole was an important era in my training as a teacher, as it led to deductions and experiments applicable to whatever teaching I did afterwards. More than that it seemed to throw into line and make available much of my already acquired knowledge, some of which was still a heterogeneous mass of unrelated facts. But for this work under Dr. Claypole, I should never have dared to undertake the teaching of natural history in the Oakland High School. This I attempted to do for seven years of the eleven spent in work there, which work, if it amounted to little in other practical knowledge, taught some students how to see.

During the winter of 1874-5 I went one night with some students and other college people to hear Bayard Taylor* at Xenia, nine miles away from the college. As I had read all of Taylor's travels and was acquainted with the look of his various portraits in which he seemed to be an alert, energetic man, I was unprepared for the fact that Mr. Taylor was at this time stout, slow, and heavy, without much movement and scarcely a gesture throughout the delivery of his written lecture. How much a curious obsession of drowsiness which I had to fight against during the whole hour had to do with the effect of the lecture, I know not; but, because of what I now know was bad ventilation, I was in a state too nearly bordering on stupor to remember even what the lecture was about. I can hardly say that I heard Bayard Taylor nor does it seem to me that I even saw him; he was so unlike the man I had met in his books.

During these two years spent as teacher in the preparatory school of Antioch College, I also frequently heard lectures by G. Stanley Hall, who was then professor of psychology and English literature, before going on to distinctions elsewhere.

My two summer vacations were occupied partly in the study of Tacitus and Plautus and partly in coaching a youth for West Point examinations. Although my second year's work was in the main satisfactory to myself, there were many reasons why it did not seem well to remain longer in a position which was not wholly congenial to me. I wanted the greater freedom of the public school, and felt that the burden of the hard climate of southern Ohio both in summer and in winter was more than I could bear much longer.

*Bayard Taylor (1825-1878) was an American man of letters, translator, traveler, and lecturer. [Ed. note]

3

A Teaching Philosophy

As soon as I had signified to the school board and superintendent of the Oakland schools my intention of returning they wrote me that they needed a teacher in the high school and that they had elected me to the position. However, when I arrived, in July, 1878, it was found that the number of classes had not been increased as was expected, so that no teacher would be needed in the high school till January.

A vacancy in the first assistant's position in the Lincoln School offered a convenient solution of the school board's problem of what to do with me for the time being. I went to work, then, on the hardest task I had had since my first experience in teaching: how to bring order out of a radical disorder produced by two entirely different bad methods of dealing with children. The first method had been that of a well-intentioned, amiable little lady who had no power of control whatever. She was a product of an eastern training school and had come with exceptional recommendations but had been a great disappointment to the school officers. The second method had been that of a teacher who used the police system excessively, and made many petty rules, which she tried to enforce by a terrible kind of patrol vigilence. The consequence was that when a new teacher came in to substitute for a few days, as the pupils then supposed me to be doing, a kind of chaotic confusion prevailed. I reported the condition of the class to the superintendent and said that I could do little for it intellectually until I had trained it to some sort of sense of moral responsibility. I added that I could not engage to keep the class along with the others of the same grade in the other grammar schools in their page-for-page work in arithmetic, history, and grammar if I took the time to teach the class how to behave and how to study. He answered, "Do as you think best. I trust the situation entirely to your judgment." I was thereby made responsible directly to the superintendent, not to the principal of the Lincoln School.

When it was understood by the class that I was to teach them for the term, there was a little abatement of the mob spirit but the mischief to the morals and manners of the class had gone too deep for immediate recovery. At the end of three weeks, by a process which involved a good deal of "Come, let us reason together," I had brought the children to a teachable frame of mind, and taught them that I was the absolute authority for them while they were in the classroom. Besides this I had taught them little else except how to study their history and reading lessons. The first of these they had been required to commit to memory, word for word; the second they had never known how to study.

It is perhaps enough to say that the work of the class, by the end of the term, was above the average in quality, though less in the number of pages covered. I had become so interested that I was sorry to leave in December. A small number of the class afterwards were pupils of mine in the high school.

Outside of my school work at this time there is nothing rememberable excepting that I saw Edwin Booth in *Hamlet*, *Macbeth*, and *Othello* supported by a stock company in the California Theatre. This was, in some senses, the real beginning of my acquaintance with Shakespeare. Somewhat earlier, also for the first time, I heard an oratorio and felt what great music, largely rendered, could make me feel then. It was Mendelssohn's *Elijah* given in San Francisco at the Taylor Street Tabernacle. An irrelevant memory connected with this concert is that of one of those unexplainable experiences which come like a shock of recollection. Though I had never seen the church or heard it described, its orchestra, as I entered, seemed as familiar as if I had seen them often. As a matter of fact, I had never before seen a church interior with such a floor arrangement and a pipe organ. I had seen a pipe organ once before at Salt Lake on my way to California. About this time also I heard the negro pianist, Blind Tom, who interested me psychologically as an example of an intellect whose expression had but one outlet, that of music.

On my return to Oakland from Ohio in August '76 I had the good fortune to be received, as a boarder, into the family of my friends, the Niswanders. Here I remained till after the arrival of my sister Adelaide a year later when we took apartments in the house of another friend and made a comfortable home for ourselves by light housekeeping, a manner of life which I followed thereafter while I lived in Oakland.

As the classes of these years came and went, new friends and new interests entered my life. I spent little time with other than students. I lived with young people, and met them where they lived. The subject of English literature gave me in the classroom many opportunities to touch upon thoughts and feelings natural to the eager and open-minded youth who studied with me. The recitations in the senior class in Shakespeare, or Wordsworth, or Lowell, were often open parliaments for the discussion of vital questions raised by the students themselves. It was thus, perhaps, that we came to know each other more intimately than is common to pupils and teachers.

In a very short time I saw that I had a new and delightful atmosphere in which to work and a class of students of a distinctly select quality. Many of those who came directly from the grammar schools were children of people who had been brought to Oakland by its educational advantages. Some were children of professional people who had themselves been educated in the east. Others still were children of prominent families in various parts of the state sent here because there were no high schools nearer. Altogether these conditions had given into the hands of the Oakland High School teachers what seemed to be almost perfect materials.

There were about two hundred and fifty students and six or seven teachers in the high school when I entered in January, 1877. At that time pupils were admitted on examination only. The preparation was better than that of later years because the curriculum was not encumbered by so many subjects as at the present time; and because the effect of political interference was as yet so slight that appointments to positions were still made on the basis of qualification. In general the principals of the various schools could ask for individual teachers whom they considered best equipped for the work they wanted done. The discipline of the

[273]

school was of the kind which makes one forget that there is such a thing as discipline; but there was no doubt as to the line of conduct to be maintained.

The high school faculty were mainly of eastern birth and education and all men and women of experience and of the true vocational calling. They loved their work and excelled in it. This gave them that confidence and tranquillity which made the sensible atmosphere of the school.

The high school curriculum in '77–'83 had very few electives, none, I think, after the course had been selected. The choice having been made of the classical, the modern language, or the scientific course, no further latitude was allowed, and students who entered the university stood examination on the subjects of their chosen course. The study of English was confined to the senior year except that the entering classes had a half year of composition, for which they were using a textbook when I entered the school.

The credit system was in use for marking both conduct and scholarship. It varied from the most elaborate to the simplest forms, but whatever the system used the moral effect was the same in the pupils; the physical effect on the teachers was an increase in the burden of clerical work.

The whole system of credit as used in schools of every kind had always seemed to me more or less mischievous. Until my connection with the Oakland schools I had never been obliged to use crediting of any kind, and the evils of it became apparent to me at once from the contrast with former schools. Here I saw the effect of putting an artificial motive into the place of the love of learning and that enthusiasm for it which leads on to a high ideal. Of course there were always a few students in each class who were but slightly affected by the numerical motive, and it may be that a few were lifted to their feet by this incentive; but in the main the loss was evident.

It may be considered that I exaggerate the effect of the credit system further when I say that it is my opinion that the present (1911) commercializing of college degrees is in part the outcome of the basal idea of the credit system. Formerly a college degree certified to a scholarship that had some breadth and solidity and gave promise of future achievement. Now while it may have such meaning, the higher college degrees often represent merely an additional amount of study in one line, valueless as a means of additional culture to the student, though it may have a technical value to be made use of in some work of the student's director. For example, a student who spends the greater part of his work for a master's degree on a study of Terence's meters, scanning every line and marking every foot to decide whether the meter depends more on quantity than on accent, does not get any very great addition to his scholarship though he may get a master's degree for his dissertation. Nor can the knowledge so acquired be of much use to anybody excepting to the person who is writing a commentary of some kind and wishes to make a statement about Terence's meters. Nor does the student who spends the time of his master's year study gain much by counting the *ut* clauses in Caesar's *Commentaries* to find out how many times the indicative is used instead of the subjunctive.

But this is not all: the degree of Doctor of Philosophy once meant so much that it was not considered attainable by the average man. Now it is considered a necessary appendage to the name of anybody who wishes to teach in college, and it may, or it may not, signify scholarship of any breadth, but it has its value in gaining a teacher's position.

My subjects were English and zoology. I had also temporarily a small class in Latin, made up of students who had fallen behind their grade and failed in examinations. I may say in passing that these five boys made up their deficiencies and reentered their class before the term's end. Among them was a boy who afterwards became a distinguished professor of psychology and later president of a college.

So far as I knew, there had not been much instruction in zoology before 1877, at least there was no tradition of method or kind of work to be done. I could hear of no field work or interest in making collections growing out of this kind of study, excepting one collection of shells. This was of such proportions and quality as to deserve mention here. It had been begun by a boy in one of the earliest classes of the high school, whose father, a carpenter, had become interested through his son's interest. After the temporary enthusiasm of the son had ceased, the father carried on the study and collecting in his lecture hours until he had brought together the best collection of marine and land shells then on this coast.

The course in zoology, as I gave it, came in the second half-year. After a somewhat condensed outline of the animal kingdom, with clearly defined differences in general structure, I passed on to a somewhat specialized study of one class of animals. Or, specializing still more closely, we spent our time studying insects, or spiders, or shellfish. The work done by the pupils gave them training, first in notetaking and careful copying, illustrating as they went along with their own firsthand drawings from the objects of study, and of copies of my illustrative drawings at the blackboard; second, in written reports of field work in which a half hour's practice a day was required in their own gardens, or in the fields and woods adjacent to town; third, in making a collection of fifty or more specimens, classified and mounted. As we had no laboratory and no microscopes except small magnifying glasses our work in dissection was limited to a single period once a week. The report of the dissection was made by drawings. We used no textbook.

Occasionally I asked for reports of observation of special organs of animals, as, for instance, the organs of locomotion. "How do all the animals that you have seen move about?" "Draw what you see, legs, feet, wings." The result was a surprising series of pictures of all kinds of feet, wings, and fins. Another observation lesson of this kind called attention to the eyes of animals. A few curious confessions, frankly made, after these lessons showed how little the habit of observation had turned toward natural objects. One bright girl, for example, said, confidentially, "Do you know I never knew before that a cow's foot was cleft. When I saw this which I drew from, I though it a deformity." The city markets offered a good deal of material for this kind of work. Many pupils in the classes below, becoming interested, made collections during their summer vacation, thus anticipating the next term's work.

At this time insect pests were almost unknown in California orchards and gardens; at least there was not as yet any commerical interest in the history of insect life, and as many of the children knew nothing about insects except as something to be afraid of or disgusted with, it happened that not a few found the compulsory course somewhat distasteful at first; but most of them became interested before the term's end to at least such a degree as to be to their advantage in learning the art of seeing. Many made large and well mounted collections of beetles. A few made at least some pretty collections of shells.

I am speaking now of the years between 1877 and 1883. A few years later, after I had left the school for a time, I had two calls from young men who had taken the course in entomology merely in a half-hearted way because they could see no commercial value in it. They came to me for information about books on insects which would help them to care properly for vineyards and orchards of which they had come into possession. One said, "There are big striped bugs in my vineyard and there are scale insects in my orchard and I don't know what to do and I don't know where to find out what to do." "Well," I said, "if you look in the back of your zoology notebook you will find that I have given you a list of the latest textbooks and the government publications on the subject. Besides, you should know from some of the things I have told you"—"Oh, but you see I took no interest in those things then and I did not know enough to be interested in subjects which I could not see affected the pocket." The next year I received a publication from the State Agricultural Department containing a lecture on scale insects by this youth and a somewhat prideful letter telling me he had read a paper before an institute in the northern part of the state.

In one of the earlier terms of this period a retired physician, whose two sons were in my classes and enthusiastic collectors of beetles, said to me one day as we walked along the street toward the schoolhouse, "What's the use of all this about bugs? Why don't you teach something about plants?—how to know, for instance, the difference between young oats and wheat, or something about the rocks?" added he, striking with his cane a piece of blue trap, the only kind of rock within sight and used for macadamizing the streets.

"I have to leave the wheat and the rocks to the teachers of botany and geology," I said. "You may hear something from the bugs if you have a farm."

Some weeks later I met the good doctor again. "A ho," he said, "I found out about the bugs. I went to visit my young apple orchard, after a windstorm and found half the trees broken off just below the first branches. They had been girdled under the bark by a beetle."

Among the students in one of my zoology classes of 18___ was a young girl of unusual gifts of intellect and character, who did all of her school work with the intelligence of purpose. She took hold of every subject as she came to it with the enthusiasm of a scholar. Before the end of her high school course I found that she had been teaching each branch of her study to an invalid brother as she went along. He had read her notebooks and among others her zoology notes and had thus become interested in spiders, or perhaps I had better say, he had begun to notice the spiders on the cypress hedge in the garden where he was taken in his chair on fine mornings.

For several years, indeed to the end of his short life at the age of twenty-four, this heroic boy, John Curtis, chained to his chair by almost utter helplessness, and able to use his hands only, found absorbing interest and occupation in the study of the only living creatures which he could observe in their own haunts. By a simple device of rolling up a little square of wire netting he furnished cage material to friends who offered to collect specimens. In this way he had brought to him some new species. By his observation and drawings he sometimes found that spiders described as three different species were really one, in several stages of growth. Some specimens he studied for several years in the larger cages made for the purpose and kept on his desk. His drawings were exquisitely done in colors.

After I left the high school in '83 the subject of zoology was dropped from the curriculum for a few years.

My English classes were a class in composition of the second half-year and a senior class in literature. The composition class had already been provided with a textbook. This I laid aside and used only for reference. At the first lesson I asked how many liked composition. One hand in a class of forty went up. "Why?" Nobody could tell me. The same question asked at the end of a month brought up almost all the hands. This change came about through the use of certain simple exercises which created in the pupils a desire for expressing their already organized knowledge. Some years later I put the results of my experience in teaching this subject into the form of a small book of composition exercises. Such success as I had in teaching composition came from the fact that I liked to teach it, and that I had in earlier years worked out plans for making this part of a child's education desirable to him, through making it possible and therefore agreeable.

As it is not possible to tell how one teaches a lesson in English literature so as to be of much use to other teachers, it does not seem worthwhile to attempt it here. Briefly and in general, my own plan was to try to put the pupil in possession of the content of a piece of English by such means as seemed best to apply to his particular case. In order to do this for the many kinds of minds in the class, various ways of awakening interest had to be found. To this end I spent much time and thought over how to make them think for themselves about whatever the subject matter was as a whole, and in parts; to make them say why they had chosen this or that passage for memorizing and these or those words or thoughts or descriptions, for examples of what they liked.

In every class, however, I made a special point of requiring memorized passages selected by the pupils for themselves. The power to see what was a detachable passage worth learning was not acquired at once but came by careful training to that end. As a result of this kind of work a large part of every class was able, for instance, to place at once any significant speech in *The Merchant of Venice*, or other Shakespearean play studied; to tell who said it, to whom, in what connection, and with what effect. Every memorized passage was selected for a reason in the pupil's own mind, which reason was in most cases come by through the lessons he had had in this exercise. He had been taught various reasons why a given passage might be liked: because of the thought, or sentiment, or because of a beautiful word or phrase, of a new word which he wished to remember, of the rhythm or the rhyme, or because it was the first or last part of a great poem, or because it contained a remarkable figure, or a beautiful description, or some remote suggestion to himself.

Throughout these seven years I made an attempt to control the outside reading of pupils by introducing them to various works of fiction, poetry, and biography, thus requiring a good deal of collateral reading laid out for each of them personally. In the Monday lesson the pupil gave an oral account of his reading for the past week in the works of the author assigned to him, with his impressions of what he had read. These oral reports awakened interest in others who in their turn sought out the books and read them. Thus the taste for what was childish or worthless was supplanted by a permanent liking for real books, as I had reason to know.

I may add here, too, the fact that I contrived to have the collateral reading selected, almost entirely, from American authors. For I believed then, as I believe now, that the study of literature, like geography and charity, should begin at home, because access to literature comes more easily by way of books containing one's own types of thought and one's own pictures of life and external nature.

Apropos of the kind of English teaching that dwells on technicalities rather than on subject matter I may give the following examples. In the late nineties, when I was examining entering freshmen in Stanford University, I picked up a textbook brought by a San Francisco high school boy for cramming to the last minute. The book opened at Shelley's "Euganean Hills," along the margin of which were written "70 synecdoches, 30 metonymies," and the like. It was the practice in the class from which this boy came to work out and count up the number of rhetorical figures of each kind in every poem studied. And, what seems beyond itself, it was necessary to make these numbers check up with what had been previously worked out by the teacher. One boy was heard to say to another, "Say, I'm great on metonymies, but I'm not much on pathos. If you'll give me twenty of your pathoses I'll give you twenty of my metonymies." Is it any wonder that many students enter the university with a positive dislike for the study of English and a corresponding ignorance of books and inability to express themselves?

4

Students and Instruction

In no other school known to me was the interest of the teachers so constantly exercised by the appearance of new types, as in Oakland High School. Yet, as I consider the first six years of my work there, I find that the larger part of these were Californians born or reared and, with very few exceptions, American, eastern or southern, in origin. But among the few exceptions were some of the strongest and highest types of intellectuality. Considering further the difference between these high school children and those of the same grade in the schools in the middle west with which I had been connected, I do not find that the intellectual development was of any higher average grade or any further advanced on account of climatic or other differences.

In the earliest years of my work in the high school I had already begun to feel that an important part of any teacher's work must always be, at least in her own mind, the attempt to bring forward the dull, commonplace, or uninteresting pupil. I had dimly felt before that it was never even right to say that this girl or boy was dull or stupid. It might be so, but there were many chances that the seeming inferiority was underdevelopment. In the course of a few year's study I found that this was true in most cases, so that I ceased myself to think, even in perplexing cases, that a given pupil was hopelessly stupid or dull past the point of awakening. I observed that among the more evident causes of what was accounted stupidity by others were too rapid growth, indifferent health, inhibitive discouragement in some branch of study, too many years of schoolroom confinement, and adolescence. I had known cases which seemed to be atttributable to nothing but poor inheritance.

One of the most interesting examples that came under my observation was a girl who may be called Hilda. I was not her class teacher though she was a member of my English class in her entering term. My attention was called to her in the very first recitation in the prescribed poem, "Evangeline." She happened to be called on to read first after the preliminaries of the lesson. She read the first few lines in a way that showed she had not a glimmering of the meaning of the simple lines. But as it turned out her reading was very little worse than that of the class as a whole.

Hilda was perhaps fifteen years old and not undersized. Her forehead was noticeably low and somewhat narrow, though her head was high above the ears; her hair was ill kept and of a rusty brown; her complexion coarse and greasy; her clothes were poorly made and of material badly chosen as to quality and color; her hands were noticeably large, and everything seemed to be wrong about her makeup excepting a smiling countenance, good teeth, and a power of attention that was absolute. She never took her eyes for one moment from the face of the teacher or from that of the pupil who was reciting and in those small but intent gray eyes was the promise of something that all the other features contradicted. She did not make any very marked advance in English during the first half of the term but came to show me her report card at the end of the second month with 96 percent in mathematics.

I kept some track of Hilda for two or three years after she passed from my recitation room and saw her gradually improve in manner, expression, and dress. She continued to excell in mathematics and advanced in other branches to something more than an average intelligence. The last I knew of her she was looking forward to preparation for a teacher's certificate. Some credit should be given to one of her class teachers for hints upon dress and other matters. I may add that this girl was motherless from her early childhood and had little help from her surroundings.

An interesting group of young people, as I place them in my own mind now, was made up of boys and girls who came from the mountains or other country districts. It must be understood that these did not appear at one time in the high school but that they are thus grouped for convenience. One, whom I shall call Geoffrey, was a tall, blond youth of fifteen, well brought up, alert-minded, deft-handed, and of good general control, physical and mental. I had early in my acquaintance two or three accidental opportunities of observing that he was very fond of his mother and unreservedly affectionate in his behavior toward her. He was emotional but had himself well in hand for so young a boy. He was soon observed to be a leader among the boys of his class and was very greatly admired by them and younger boys. He led in scholarship and began rather early to show signs of a judicial temper. He weighed people and things and formed judgments concerning them as if consciously doing so to acquire the habit. His subsequent career at the university, in the law school, in legal practice, and as a husband and father fully confirmed this promise. He was always the object of respect and admiration in his fellows and through this he had, and still has, an extraordinary personal influence.

Another of this group of country boys, whose name may have been Peter, was evidently a boy who had more than a boy's share of responsibilities at home and other limiting conditions to contend with. He was a little under medium height for his age, very quiet in manner, and agreeable though inconspicuous in facial expression. He lived at home at a distance which made daily attendance difficult and seemed very often weary as if driven by circumstances, but he was always in his place and always prepared in his lessons.

Very soon after his entrance to the school he became one of a group of boys who were evidently attracted to him by his lovable qualities and whose friendship with him continued throughout the three-years' course. Among so many pupils such a boy was little noticed by the various teachers for some time; but as term after term passed by one heard teachers remarking how greatly Peter had improved and how thoroughly trustworthy he was. At such times too one might hear of his achievement in the school debating club. In the last term of his senior year we suddenly became aware that Peter was showing the effect of the long strain on his health and strength and, with some feeling of blame to ourselves that we had not noticed earlier, we took steps to make conditions easier so that he finished without breaking down.

More than this, I remember with what genuine pleasure both the faculty and the members of his class received the announcement that to Peter was awarded the gold medal offered that year by the president of the school board to the student who should have shown the greatest improvement in all respects during the three-years' course. And I cannot forget with what modesty and manliness the surprised boy arose in his place after the president's presentation speech and said with a smile, "If there has been the greatest improvement it is because there was greatest room for it."

I may class with these another boy of very different make-up and temperament whose situation in life was somewhat similar though of less narrow conditions. In order to come to school at all he had to be at home nights to run his widowed mother's farm. He rode several miles on horseback every morning to reach a suburban horse car line that would bring him near the school. But as he was of exceptional strength and sound health this hardship left no mark on him. His work in school was uniformly good and he had a certain amount of dynamic force that carried with it a kind of influence difficult to describe. Both boys and girls admired his power but somehow the best stood aloof from his influence. I knew very little about his career subsequent to his university life excepting that he became a successful lawyer.

So far as moral characteristics of these and all other boys of the high school were concerned, I observed that what they showed themselves to be in these formative years that they continued to be in the university and afterwards. In a large number of cases, especially observed, I remember no exception to this but two or three who were called lazy. This, however, was on account of their too rapid growth and a consequent inability to be mentally active. Their growth once attained, they fell to work with vigor.

When I sit, in imagination, on the schoolroom platform, I see, crowding to their places at their own special desks, one and another vividly remembered face. A strongly built, broad-shouldered, black-haired mountain boy with a practical, unimaginative mind excepting in mathematics comes first. His direct gaze, impatience with what he considered to be false or useless, and his rather autocratic small class of which he was a member. A slender, beautiful brunette girl, at another desk in another year, sits over her books or rises to recite with that kind of gentle dignity which shows self-possession and a respect for one's own powers without lack of modesty. Whether one admired her more for these qualities than for her beauty it would be hard to say. The last time I saw this girl, after ten years in Japan as the wife of a missionary, she had added much to her early charm.

At this moment I see another slender girl with brown hair and delicate features so beautifully moulded as to express a harmony of nature that made itself felt in her movements, her pleasant laughter, and her invariable good nature. Many times since I have had the opportunity of observing that this lovely harmony of character pervaded and ruled in her home and renewed itself in her children.

Now comes before me a youth, Boston-born but Californian in school training, showing qualities of a kind not found in any other who came under my care. He had evidently inherited, as well as acquired by the early training of a refined and cultivated mother, certain characteristics that set him apart as unusual at least in the minds of those who taught him. His intellectual grasp was quick and firm. He was greatly admired by his boy classmates.

Unfortunately, as it seemed at the time, he was obliged to leave school and go into business; but, determined to have an education, he made the most of every interval by reading and study of literature, science, and modern languages. By the time he was twenty, he was better educated than many a college man. Although as a boy he had not seemed to be an artistic temperament, the outcome of his study in more than one direction appeared to indicate that the bent of his mind was artistic. But the truth is that it was scientific rather, and that when circumstances brought him into contact with art from the business side his approach was scientific and gave him an orderly knowledge and appreciation of certain art forms to such a degree as to make him an acknowledged authority. This must be understood, however, to imply that he had not an essentially esthetic mind.

Among other observations made in the course of my high school work none interested me more than the study of family traits as they appeared in successvie or contemporaneous members of the same families. In the earlier years of my teaching in an old and settled community I had unavoidably acquired facts which led to definite conclusions and, although I had not always generalized from this knowledge, it now formed the basis of some inevitable educations.

I may give place here to one or two of these studies of family traits: I had, at nearly the same time, in my various classes, eight children who were cousins and the sons and daughters of three sisters of Irish birth and education. The three sisters, I may add, with their mother and her three other daughters, had come to California in earlier times. Four of these eight children, two boys and two girls, belonged to one family; two boys and one girl to a second and one girl to the third. All of these children had been thoroughly trained at home to habits of obedience and responsibility. They were all keen-minded, quick-witted, and studious. Two of them, whom I had most opportunity of observing, excelled in power of application. They could learn a given lesson in much less time than their classmates because of this power.

I made a special study of these two lads to find out what, beside their unusual intellectual gifts, gave them the first rank as students in all their classes in every subject. When I expressed to their mother my fear that they were overworking, she said they did no study at home and that, so long as they played so much out of doors, ate so much beefsteak and bread and butter, and slept so soundly she thought there was little danger, although they were much younger than the average of their classmates. But clearly their advantage lay in the fact that they were the children of women of intellect and culture. All the boys of this family connection are now men of distinction in their several professions and at least three of them are benefactors of their day.

Another family of entirely different origin is represented in my experience by five of its nine members, all children of the same father and mother, the one of German and the other of Latin-European birth. Through a somewhat intimate acquaintance with the family I had numerous chances, extending over a long period of years, of studying them all. Though they differed greatly in talent as to kind, they all excelled in one or more directions: language, mathematics, music, histrionics, handicraft; in short, in any means of expression they saw fit to choose, they showed unusual gifts.

Most of these children read at a very early age. Several of them read Dickens and Scott at seven. The youngest child, Alex, taught himself to read between the ages of three and four. He would have learned earlier except for discouragement put into his way by the family on account of his precocity. He read *Hamlet* at five. At seven he was reading fiction, history, physiology, and zoology; a little later he was writing original stories, teaching himself to play on the guitar, for which he transposed songs that he might sing them himself. He might easily have entered the high school at ten if it had been thought wise to send him. He was taught at home until he was ten and was allowed to enter the high school at twelve with the understanding that he was to take four years for the three-years' course. This he did, in a sense, but it was found that he was quietly taking other studies than those prescribed for him and coming up to ask for examination with the classes at the term's end.

It was not an uncommon sight to see this child surrounded, before school hours, by a group of young men who had failed to do the difficult problems given in addition to textbook work, and were asking help of this boy who was doing the work outside the class for his own satisfaction. While this child was directly under my tuition I had many misgivings as to his chances of growing up, as he lacked in physical vigor, but contrary to expectation he had improved in health so that he seemed at sixteen, when he entered the university, to have more than a chance of a vigorous manhood. After distinguishing himself in mathematics and philosophy in both of which he did brilliant original work, he was graduated at the age of twenty without any disadvantage to his health. After several years of advanced study he was called to a professorship in an eastern college.

Many years of observation of ordinary children and precocious children have led me to the opinion that no amount of careful early training could make out of the ordinary boy what Alex made of himself by his own efforts in his early years. Alex, like every other precocious child I have observed, lost much that belongs to childhood in that he was without playmates. Boys of his own age thought him queer because he wanted to play games that they didn't understand. Older boys, naturally, would not play with a little child, and he himself did not wish to play with younger children.

This lack of adjustment continued to a greater or less degree through the high school but began to be modified by the time he entered the university. Through some unusual power of his own he was able to complete the adjustment by the time he entered into active life, so that he escaped eccentricity. Other cases I have known of precocious children whose precocity was exploited and encouraged by injudicious parents. They failed of adjustment to conditions of life around them and so disappointed their friends and themselves. The truth is, children at birth are differently endowed and this difference must be recognized in their training, which platitude would not be set down here except for the now common contention to the contrary.

Although there were children from Roman Catholic and Jewish families in the high school no objections were made to the simple religious exercises held in the assembly every morning. The reading of a selection from the Bible, the singing of a hymn, and the recitation of the Lord's Prayer made the ordinary form followed in these exercises. There was no formal instruction in morals, except that at one time teachers were expected to lecture to their own classes on such topics as the care of the health, behavior in public places, manners and language, and use of tobacco and alcohol.

But the more important part of the instruction in these matters was done at other times than in the hours set for formal lessons. The apt word spoken privately to the individual boy or girl at the right moment, and sometimes even the mere glance or gesture or expression of surprise or other emotion on the part of the teacher did more than pages of lecture. The best moral and religious instruction possible in the schoolroom is that which is given at the moment of contact with a new thought suddenly made inadvertantly in the course of a lesson either by teacher or pupil. As in a flash the teacher sees the new idea awakening, sees the source from which it came, and meets it with a word which gives it significance. Often in preparation for the lesson the teacher finds many a door ready to open to her touch and many a way to work out problems which come to her from every desk in the class before her.

Since religion does not consist in the knowing of a body of doctrine or a set of dogmas but in the realizing of the soul's relation

[288]

to God and to humanity, there is no reason in the nature of things why instruction in religion should not be a part, and an important part, of public school training. Indeed it seems to me that before many of the wrongs which now exist can be righted the public schools must undertake this responsibility. And if this should ever be so, those who train teachers will be obliged to discriminate between those who have and those who have not that larger life which is expressed in terms of what we mean by the word religion.

There is no doubt that the teacher of English literature has more material at her command for use in teaching religion and morals than the teacher of any other branch. This is, of course, because literature is life and contains all the recorded experiences of the human soul: its hope, fears, triumphs, failures, ambitions, and above all its deals and aspirations.

When by the leading of one who has herself been led by the ideals therein expressed, real books become a part of the child's possessions, he has been instructed, thereby, in religion and morals. All the other parts of the content of these books have been added in the process. This does not mean, necessarily, that he could pass an examination in the technical details of form, and other mechanical matters, now so much insisted upon as often to lose sight of the thing of most value; but it does mean that he has a permanent acquisition of permanent values of life, which things do not come through drill in rhetorical figures, balanced or loose sentences, "end-stopped" lines, feminine endings, or etymologies. Nor do they come by forcing an interpretation on some isolated thought in order to preach through it or by means of it. When the moral or religious idea is obvious, it had best be left to make its own way, for hardly a worse mistake can be made than to try to force attention to the sense of what cannot be mistaken by the average intelligence. In other words, let the preaching do itself.

Among the opportunities of influencing students none were more effective than private conferences, especially those sought by the students themselves. Everything personal, grievances against other teachers, difficulties with studies, misunderstandings connected with home life, ambitions, religious doubts, and even love affairs were brought to me, sometimes after school in the schoolroom, often as we walked home, and not infrequently in my own rooms at

[289]

home. Now and then a mere desk interview over a lesson question prolonged itself into something of a personal nature. Sometimes students used their composition exercises or notes appended thereto as means of personal communication. These latter were answered either by a personal interview or on the returned exercise as the case demanded. Of course I would not discuss a grievance against another teacher but usually succeeded in persuading the aggrieved boy or girl to go at once to the teacher concerned and talk it over frankly. This nearly always resulted in a better understanding on the part of each.

Sometimes pitiful revelations came to light about the lack of sympathy or wisdom exercised by parents in dealing with their children. When I sometimes asked of a girl, "Why don't you tell this to your mother?" she would say, "Oh, I wouldn't tell my mother that for anything." More than once when I have asked the same question of a boy with respect to telling his father, he would say, "My father would kill me if he knew that." One such boy had been going, without his father's knowledge, to a billiard saloon where there was drinking and had got into debt at the billiard table.

The graduating essay in the earlier years of the high school was a formidable undertaking—especially to the teacher. While the classes were still small every pupil was expected to read an essay or deliver an oration which must be original so far as its composition was concerned. As may be supposed there were but few, if any, at this time who had had training enough in the lower grades to know how to use their own already organized knowledge in independent expression. Tradition and observation of other schools had led them to suppose that they must write something very wise and profound. Occasionally one or two had ideas so new under the sun that they expected to reform the world.

When the graduating paper had been written and submitted to the various teachers to whom they were assigned, it was generally found that two or three or more were impossible in subject, treatment, and quality. These cases were reported to the principal with the suggestion that the writers had better be excused from taking part. "Oh, they will have to read something. Their folks are all coming to see them graduate." To drag by a painful series of questions from the docile victim some ideas that could be put together consecutively was the difficult task of the teacher. A girl who thought she wanted to write on, "Keep Step to the Music of the Union" and who had not the vaguest idea of what that meant or what she wanted to say about it, was led by long-continued questioning to bring into written shape the simple experiences of a horseback ride in the spring in the country surrounding her home. Paragraph by paragraph I made her recall and evolve the bare facts of that experience and set them down in readable form.

I give this as an example of that period of high school history. Later, when the classes were larger, a place in the graduation exercises was made a matter of percentage, so that not more than one third of the class took part. And, later still, much to the relief of everybody concerned, the essay and oration were abolished and graduating exercises took the form which they now have.

The weekly rhetorical exercises held on Friday afternoons in each class consisted of compositions, recitation of memorized selections, and talks on subjects chosen by the pupils out of their own experience. The talks were sometimes illustrated by drawings at the board or by specimens of their own handiwork. Occasionally there were crude attempts at elocutionary display of kinds which I discouraged in my class. For these were the days in which it was the fashion to take "elocution lessons" and a number of students were learning to recite highly colored dramatic compositions after the pattern set by artificially trained teachers. To avoid too great an infliction of this kind of entertainment I had finally to make a list of poems which could not be recited in my class, among which were "Curfew Shall Not Ring Tonight," "Bernardo del Carpio," "Maclane's Child," and several other which lent themselves to similar aritificial interpretation. But usually good taste was shown in the selections and advice was asked for in cases of doubt. Perhaps the most interesting part of these exercises were the original talks. I recall one afternoon in which a fifteen-year-old boy rose and said, "I'm going to tell you about when I received the Emperor of Japan at the University of _____ of which my father was the president." He then explained how he, a boy of thirteen, his father's oldest son, had, according to Japanese etiquette, to receive the Emperor in the place of his father, who was ill. Another boy who had been to school at Brighton gave an account of his visit to the tower of London.

The only other special lessons given in this period of the high school were music and drawing, both of which had been taught in the grammar and primary grades for some years. Judging from the results of the work in both, the teaching had been excellent; for there were many whose natural talent showed evidences of good instruction. The singing was remarkably good and, according to visitors from Boston on their way to Japan to introduce Boston singing books into the schools of that kingdom, surpassed anything done in the Boston schools at that time. About three hundred pupils, made up of all the high school grades, sang the words of new choruses at sight under the direction of the teacher.

5

Thoughts and Memories

Among the memorable events connected with my high school life of this period was the reception given to General Ulysses S. Grant by the Oakland School Department on his return from his trip around the world in September 1879. The preparations for the reception had been admirably managed by Superintendent Campbell, who massed all the children on bleachers on the sidewalks of Fourteenth St. between Clay and Broadway. A carriage drawn by four white horses decorated by festoons of flowers entered Fourteenth Street from Clay. As soon as the two men who occupied the carriage came in view the children rose and waved their bouquets of flowers.

The carriage moved slowly up one side to Broadway and back on the other side to Clay. It stopped and the two men alighted and walking, bare-headed, General Grant leaning on the left arm of Charles Fox, president of the school board, passed up the street near the children, who after untying their bouquets scattered the loose flowers before the feet of the two so that they literally walked on flowers. The two men were so close that we could see perfectly the expression of the face so familiar to us from prints in school histories and the magazines. The General's close-cropped gray head, slightly bowed as he walked, the pleased expression of his eyes, the short sturdy figure, plainly dressed, had in them something pathetic or otherwise so appealing that tears stood in the eyes of many as the old hero moved along up one side and down the other back to the carriage. He is reported to have said that nothing in all that happened after he landed in San Francisco pleased him so much as this reception by the Oakland school children.

After a little more than seven years of work in the Oakland schools I found myself again in a state of nervous exhaustion. The work had grown increasingly heavy year after year so that the short vacations failed to restore my strength before it was time to begin again. Having thus to draw upon my reserve of health I came to a place where it was necessary to halt. With my sister Adelaide's emphatic help I decided to resign and go back to Ohio. This I did in September, 1883, leaving behind me the school and the friends and the country I loved not only without regret or emotion of any kind but as if escaping from some inevitable threatening fate. I was too weary to think or to feel except that I was to be released from some overburden that I could no longer bear. However, after two or three days rest there came to me as I journeyed eastward out on the Nevada desert, a feeling of intense grief at the thought of all I had left behind me and the friends I might never see again. I had no plans for the future excepting the intention of staying in Ohio and a determination to rest for at least a year.

My father, my two sisters, Laura and Caroline, and my brother were living in Yellow Springs, Ohio. The first event of the year after our arrival was the marriage in October of my sister Caroline. The autumn and winter went by quietly and without incident, until January when we had news of the death of our friend Lucy Emma Temple, my colleague in the high school and our intimate house neighbor. Nothing more of especial note broke the even passage of time excepting a visit to my friends, Major and Mrs. W. L. Shaw who were then superintendents of the Soldiers' and Sailors' Orphans' Home at Xenia, Ohio. What I had already seen of Major Shaw's work as teacher and superintendent of schools hardly prepared me for what I saw of his management of this great institution. No less admirable was Mrs. Shaw's handling of her part of the work. Omitting much detail that would really be of interest to teachers and other trainers of the young, I must content myself with giving the vital points of my observations on the education of these orphaned and half-orphaned children. When they left the institution at the age of sixteen they were possessed of three essentials of successful living: a thorough grammar school education, the elements and practice of a good trade, and, best of all, "habits of industry," to quote Major Shaw. This had been accomplished in the time by requiring the children from twelve to sixteen to spend but half a day in school and the other half day working at their trades. All were early trained to responsibility in the details of their daily life, and all were aware of the presence and interest of the heads of the institution.

Some correspondence with Professor Sill on my projected composition book I remember with satisfaction. Some letters from California friends, a little reading, a little housework, a little visiting of neighbors, and a good deal of comfortable companionship with my own people made up the sum total of my experiences.

Perhaps I need to mention here also that the new president of Antioch College, having interested himself in looking up the records of students who had nearly finished their courses but had not taken their degrees, offered to give them that opportunity. I was one among these and without working directly in all the lines of the curriculum I had done much more than was required. I, therefore, on this invitation joined the number of those who were to take degrees in 1885, and then received my belated degree of Bachelor of Arts. This was of little moment to me as then comparatively little importance was attached to the possession of a degree in public school work. And such reputation as I had as a teacher was made without literary appendix.

An unusually hard winter and a heavy cold in February made it unadvisable for me to spend another winter in the climate of southwestern Ohio. Accordingly I decided to return to California, and again in August, with a greater wrench than I had yet felt at separation, I left my family, friends, and home. Such an experience as this has frequently made me question whether after all it is worthwhile to bring upon oneself separations which are not inevitable. But this is a world problem as old as family life.

Among the minor recollections of this year, 1883-4, is that of a mental phenomenon which, for want of a better name, I have called "processions." It appeared to be a symptom of the period of convalescence from an extreme case of nervous breakdown and was of very frequent occurrence during the earlier months after my return home.

As soon as I had settled myself in bed at night, and while yet awake, or immediately after waking in the morning, there seemed to pass before me, from right to left, long processions of people who turned smiling faces toward me as soon as they came opposite. It was as if I were looking at passing crowds near enough to see their expression. They seemed to be no larger than the heads and shoulders of cabinet photographs and were all dressed in bright colors, cherry red, light blue, and crocus yellow, all made still brighter by the sunshine which poured down upon them from an unseen sky. The same face never appeared twice, nor did I ever recognize anyone that I had known in real life. I remember but one, a round, ruddy face of a smiling blue-eyed man whose broad-brimmed light hat was pushed back so as to make a sort of halo around his head.

I was subject to these visions at intervals for three or four years. As my health improved they disappeared, to return again a few years later under similar conditions.

Although I enjoyed these visionary friends I had no power of calling them up and they were gone in a flash if I made the slightest movement.

Why did they pass from right to left? Why were they always dressed in the three primary colors and always smiling? Why were they all the faces of strangers and never of anyone that I had ever seen? Why did they disappear at the slightest movement on my part? I must leave these questions to the psychologist. But I was as much interested in studying these phenomena as if they had been the experiences of someone else.

My plans for work on my return to California did not consider teaching in the public schools, for as yet I thought of such work with an aversion too strong to be set aside. Unexpectedly enough however, and without any seeking of my own, I found myself in the Sacramento High School in December. The high schools had but very recently been connected with the State University in a preparatory relation, and this school had not yet been accredited for entrance without examination. I was called to the position to put the English Department into line with the requirements to this end. After three month's work in this small but interesting school I resigned in favor of a former pupil of mine who was well equipped for the work. The pleasantest part of my life here was in the classroom. The climate was not suited to the condition of a nervous convalescent and I made no acquaintances that added much in the way of cheerfulness to what was really a lonely period of my life.

I had been urged by a number of my former Oakland pupils to take private classes in English literature. Some of these were in the university but wanted additional work in studies already begun with me in the high school. I therefore opened classes in literary study and soon found my time very pleasantly and profitably occupied. Classes of young women in Shakespeare, in 19th-century prose and poetry, in Milton and Wordsworth, and in American literature, two or three pupils in Latin, and several in rhetoric and grammar brought me into contact with many of my old pupils and a number of new ones of varied stages of mental growth. Two or three classes were made up of young society women the greater part of whom took but a transient interest in study; but I am glad to remember that to two others of these came an awakening that meant for them, though they themselves did not then know it, a soul-saving process. In another class were several business young men and women whom I met on Monday nights for three years and with whom I enjoyed explorations into the fields of poetry. Public school teachers, elocution teachers who could not read and wished to learn, two or three whose opportunities had been very limited, a young newspaper man or two, were among these who gave interest and variety to private tutoring.

Four years of this work gave me intervals of leisure for rest and such recreation as I had not been able to take during my life in the public schools. I went occasionally to San Francisco to see Shakespearian drama. I belonged for the first time in my life to a Shakespeare Club. I went to lectures and concerts, regularly to church and Sunday school. I visited and received visitors, and in many ways found life fuller than when its experiences were bounded almost exclusively by professional demands.

In 1880, by change of residence and church connection I came under the intellectual and religious influence of John Kimball McLean, the pastor of the First Congregational Church. Dr. McLean was then in the prime of life, and, to quote one of his admiring young men followers, "easily the first citizen of Oakland," which estimate may serve to show the breadth of his interests outside of his parish people. For he was counselor and friend to all sorts and conditions of men of all or no sorts of religious convictions. It was this, perhaps, that gave him the power evident in all his relations to his church as well as to the public. His style of preaching was simple and direct from man to man without the interposition of writing. He was a great teacher, not only in the generally accepted sense of that word but literally.

It was my good fortune to be often included in the smaller circle of those who came in contact with the family life of the McLean's. It was at these times that I saw and felt the beauty of life as illustrated in a perfect companionship of father, mother, and child. It was at these times too that I came to know how near a man can come to God in his office as priestly head of his family, on his knees at morning prayer, for I had never known that there could be such intimate communing with God.

In one of the earlier summers of this time I took a position as governess in a family who spent the months of the long vacation and on till late in September in the Sierras in a mining camp. Here for the first time I experienced the delights of mountain life in the pine woods. Among the ridges of the American River region are long stretches of unbroken forests of sugar-pine, spruce, fir, white cedar, and other evergreens interspersed with oaks, maples, dogwoods, and various other deciduous trees. Our transient home in this region was surrounded by great forests, yet commanded distant views of blue ridges and deep canyons whose constantly changing shadows created an every varying picture for our occupation. It was enough to do, to sit on the porch and look at it.

Here too at her daughter's house I made the acquaintance of the widow of J. Ross Browne, the traveler and author, and American Minister to China, a lady whose eventful life of travel and residence in the capitals of many countries as well as in that of our own gave to her conversation most extraordinary variety and picturesqueness. Anecdotes of distinguished persons, descriptions of people, customs and scenery, brought to her memory by any trivial commonplace of conversation, flowed from her lips in delightful profusion of color and variety. Besides all these, her reminiscences of early years in Oakland, California, during her husband's lifetime, and her stories of Mark Twain, Joaquin Miller, and other early Western writers whom she knew, were full of history for me. On many other accounts this was one of the happiest summers of my California life.

Among the events of this period was my meeting with Mrs. Julia Ward Howe who talked with me about Antioch College and Horace Mann. Another recollection is of going with fifteen of my Shakespeare students, then studying *Macbeth*, to see Madam Ristori and Lady Macbeth. The actress was then seventy years old but was very great in the sleep-walking scene. Indeed I have never so completely lost the stage illusion as during this act. Briefly, this period of my life might be characterized, so far as my intellectual growth was concerned, as the period of my real acquaintance with Shakespeare, for though I had read and studied many plays before and during my years in the high school, I had never had time to make any comparative study, nor opportunity to realize the Shakespearean world. The interpretations of the distinguished Shakespearean reader, Mr. Locke Richardson, gave a fresh impetus to the study, an interest which was illuminated by the occasional presentations of the great actors Booth, the elder Salvini, Sheridan, and Barrett. The organization of the Locke Richardson Shakespeare Club, as the outgrowth of these events, gave some permanence to the interest which led a group of professors, teachers, and others to continued study for several years.

Two or three times after my return from Ohio I had invitations to go back to the high school and a call to the position of Professor of English at the opening of Mill's College, but I still preferred my new way of life and hesitated to take up in either place what I knew would be heavier responsibilities. Besides at this time I was at last engaged in the work of writing the composition book undertaken at Professor Edward Rowland Sill's suggestion some time before. Professor Sill's death in Ohio in February, 1887 had awakened in me a desire to do what he had seemed to believe me so well prepared for through my work in the Oakland High School.

The tranquillity of this period was broken by the sudden death of my father at his home in Ohio, March 14, 1888. This event ended for a time my interest in plans for carrying out certain wishes of my father with respect to literary work. And it seemed to end other ambitions involving intellectual activity. Soon afterwards I was called on to mourn the death of my friend Nancy Van Mater, Nelly's mother, whose kindness had been so much to me during my college life.

In September, 1888, after some hesitation, I decided to accept a third call to return to the Oakland High School. The four years following, although in many ways filled with satisfactory work, gave me less opportunity for individual expression on account of the larger numbers and the restrictions of new university requirements in English. Certain exactions of that institution in the teaching of technical details and a too rhetorical method in the selection of pieces of literature interfered with my ideas of a rational order in the presentation of literary study. However, during these years I had the pleasure of dealing with a goodly number of very interesting young men and young women, some of whom later arrived at a distinction which their gifts seemed to me then to foretell.

To this period also belong the recollections of seeing and hearing several persons of greater or less distinction in the world of letters and other achievement. Among these was my last meeting with Dr. Edward Everett Hale. The benevolence and universality of Dr. Hale's spirit were as strongly evident then as they were in the seventies when I had met him in Antioch College. But at this time he was less enthusiastic as shown in his public readings.

The meeting of Clara Barton and listening to her reminiscences of the Civil War made a vivid mark in my memory, emphasizing as it did many of my own recollections of that time. Mental portraits also I have of the historian John Fiske and the novelist George W. Cable and perhaps something more than mere portraits though it would be difficult to separate that residue from the personalities of the two men as they appear in their books. Toward the end of this time I first saw David Starr Jordan,* to whose lecture, "The

---

*David Starr Jordon (1851–1931) was president of Indiana University from 1885 until his appointment as the first president of Stanford University in 1891, where he served until his retirement in 1913. Jordan was a distinguished

Ascent of the Matterhorn," I went with indifferent interest as I had deprecated the risking of life in mere climbing for the sake of climbing since I had read of Whymper's exploits in the Alps. But before I had gone with the lecturer much above Zermatt, I was climbing with his enthusiasm which expressed itself not in rhetorical terms but in the stirring of the man's soul at the recollection of the adventure.

But of all the persons of distinction who came into my horizon in these years, the deepest impression was made by the great traveller, Sir Henry M. Stanley. What there was in the sight of a man who had lived through such hardships and performed such tasks to awaken the deepest emotion would be difficult to say; but the dark face, the close-cropped head of noble proportions set sturdily on a sturdy, full figure, but most of all the steady gaze of the dark eyes, which had looked fearlessly upon the huge, the insurmountable, the terrible, and even the unspeakable, stirred the feelings and the imagination profoundly. The simple plain speech, the undramatic delivery, carried this effect through the whole of his narrative, while, like Othello, he seemed to speak straight on.

The effect of an increasing pressure from without, which had its origin in political interference with school appointments, had gradually changed the personnel of the high school faculty in such a way as to create an atmosphere of unspoken, but nevertheless appreciable, unrest. While there was no open discord, that tranquil spirit which had characterized the school in the earlier years was lacking. Partly owing to this and partly owing to the fact that the work was growing beyond my strength, for at the beginning of the fifth year, I was teaching two hundred pupils in English, I decided to take a leave of absence. The mere mathematics of English composition correcting for such a number of students even of one paper a week will be seen to have a discouraging aspect. Moreover it is impossible, for me at least, to work in a constantly baffled state of mind, for I could but feel that I was doing little of what I called teaching under this imposition. But the experience of the last year or two of this time made it possible for me to understand the

---

scientist, an early conservationist, and an important figure in the World Peace movement. [Ed. note]

6

Epilogue

The remainder of my story, more interesting to me in some respects, is too near and therefore too intimate to be recorded. Its outline may be set down thus: In 1892 I took a six-months' leave of absence from the Oakland High School and came to Stanford University to rest. At the end of that time I was assured of an appointment as instructor in English literature, a position which I held until January, 1900, at which time I was appointed assistant professor in the same department. My work, however, during all these years was in the main as a teacher of composition. This involved the correcting of not less than a thousand pages of manuscript a month besides other work. After a year's leave of absence I resigned on account of ill health and permanently left the business of teaching except for a year or two of light work in a small private school in the Sierras. Failing sight made it necessary for me to give up even this light work and, later, to be largely dependent on a secretary for much of the writing I have done.

A friend who has read these pages objects, "But you have not after all, in the chapters in which you have written of your life as a teacher, told how you taught so as to influence character." Nor can I, nor, I think, can anyone else tell of her own work as it affects others. I wanted to help them. Some said that I did. That is all I can tell.

Bibliographical Note

Although Miss Hardy's memoir has unique traits of sensibility and observation of people and locale, it is far from alone in early Ohio history. Those wishing to look further into aspects of her narrative can enjoy the accounts of others who were part of Ohio's past or its historians.

Francis P. Weisburger, *The Passing of the Frontier, 1825–1850* (1941), is Volume III in *History of the State of Ohio*, edited by Carl Wittke. Volume IV, Eugene H. Roseboom's *The Civil War Era, 1850–1873* (1944) touches on events in the preceding pages, such as the "Squirrel Hunters." Much diverse and relevant material is contained in Ohio State Archaeological and Historical Society *Publications* (1886–1887 *et seq.*). They were succeeded by the *Ohio Historical Quarterly* and then *Ohio History*, which modernized and maintained the Society's mission.

There are massive individual enterprises in the field, most notably Henry Howe's *Historical Collections of Ohio* (1904), which includes a short, enlightening section on Preble County in Volume II, pp. 446–63, with an illustration of the Lowery Monument of Miss Hardy's memory. The scenes and spirit of her youth are fully displayed in *History of Preble County, Ohio*, published in 1881 by H. Z. Williams & Bro.; and in *Directory of Preble County, O. for 1875, Historical Sketches and Biographies of Eminent Pioneers*, published in Eaton in 1875. The latter contains woodcuts and other matter concerning businesses, banks, and personalities.

Many other works bring the era closer, for example, Rev. Elnathan Corrington Gavitt's *Crumbs from My Saddle Bags or Reminiscences of Pioneer Life and Biographical Sketches* (1884), by a traveling Methodist preacher, and Mrs. Elizabeth Fries Ellet's *Pioneer Women of the West* (1852). Barbara M. Cross, ed., *The Educated Woman in America* (1965), a volume in the Teachers College "Classics" series, prints excerpts from the writings of prominent woman educators and gives a sense of the intellectual climate of the time, within which school teachers were required to build their professional careers.

Particularly valuable is E. O. Randall, ed., *Ohio Centennial Anniversary Celebration at Chillicothe, May 20–21, 1903* (1903), and especially the survey by William Henry Venable, whom Miss Hardy knew, "Ohio Literary Men and Women," pp. 582–663. Venable here notes Daniel Vaughan, whom Miss Hardy so much admired. An overview is contained in James M. Miller, *The Genesis of Western Culture... 1800–1825* (1938).

Revivals have received due attention from historians as great human and religious events; see W. W. Sweet, *Revivalism in America* (1944), Charles A. Johnson, *The Frontier Camp Meeting; Religion's Harvest Time* (1955), John B. Boles, *The Great Revival 1787–1805* (1972), and William G. McLoughlin, *Revivals, Awakenings, and Reform* (1978). William Spier's *The Great Revival of 1800* (1872) provides a closer religious perspective.

Horace Mann is a central figure in this work. The definitive biography, which covers the old Antioch College as well, is Jonathan Messerli, *Horace Mann* (1972). The Antioch Miss Hardy knew is warmly captured by the college's great alumnus, Robert L. Straker, in his *Horace Mann and Others* (1963).

Finally, McGuffey, so central to culture and education as Miss Hardy knew it. A sampling of his work is contained in Stanley W. Lindberg, *The Annotated McGuffey: Selections from the McGuffey Eclectic Readers 1836–1920* (1976), which includes a bibliography. A somewhat critical view of McGuffey and his influence is John H. Westerhoff III, *Piety, Morality, and Education in Nineteenth Century America* (1978).

Index

LOUIS FILLER's long and distinguished career has involved him in many aspects of American life and letters, and his publications have ranged from books to bibliography, from articles to edited documents. He has taught in and visited literature and history departments from New York to San Francisco and has served as a Fulbright Professor at the University of Bristol and Erlangen University.

He has been called "the Dean of American reform historians" because of such works as *Crusaders for American Liberalism* (now titled *The Muckrakers*), *Crusade Against Slavery*, and his *Dictionary of Social Reform*. His interest in biography has resulted in many articles and the books *Randolph Bourne*, *The Unknown Edwin Markham*, and *Voice of the Democracy*, the last a study of David Graham Phillips, the novelist and Progressive. He seeks continuity in our cultural heritage, as in his recently edited *Seasoned Authors for a New Season*.

He has collected materials about American women for many years, served as a consultant to the long-term *Dictionary of Notable American Women*, and has pioneered the study of their roles in American affairs. An earlier edited memoir of a nineteenth-century woman was *The New Stars* by Manie Morgan, an account of life on the Missouri-Kansas frontier in the 1850s and Civil War years.

Filler lives in Ovid, Michigan, with his wife, Saralee R. Howard-Filler, an editor of *Michigan History*. Their home, The Belfry, is an 1872 church listed on the National Register, which they have partially converted into living quarters but without infringing on its spirit symbolized by stained glass and belfry.

OTHER WRITINGS IN HISTORY AND LITERATURE BY LOUIS FILLER

BOOKS

The Muckrakers (formerly *Crusaders for American Liberalism*) (1978 ed.)
Appointment at Armageddon (1976)
Randolph Bourne (1965 ed.)
The Crusade against Slavery, 1830–1860 (1960 ff.)
A Dictionary of American Social Reform (1970 ed.)
The Unknown Edwin Markham (1966)
Muckraking and Progressivism: an Interpretive Bibliography (1976)
Voice of the Democracy: a Critical Biography of David Graham Phillips (1978)
Vanguards and Followers: the Youth Tradition in America (1979)

EDITED WORKS

The New Stars: Life and Labor in Old Missouri, Manie Morgan (1949)
Mr. Dooley: Now and Forever, Finley Peter Dunne (1954)
From Populism to Progressivism (1978)
The Removal of the Cherokee Nation (1978 ed.)
The World of Mr. Dooley (1962)
The Anxious Years (1963), anthology of 1930's literature
Horace Mann and Others, Robert L. Straker (1963)
A History of the People of the United States, John Bach McMaster (1964)
The President Speaks (1964), major twentieth-century addresses
Horace Mann on the Crisis in Education (1965; Spanish translation, 1972)
Wendell Phillips on Civil Rights and Freedom (1965)
The Ballad of the Gallows-Bird, Edwin Markham (1967)
Old Wolfville: the Fiction of A. H. Lewis (1968)
The Rise and Fall of Slavery in America (1980)
Abolition and Social Justice (1972)

INTRODUCTIONS

Chatterton, Ernest Lacy (1952)
Plantation and Frontier, Ulrich B. Phillips, in new edition, John R. Commons et al., *A Documentary History of American Industrial Society* (1958)
The Acquisition of Political, Social and Industrial Rights of Man in America, John Bach McMaster (1961)
My Autobiography, S. S. McClure (1962)
A Modern Symposium, G. Lowes Dickinson (1963)
A Statistical History of the American Presidential Elections, Svend Petersen (1963)
Samuel Gompers, Bernard Mandel (1963)
The Political Depravity of the Founding Fathers, John Bach McMaster (1964)
Democrats and Republicans, Harry Thurston Peck (1964)
A Political History of Slavery, W. H. Smith (1966)
Georgia and States Rights, Ulrich B. Phillips (1967)
The Pantarch: a Biography of Stephen Pearl Andrews, Madeleine B. Stern (1968)
Forty Years of It, Brand Whitlock (1970)